FROM THE INSIDE OUT

A Self-Teaching and Laboratory Manual for Biofeedback

FROM THE INSIDE OUT

A Self-Teaching and Laboratory Manual for Biofeedback

Erik Peper

Center for Interdisciplinary Science
San Francisco State University
San Francisco, California
and
Biofeedback and Family Therapy Institute
Berkeley, California

and

Elizabeth Ann Williams

Center for Interdisciplinary Science
San Francisco State University
San Francisco, California

Illustrated by **Demetra Paras**

Plenum Press · New York and London

Library of Congress Cataloging in Publication Data

Peper, Erik.
From the inside out.

Includes index.
1. Biofeedback training – Study and teaching. 2. Biofeedback training – Problems, exercises, etc. I. Williams, Elizabeth Ann, joint author. II. Title. [DNLM: 1. Biofeedback (Psychology) – Laboratory manuals. WL25 P421f]
BF319.5.B5P46 152.1'88 80-20551
ISBN 0-306-40535-0

Plenum Press is a Division of Plenum Publishing Corporation
233 Spring Street, New York, N.Y. 10013

Printed in the United States of America

Acknowledgments

We would like to thank Tony Hughes and Lorna Sandler for their many helpful suggestions; David Wise for introducing us to the cardiac awareness exercise; and Lori Divine, Adele Dypdahl, Michael James, and Karen Jungery for their important feedback. Our special thanks to Barbara Tandy, whose organizational ability helped make our work possible, and to the many students, clients, and experimental subjects who helped make this manual a reality.

We thank Kathleen Parks for her very creative cover design.

Finally, we wish to extend our appreciation to all those at Plenum Press who assisted in the rapid development and production of this volume, and especially to Peter Strupp, Assistant Managing Editor, and Leonard R. Pace, Senior Editor, whose sensitive professionalism truly comes from the inside out!

Contents

Introduction ix

Note to the Instructor xiii

Note to the Student xv

□Instruction Set A Guidelines for Learning Unstressing and an Introduction to Modified Progressive Relaxation 1

Section 1 Electromyograph

Lab I Understanding Biofeedback Equipment and an Introduction to the Electromyograph 45
Lab II Location of Muscle Tension 57
Lab III Experience of Imagined Stressor 81
Lab IV Experience of Imagined Stressor with Feedback 105
Lab V Home Practice: Awareness of Thought Patterns and Muscle Tension 117
Lab VI Dysponesis 123
Lab VII Home Practice: Dysponesis 151

□Instruction Set B Meditative Unstressing Techniques 157

Section 2 Temperature Unit

Lab VIII Introduction to the Temperature Unit 179
Lab IX Techniques of Learning Temperature Change 187
Lab X Home Practice: Learning Temperature Awareness 221
Lab XI Home Practice: Learning Intervention 227

Section 3 Electrodermograph

Lab XII Introduction to the Electrodermograph 235
Lab XIII Systematic Desensitization 269
Lab XIV Home Practice: Densensitization 285

Section 4 Electroencephalograph

Lab XV Introduction to the Electroencephalograph 293
Lab XVI Home Practice: Theta 313

□Instruction Set C Long-Term Biofeedback Training 319

Section 5 Generalized Use of Biofeedback

Lab XVII Economical Biofeedback 329
Lab XVIII Home Practice: Language Use 355
Lab XIX Home Practice: Breath Awareness 361
Lab XX Physiological Effects of Some Common Activities 367
Lab XXI How Do You Respond to Stress? 389

Appendices

Appendix A Introduction to Electricity 411
Appendix B Graphing Your Data 415
Appendix C Using the Sphygmomanometer 419
Appendix D Equipment Problem Solving 421
Appendix E Biofeedback Resources 423
Appendix F Biofeedback Equipment and Supplies 425
Appendix G Glossary 427

Introduction

You have just received your new biofeedback device with its instruction manual. You ask yourself: How can I personally use the equipment to encourage my self-growth? How can I help my patient to relax his spastic colon? How best can I use the equipment with my client who has chronic anxiety? How can I use this equipment in my research examining the correlation between location of muscle contraction and specific emotions? What is the best way to teach my students an understanding of the basis of the signal and the problem of artifacts? Should I have purchased this device or would I have been better off with another type of biofeedback equipment? How can I integrate the use of this device and other biofeedback equipment with such techniques of unstressing as progressive relaxation and meditation? Can I harm myself or others, either physically or emotionally, with the equipment? Where can I look for additional information regarding the use of biofeedback equipment?

These questions and others have been raised over and over in our teaching of biofeedback to both students and professionals. This manual has been structured so as to provide both background information and experiences that will allow the user to answer these questions.

The manual is based on the premise that the only way to really learn ("know") about biofeedback is through *self-experience*. Hence the book is organized as a set of structured experiences that provide the user with an understanding of

1. How the biofeedback signal is generated and processed and how to use the biofeedback equipment
2. A format to record, collect, and analyze data
3. How biofeedback can be used in a variety of situations inside and outside the laboratory
4. Other unstressing techniques and how biofeedback can be integrated with them
5. The attitudes and methodology important for the use of biofeedback and other self-training techniques
6. Mind/body integration and techniques of enhancing self-awareness
7. The fundamental concept of feedback and how its usefulness goes beyond traditional modes of biofeedback
8. The rich variety of individual experiences that may occur during biofeedback training

The manual consists of three different types of procedures: *instruction sets, laboratory exercises,* and *home practices*. The *instruction sets* include directions for learning unstressing techniques and long-term biofeedback training. In addition, they provide background information regarding such important issues as problems that may arise during unstressing procedures as well as during biofeedback training, and attitudes strategic for learning control over psychophysiological functions. The unstressing techniques are included in the manual because often they are used as adjunctive techniques during biofeedback training, and also because they are well suited for home practice.

The *laboratory exercises* are designed to provide actual experience with biofeedback equipment. Information providing an understanding of the basis of the signal, instructions on the application of appropriate sensors, and directions for operating the equipment are included.

The *home practices* are exercises derived directly from the labs. They are designed to encourage the transfer of skills learned in the biofeedback lab into daily life.

The three different types of procedures are interwoven and presented in the order through which it is recommended that one proceed. Labs using the electromyograph (Section 1) are presented first, followed by those using the temperature unit (Section 2), electrodermograph (Section 3), electroencephalograph (Section 4), and, finally, a variety of feedback devices (Section 5). If, as a result of equipment limitation, it is not possible to follow this recommended sequence, one may proceed through Sections 1-4 in another order. However, the information contained in Instruction Set A and Lab I is *vital* for the use of biofeedback equipment and the reader must be familiar with these concepts *before* proceeding to any other labs, regardless of the order in which subsequent labs are done.

In addition, Instruction Sets B and C contain information that is *basic* to biofeedback training; hence these should be read thoroughly at some time as you proceed through the manual.

Each of the procedures (instruction set, lab, or home practice) includes both a statement of the objective and explicit instructions for completion of the procedure. Also included are a list of equipment needed and directions for prelab preparation, when required. It is important to read these sections of the lab *before* the lab period, both to collect the equipment and to complete the prelab preparation.

The procedures also include data collection forms, graphing forms, and questions to be completed by each trainee regarding his/her data. In addition, the instruction sets and labs contain a Discussion and Conclusions page. In order to complete this page, the trainee must meet with individuals who also have completed their data collection. Therefore, time during your lab period should be scheduled for the sharing of data, which will provide the basis for the completion of this page. This sharing of individual data is important in that it provides an opportunity to see how others respond to the same learning experience: one may observe both idiosyncratic behavior and the emergence of common patterns of behavior. If it is not possible to meet with a group, skip the Discussion and Conclusions page.

A number of the labs assume familiarity with certain concepts or procedures such as electricity and graphing techniques. The appendices provide information helpful to the understanding of these concepts. For the individual who wants more background information, additional references are provided in each of the procedures. Specific page references for the text *Mind/Body Integration: Essential Readings in Biofeedback,* edited by E. Peper, S. Ancoli, and M. Quinn, are also provided.

Each of the lab exercises should be done with a partner. Each individual should have his/her own lab book for recording his/her data, and completing the Questions and Discussion and Conclusions pages. Working with a partner allows one to complete the lab *both* as a trainee and as a trainer.

The length of time required for each of the lab exercises will vary—some will take longer than a three-hour lab period, some less time. Take as much time as is needed for mastery of the skills, and then go on to the next lab. The labs introducing biofeedback equipment (Labs I, VIII, XII, and XV) were not written with a specific manufacturer or machine in mind. These exercises discuss the major functions of the equipment. Your specific instrument may or may not have all the functions that are described. Complete those sections of the lab applicable to your equipment.

We hope that as you proceed through this lab book you will experience the richness of the field of biofeedback. We hope you will share our enthusiasm for its potential as a tool for scientific study, as a procedure with clinical applications, and as a methodology for experiencing mind/body integration and fostering self-awareness and growth.

Erik Peper
Elizabeth Ann Williams
Berkeley, California

Note to the Instructor

This manual has been divided into sections according to the biofeedback equipment required; thus any one section may be done with only one piece of equipment. However, in order to complete all the sections of the manual, one needs at least one unit of each of the following biofeedback devices and its instruction manual: electromyograph, temperature unit, electrodermograph, electroencephalograph. Appendix F lists several manufacturers of biofeedback equipment and their addresses. Although the units vary in sophistication and price, it is possible to purchase all four units appropriate for a biofeedback class for less than $2000.

In addition to the biofeedback equipment, other supplies will be required. At the beginning of each lab, there is a complete list of materials that are necessary in order to complete the lab. Most of the labs will require alcohol, tissue, a watch with a second hand, adhesive electrode collars, tape, and electroconductive paste. Electrode collars and paste may be obtained from the manufacturers of biofeedback equipment. Certain labs also require specific items. The following is a list of these labs and the specific equipment needed:

Lab or instruction set	Equipment needed
Set A	*Optional:* Tape recorder and tape of scripts (see Appendix F for source)—one set per student
Lab I	10,000-ohm (10-kΩ) resistors—two per piece of equipment
Lab VIII	Beaker, plastic bag, lab thermometer—one of each per piece of equipment
Lab X	Small thermometer for hand or thermosensitive paper (see Appendix F for source)—one per student
Lab XII	10- and 50-kΩ resistors, connecting leads with alligator clips—one of each per piece of equipment. Bottle of detergent, jar of hand cream, ski hat, parka—one of each per class. *Optional:* resistors of 15, 20, 25, 30, 35, 40, and 45 kΩ
Lab XV	Metric tape measure—one per piece of equipment; grease pencil. *Optional:* styrofoam wig holder
Lab XVI	Tea bell—one per student

Lab or instruction set	Equipment needed
Lab XVII	Two bathroom scales, stethoscope, and sphygmomanometer—per group of students; paper bag
Lab XXI	Ice bucket and ice—one per set of equipment

The organization of the class will depend on the number of students and the space and equipment available. Students should work in pairs, and, ideally, at any one time there should be only one pair of students per piece of equipment, allowing eight students to work simultaneously with the minimum equipment. To accommodate more students, the time during which the equipment is available must be well managed, with sign-up sheets for each piece of equipment.

With regard to the instruction sets, we recommend that the instructor begin by checking the history forms in Instruction Set A for any questions answered in the affirmative, in order to be sensitive to problems that may arise during relaxation and biofeedback training. Next, the scripts of this instruction set should be introduced to the class as a whole during the first four laboratory periods. Time should be allowed for discussion and completion of the questions on the Discussion and Conclusions page of each week's practice before the new script is introduced.

Instruction Set B should be started during the fifth laboratory period (or after completion of Lab VII), and Instruction Set C during the eleventh laboratory period (or after completing Lab XVI). Again allow for group discussion when so suggested in the text of the instruction sets.

We have found the following procedures helpful with our own students:

1. Demonstrate use of each piece of equipment before students start a lab requiring this piece of equipment; always have the manufacturer's instruction manual present during laboratory period.
2. Remind students to read the laboratory instructions before coming to class so that they are ready to begin immediately and have completed any necessary prelab preparation.
3. Collect Data sheets, Graphs, Questions, and Discussion and Conclusions pages on a specified due date.
4. Observe students while they are using equipment to check set-up; periodically attend different group discussions; leave time available to act as consultant and problem solver.
5. Keep noise in the lab to a minimum. Use room dividers or multiple small rooms to reduce distractions.
6. Divide the class into groups of six (i.e., into groups with three pairs of students), all members of which should work on the same lab. Have the group meet for discussion *immediately* after all the members have completed their data collection, graphed their data, and completed the Questions page.

In addition to the labs, the lab book provides other useful information. For independent research projects, suggested topics are provided at the end of most labs. Appendices are provided for students with little background in electrical concepts and graphing.

Note to the Student

If you are proceeding through the manual without an instructor, be sure to read ''Note to the Instructor,'' paying special attention to equipment and materials needed. Make sure you have assembled the materials necessary, are familiar with the procedures, and have completed any prelab preparation before commencing each lab.

This lab manual contains terminology from a variety of sources, reflecting the interdisciplinary nature of biofeedback. Many of these terms have been defined in the body of the text or in an appendix.[1] Don't be intimidated by new concepts; enjoy the interdisciplinary richness of biofeedback.

The manual is organized into sections, the first four of which each explore a different physiological system. Different individuals respond in different physiological systems; therefore, it is possible that you may not show a response in some of the labs. In addition, you may find the time allotted for recording baseline or learning periods to be either too long or too short for your response pattern. Do not be constrained by the instructions; adapt the lab so that you are comfortable.

In order to get the most out of the labs, make sure your data are graphed before completing the Questions. Often trends become obvious only once they are graphed. You may have experiences during the lab exercises that are not specifically mentioned in the Questions. Don't be constrained or limited by the questions; use the space under ''Comments'' to record your experiences.

In addition, make sure you meet with your small group and complete the Discussion and Conclusions page of one lab before going on to the next.

[1]Terms defined in an appendix are *italicized* in the text.

INSTRUCTION SET A

Guidelines for Learning Unstressing and an Introduction to Modified Progressive Relaxation[1]

EQUIPMENT

Tape recorder and tapes (*optional*).

OBJECTIVE

The objectives of this instruction set are to become familiar with the procedures and variables essential to learning unstressing (relaxation),[2] and to learn a specific unstressing technique, Modified Progressive Relaxation (MPR).

Learning an unstressing technique is important both for its intrinsic value in promoting health (e.g., eliminating such stress-related diseases as hypertension, ulcers, asthma, and anxiety states) and for its value in biofeedback training. Unstressing techniques are often directly integrated into biofeedback training by providing a skill (1) to enhance learning during training sessions and (2) to encourage generalization (i.e., transfer from the lab to "daily life") by providing a technique of home practice. Furthermore, many of the procedures and variables discussed in the following sections that have been found to be important in learning an unstressing technique are equally important for successful biofeedback training.

PROCEDURES IMPORTANT FOR LEARNING UNSTRESSING

Pretraining Screening

General unstressing may have profound psychophysical effects. Experience with unstressing techniques has shown that persons with specific characteristic symptoms or histories are susceptible to these possible effects. Generally a history form is used to screen for these persons. The following list of conditions (characteristic symptoms or history) is derived from the systematic observations of Autogenic Therapy.[3] It has been observed that persons with these conditions may have problems in learning an unstressing technique. Included with each condition are suggestions for how to manage the possible problems.

[1]REFERENCE: E. Peper, S. Ancoli, & M. Quinn (Eds.), *Mind/body integration: Essential readings in biofeedback,* New York: Plenum, 1978, pp. 68–78; 163–200.

[2]A useful guide to the literature on relaxation: D. Waterman, B. Tandy, & E. Peper, *Relaxation: A bibliography,* Denver: Biofeedback Society of America, 1978.

[3]W. Luthe & S. Blumberger, Autogenic therapy. In E. D. Wittkower & H. Warnes (Eds.), *Psychosomatic medicine: Its clinical applications,* New York: Harper & Row, 1977, pp. 146–163.

Condition	Suggested management
1. Trainee is not capable of following instructions or willing to provide feedback of home practice experiences to trainer (i.e., to maintain a log). EXAMPLES: schizophrenic, severely mentally retarded, individual who does not speak language in which instructions are given.	Do not do training with this individual.
2. Trainee is taking medication for some physical or psychological problem. EXAMPLES of medication: sleeping pills, antihypertensive medication, tranquilizers, antidepressants, insulin, thyroid supplement.	System for which medication is being taken *must* be monitored daily following training and dosage of medication altered if necessary. If trainee is unwilling or not capable of monitoring system, do not do training. This is *crucial* with certain medications, such as insulin, where relaxation may alter requirements in a brief period. Also, during the beginning of training, do not focus on the area of concern (pathology) as this often increases anxiety.
3. Trainee has some physical pathology or history of pathology. EXAMPLES of pathology: asthma, ulcer condition, heart condition.	Avoid focusing during the beginning of training on the area of concern. For example, an asthmatic should not focus on breath or chest.
4. Trainee has had traumatic or consciousness-altering experiences. EXAMPLES: anesthesia, automobile accidents, near drowning, rape, experiences with psychedelic drugs.	Provide support and opportunity to "discharge"[4] the emotions associated with these experiences. Encourage trainee to let these feelings be without becoming involved in them. (Often individuals with these kinds of experiences find it difficult to relax.)
5. Trainee has some other unusual physical condition. EXAMPLES: pregnancy, narcolepsy.	Modify training as appropriate. If trainee is pregnant, do not focus on abdomen; a narcoleptic trainee should be lying down.
6. Trainee has some other unusual psychological condition. EXAMPLES: anxiety-provoking life situation such as dealing with death of a loved one, history of lapses of attention such as fugue states, experience of depersonalization.	Provide emotional support; follow trainee closely and if conditions worsen, terminate training.

[4]*Discharge* refers to the spontaneous occurrence of sensations, images, feelings, thoughts, or movements while relaxing.

Condition	Suggested management
7. Trainee has had prior experience with another relaxation or meditation technique or hypnosis.	Instruct trainee as to difference of techniques and encourage trainee to follow instructions carefully and avoid falling back into the old technique.
8. Trainee generally controls (blocks, suppresses) a need to cry or vomit.	During training, watch for responses such as headache, gagging feeling, or nausea. If present, encourage and support crying or vomiting.

Monitoring during Training

There are certain responses that may occur during training that indicate the possibility of a problem. The following is a list of what to look for as well as how to respond to these behaviors:

Response	Suggested management
1. Response incongruous with instruction. EXAMPLES: trainee reports pain during "letting go" instruction; trainee becomes panicky when imagining a "relaxing" scene.	Check in detail what trainee is doing and, if necessary, instruct trainee in correct procedure; check personal association trainee has to instruction or image; if incongruous response continues, discontinue training.
2. Excessive or unusual physiological response. EXAMPLES: flushing of face, sweating palms, heart palpitations, headache.	Do exercises for shorter time period; if exercise directs attention to body part responding excessively, avoid that focus; encourage attitude of "letting be"; if response continues, discontinue technique; if appropriate, refer to doctor.
3. Excessive or unusual psychological response. EXAMPLES: disorientation in time and space; "discharge" of emotion such as crying; intense dynamic changing of image, which is predominantly red.	Provide supportive environment for trainee to become oriented or calm down before leaving session; check in detail what disoriented trainee is doing, making sure trainee is not giving "posthypnotic-like" suggestion to him/herself. Encourage attitude of "letting be" and detachment. Do exercise for shorter period of time: if response continues, discontinue training; if appropriate, recommend counseling.

VARIABLES IMPORTANT TO OPTIMIZE TRAINING

In order to learn an unstressing technique, one needs to optimize the conditions under which one may relax. These conditions involve the reduction of stimuli impinging upon the trainee—both environmental and proprioceptive.

Physical Variables

1. Select an environment:
   a. Where, once commenced, training will not be interrupted (unplug phone, put note on outside of door, inform others that you are going to begin training, etc.);

b. Where noise is minimal (not next to TV or recreation room);
c. Where lighting is subdued, not harsh or glaring;
d. Where temperature is comfortable (a cold room makes it difficult to relax); and
e. Where chair or bed on which training is done is comfortable and provides good support.

2. Choose the position for training that is most comfortable for you—either lying down (Figure 1) or sitting (Figure 2A,B).
   a. If lying down, place a pillow underneath the head so the neck and shoulders are comfortable. Place pillow underneath knees so lower back is not strained. Be sure surface beneath is comfortable (use carpet or foam). Make sure legs are not crossed and that toes are pointing outward. Keep arms at side, not touching trunk.
   b. If sitting, make sure chair offers sufficient support so you don't fall over when you relax. Make sure height of chair is such that your feet are flat on the floor and there is not undue pressure on your thighs (if chair is too high, place a telephone book under your feet). Sit with legs and feet uncrossed and with thighs relaxed so that legs are slightly separated. Let arms rest on arms of chair (if present) or rest gently on lap. Let head either hang forward (Figure 2A) or be supported by back of chair (Figure 2B). Be sure neck is not strained.
3. Scan your body and check if there is anything impinging upon and/or constricting the body; if present, loosen or remove the constricting or impinging items.
   a. Often we become unaware of the constricting nature of our clothing. For example, when you first put on your shoes in the morning, you may "feel" the shoe enclosing your foot, yet after a few minutes you are unaware of the shoe. When you scan (i.e., feel what's going on inside) your body and attention is brought to your foot, you again become aware of the shoe. During relaxation, one often becomes aware of the constricting sensation and is distracted from the process of relaxation. Check for such items as shoes, a tight collar, tie, wig, glasses, contact lenses, socks with elastic tops, watch, ring, heavy pendant, wallet or keys in pocket, belt, bra, or girdle. If you are working in a group and are uncomfortable about loosening personal items, go through the exercise as best you can and next time you practice make sure to dress so that these items are not a problem.
   b. An item that appears comfortable in one's normal posture may physically prevent the process of relaxation. For example, jeans that are tight across the abdomen prevent the letting go and relaxation of abdominal muscles. They force thoracic breathing and prevent the more relaxing abdominal breathing. Check for such items as belt, tight pants, or a tight corset.

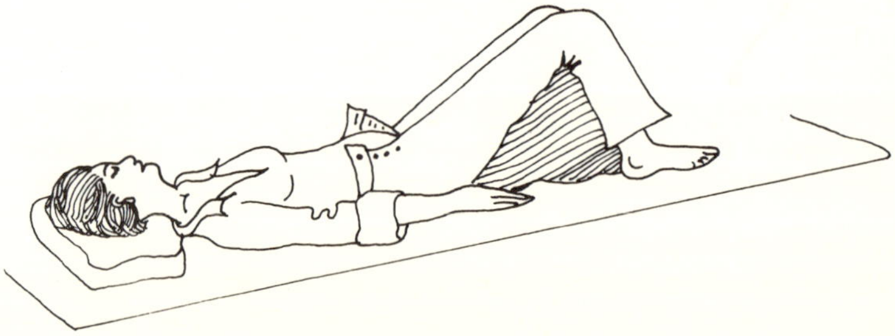

FIGURE 1. Relaxed position, lying down.

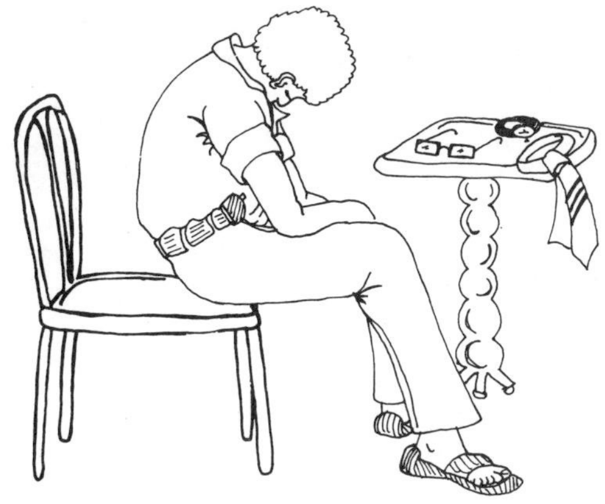

FIGURE 2A. Relaxed position, sitting on a straight-back chair.

FIGURE 2B. Relaxed position, sitting in chair with support for head and arms.

c. An item that appears comfortable in one's normal posture may demand bracing while relaxing. For example, if one is wearing glasses and the head tilts forward during relaxation, one may tend to tighten the neck muscles to prevent the head from nodding and the glasses from falling. Similarly, a woman with a short skirt may hold her knees together and not let her legs relax, and someone with dentures may tighten his/her jaw because of the fear that the dentures may fall out.

d. A physical state may also distract one from relaxing. For example, a full bladder or being either very hungry or very full may make it difficult to relax.

Psychological Variables

1. There are certain attitudes of the trainee that encourage relaxation. These include:
   a. Passive attention. This is an attitude of nonstriving, of allowing versus forcing, and characterized by the absence of concern for performance and end result.
   b. Nonjudgmental acceptance. This attitude includes not explaining, interpreting, or labeling an experience as good or bad, but letting it be and describing without judgment. This implies not comparing an experience to another but

rather experiencing each new situation afresh. This means not using words like "because . . .," "the reason is . . .," or "should. . . ."

c. Mindfulness. This is an attitude of remaining present, watchful, and aware of what is happening without becoming involved or captured by the images or feelings. Being truly present implies the absence of either anticipating or ruminating.

2. There are trainer-trainee variables that influence the learning of relaxation.
   a. The trainer should be self-experienced in the technique s/he is teaching. This "knowingness" or belief in the efficacy of the procedure is subtly communicated to the trainee.
   b. The trainer should be sensitive to other trainer-trainee interactional issues, such as power, authority, and sexuality. A respect for the trainee is implicitly assumed, so that abuse and exploitation would never arise.[5]
3. There are a number of strategies that facilitate home practice and generalization of relaxation skills. The following are a few suggestions:
   a. Keep a log of situations when practice is done and when it is not done. This enables one to select those situations that encourage practice. For example, you may find that you practice a relaxation skill with another person more often than by yourself—hence, you structure your practice time with a friend.
   b. Schedule a regular practice time and associate it with an existing behavior. For example, you may practice after watching the evening news or before dinner.
   c. Give yourself a reinforcer meaningful to you when you practice. For example, if you practice for a week, treat yourself to a movie or special meal.[6]
   d. Develop cues to remind yourself to do the relaxation technique (or a modified portion of it) in situations where you often are not relaxed. For example, if you tend to tighten up when you are late or in a hurry, put a dot on your watch. Each time you glance at your watch and see the dot, say "relax" and practice part of your relaxation technique. Other situations you may consider: standing in a long line at the bank or supermarket, driving in traffic, or answering the phone.

INSTRUCTIONS

History Form

Before commencing the relaxation exercises, complete the History Form. An answer of "yes" for any of the questions indicates a condition to which you should be sensitive—known as a "red flag." Check the section on Pretraining Screening (pp. 1–3) for what to do.

[5]For a detailed discussion of ethics, see the American Psychological Association's *Ethical principles in the conduct of research with human participants*.

[6]For a detailed discussion see C. E. Thorenson & M. J. Mahoney, *Behavioral self-control,* New York: Holt Rinehart & Winston, 1974; D. Watson & R. Tharp, *Self-directed behavior: Self-modification for personal adjustment,* Belmont, California: Brooks/Cole, 1977.

Trainee ____________________

Date __________

INSTRUCTION SET A HISTORY FORM

1. Are you unable or unwilling to do the home practices and keep a detailed daily log (diary) of your experiences? Yes___ No___

2. Are you taking any medications? Yes___ No___

   If so, which ones?

   ____

   For what?

   ____

   Dosage?

   ____

3. Do you have any physical problem(s) or a history of a problem(s)? Yes___ No___

   If so, what is the problem?

   ____

   ____

4. Have you ever had a traumatic or consciousness-altering experience such as an accident, use of anesthesia, or mood-altering drugs? Yes___ No___

   If so, describe:

   ____

   ____

5. Are you pregnant? Yes___ No___

6. a. Are you presently experiencing a great deal of emotional stress or problems in your life? Yes___ No___

   If yes, describe:

   ____

   ____

b. Have you recently experienced lapses of attention or memory or a sense of depersonalization? Yes___ No___

If yes, describe:

___

___

7. Have you had prior experience with meditation, hypnosis, or any other relaxation technique? Yes___ No___

If so, describe:

___

___

8. Do you find it difficult to let yourself cry or vomit? Yes___ No___

LEARNING MODIFIED PROGRESSIVE RELAXATION

Progressive Relaxation was originally developed and systematically researched by Edmund Jacobson.[7] The technique was based on the observation that anxiety was manifested by muscle tension and that such anxiety could be removed by eliminating the muscle tension. The relaxation technique to be introduced has been adapted and modified from Jacobson's work.

The following four scripts guide you through the steps for learning a modified form of Progressive Relaxation (MPR). Each script is to be practiced once each day for a week. You may either memorize them, have a friend guide you through them, or tape record the script and play it back during your practice. Both timing and quality of voice should encourage relaxation. You can monitor the effect of your voice by monitoring your own reaction—e.g., did I have enough time to become aware of the sensation of tightness? After each daily practice, note your experiences on the appropriate Weekly Log Sheet and at the end of each week complete the appropriate Questions. If possible, meet with your group and complete the Discussion and Conclusions section. For example, during the first week of practice, you will follow Instruction Set—Week 1, make your daily entries on Log Sheet—Week 1, and at the end of the week complete Questions—Week 1 and Discussion and Conclusions—Week 1.

In learning MPR, it is helpful to have a skilled person guide you through the scripts for the first time. A skilled trainer may also lead the group discussion, scan log sheets, and observe reactions during sessions for unusual physiological or psychological reactions.

If you are learning these scripts on your own, monitor yourself for unusual reactions. Refer to the section Monitoring during Training (p. 3).

Complete the following exercise to experience the basic processes involved in Progressive Relaxation—tensing and letting go:

> Choose a comfortable position. Close your eyes. Bend your hand back at the wrist with your fingers pointing upward. Hold this position for 5–10 sec. Check that you are not tightening any other part of your body—check your shoulders and your jaw.[8] Are you breathing comfortably? Bring your attention to your forearm. *Observe the sensations of tightening.* What are they? Describe sensations nonjudgmentally in the present tense. If your attention drifts away, bring it back to the forearm. Let gravity pull your hand down; do not actively "put" it down. Let your hand and arm relax for at least 20–30 sec. Relaxing is not "doing." *Observe the sensations of relaxing,* "letting go." What are they? How do they differ from those of tightening? If you do not feel any sensation, hold the muscle tight until you feel something such as pain or discomfort. If you find it difficult to "let go," try the exercise either during or after a sauna, hot tub or massage.

Before commencing the scripts, read through the following list of problems that commonly occur during practice, and their suggested solutions. If you encounter any of the following problems, refer back to this section.

Problem	Suggested solution
1. Muscle cramps.	Stop tightening muscle when you begin to sense cramping; massage or move cramped muscle while keeping rest of body relaxed.

[7]For a more detailed discussion, see E. Jacobson, *Progressive relaxation* (3d ed.), Chicago: University of Chicago Press, 1974 (originally published, 1938); E. Jacobson, *Modern treatment of tense patients,* Springfield, Illinois: Charles C Thomas, 1970; D. A. Berstein & T. Borkovec, *Progressive relaxation training: A manual for the helping professions,* Champaign, Illinois: Research Press, 1973.

[8]During this exercise, or during later practice of MPR, electromyographic (EMG) feedback may be helpful in confirming that other body parts are not being tightened.

Problem	Suggested solution
2. Laughter or feeling self-conscious.	Practice in private place; or just let feelings be and return attention to practice.
3. Difficulty maintaining attention.	Describe changing sensations out loud during tension and relaxing.
4. Tics or spasm.	Allow to continue as this indicates relaxation is occurring.
5. Sleepiness.	Practice at different times of day, sitting up, or for shorter periods of time; may indicate need for more sleep.
6. Experience of body part changing, e.g., becoming dissociated or increasing in size.	Allow to continue, as this indicates relaxation is occurring; if necessary, open eyes to check out body part.

Instruction Set—Week 1

The following is the script for Week 1. As described in the previous section, Variables Important to Optimize Training, one may complete the exercises either lying down or sitting in a chair. If your position inhibits the tightening and letting go of a muscle group, or the directions do not feel quite appropriate or clear, modify the script to make it appropriate for you. As a general reminder:

1. Keep your attention on the muscle group being tightened and relaxed.
2. Breathe easily and smoothly.
3. Tighten only the muscle that you are being directed to tighten, letting the rest of the body stay relaxed.

Each day, 20–30 min should be allotted to go through the script. This time period may be perceived as a "time-out" period during which the body/mind is allowed to totally relax.

Script 1

Shift to a comfortable position. Be sure your belt is loose, your shoulders are loose, your legs uncrossed, your glasses off. Close your eyes. Clench your right fist . . . tighter and tighter. Be sure you continue to breathe, allowing the lips to be slightly parted.

Exhale through the mouth, whispering *HA*. Be sure the rest of the body is relaxed. Observe the sensations of tightening.

Now let go and relax. . . . Observe the contrast in feeling between your right fist tensed and relaxed. Observe the difference in the way your right and left hands feel now.

Now tighten your left fist. . . . Observe the sensations of tightening. Be sure you keep breathing, and that the rest of the body is relaxed. Now let go. Observe the sensation and feeling of letting go. . . . If your attention wanders to other things, gently bring it back to the sensations in your arm.

Now tighten both fists. Observe the sensation of tightening. . . . Then let go and relax all over. Enjoy the sensation. . . .

Now bend the elbows. Tense both biceps (in the front of your upper arms). Let your hands and fingers be relaxed. Observe the sensations of tightening. . . .

Keep breathing. Be sure your neck, your jaw, and the rest of your body are relaxed.

Now relax and let your arms drop either to your side or to your lap. Notice the difference in feeling between tensing and letting go.

Straighten your arms so that you tense your tricep muscles (in the back of your upper arms), again keeping your hands relaxed. Keep breathing smoothly. . . . Observe the sensations of tightening. Relax your arms at your sides or on your lap. Relax all over. . . .

Notice that your arms feel comfortable and heavy. Feel the relaxation spread up your arms. Notice that your arms feel heavier and heavier as you relax more and more.

Frown hard. . . . Be sure the rest of the body is relaxed. Relax and let go. . . . Now wrinkle your eyebrows up toward your scalp. Be sure your tongue, jaw and neck are loose and you are not holding your breath. . . . Observe the sensation of tightening. Relax and let your brow be smooth. Observe the sensations of relaxation. . . .

Now tighten your eyes. Tighten the muscles deep in your eyes as well as the facial muscles around your eyes. Be sure your tongue, your jaw, the back of your neck and the rest of your body are relaxed. . . . Relax and keep your eyes gently closed. . . . Observe the sensations of relaxation and how they differ from those of tightening.

Clench your jaw and clench your teeth. Study the tension in the jaw. Be sure you keep breathing. . . . Relax and let go. . . . Slightly part your lips and as you exhale, let the air go out your mouth in a soft whispered *HA*.

Press your tongue hard against the roof of your mouth. Observe the tension. . . . Relax and let go. Feel the relaxation in your cheeks, scalp, eyes, face, arms, hands. . . .

Now tighten your neck by tilting your head backwards. Be sure you keep breathing and the rest of the body stays relaxed. Feel the tension in your neck. . . . Relax and let go.

Breathe comfortably and let your jaw be relaxed. Bring your head foward toward your chest. Feel the tension in your neck. Relax and let go. . . .

Raise your shoulders to your ears. Be sure the neck and the rest of the body are relaxed. Notice the contrast between how your shoulders feel and how the rest of your body feels. . . . Relax and let go. . . .

Let the relaxation flow into your back, neck, throat, jaw, and face. Let it spread and go deeper and deeper. . . . Feel the force of gravity pulling on your body. . . .

Breathe deeply and hold your breath. Note the tension in your chest and shoulders. Be sure your eyes, your jaw and the rest of your body are relaxed. Exhale and observe the feelings. Breathe in and out normally. Notice how on each exhalation you feel more and more relaxed. Let the chest walls be loose and soft as you breathe out. . . .

Now take another deep breath. Hold your breath. Be sure the neck is relaxed. Exhale. Feel the release of tension. Let the relaxation spread to your shoulders, neck, back, and arms. . . .

Tighten your stomach as if you were receiving a blow there. Make it solid. . . . Relax and notice the well-being that accompanies your relaxation. . . .

Now suck your stomach in. Hold it. . . Relax and let go. Let your breathing go smoothly and easily. Note that you can feel the whole lower abdomen move out as you inhale. Notice how exhaling relaxes your shoulders, chest, and stomach. Let go of all the contractions in your body. . . .

Arch your lower back so there is a space between it and the floor or the chair. Feel the tension along your spine and back. Be sure your legs and the rest of your body are relaxed. . . . Relax and let go. . . . Relax the lower back, upper back, stomach, chest, shoulders, arms, face. Relax further. . . .

Tighten your buttocks. Be sure your abdomen and the rest of your body are relaxed. Keep breathing. . . . Relax and let go. . . . Feel how different the sensations of relaxation are from those accompanying the tightening. . . .

Now point your toes and feet downward to tighten your calves and the arches of your feet. . . . Be sure you keep breathing. . . . Relax and let go. . . .

Curl your toes toward you to create tension along your shins and the top of your feet. . . . Relax and let go. . . .

Now let go more and more of each of the parts of the body: feet relax . . . ankles relax . . . calves and shins . . . knees and thighs . . . buttocks and hips. . . . Feel the heaviness of your lower body . . . stomach relax . . . waist relax . . . lower back. . . . Let go more and more. . . . Upper back relax . . . chest relax . . . shoulders . . . arms. . . . Let relaxation take over . . . throat relax . . . neck . . . jaws and face—all relaxed.

When you are ready, take a deep breath, sit up and gently open your eyes. Observe how you feel and how the world looks. Do you notice a difference in brightness, clarity, vividness, aliveness, depth in vision . . .?

Each day, after you have gone through the script, complete the Log Sheet—Week 1. Again, if you have experienced an incongruous response or an "excessive" physical or psychological response, refer to Monitoring during Training (p. 3). At the end of the week, answer Questions—Week 1. Meet with your group and complete Discussion and Conclusions—Week 1.

Trainee ______________________

Date ____________

INSTRUCTION SET A LOG SHEET—WEEK 1

After each practice, describe (a) the practice situation (your mood, the place, your physical position, etc.) and (b) experiences (both physical and subjective) both during and directly following MPR.

Day 1 a. ______________________

Date______ ______________________

b. ______________________

____

____

Day 2 a. ______________________

Date______ ______________________

b. ______________________

____

____

Day 3 a. ______________________

Date______ ______________________

b. ______________________

____

____

Day 4 a. ______________________

Date______ ______________________

b. ______________________

____

____

Day 5 a. ________________________________

Date________ ________________________________

b. ________________________________

____

____

Day 6 a. ________________________________

Date________ ________________________________

b. ________________________________

____

____

Day 7 a. ________________________________

Date________ ________________________________

b. ________________________________

____

____

Trainee ______________________

Date ___________

INSTRUCTION SET A QUESTIONS—WEEK 1

1. What, if any, were the problems that occurred during your practice?

2. Did your experiences with MPR vary during sessions? If so, how did this relate to the conditions under which you practiced? (EXAMPLE: It was difficult to maintain attention during practice at the end of the day.)

3. Did you find that you held your breath and tightened muscles other than the intended muscle during your practice? Which ones? How did your ability to selectively tighten muscles change over the week?

4. In what ways did your practice of MPR affect other aspects of your life? What were some of the benefits?

5. Comments:

Trainee ____________________

Date __________

INSTRUCTION SET A DISCUSSION AND CONCLUSIONS—WEEK 1

1. Among group members, were there common problems that occurred during practice? What are some possible solutions?

2. Did the kinds of experiences that occurred during and following MPR vary among group members, and how were they related to age, sex, medical history, previous experience with relaxation techniques, etc.?

Instruction Set—Week 2

Often we chronically tighten certain areas of the body and are unaware that we do so. During the practice of Script 1, did you notice, for example, that you tightened your shoulders or jaw when intending to tighten other muscles? One can learn to let these areas relax through selectively tightening and letting go the different muscle groups around them. Two areas in which we often unknowingly hold tension are the eyes and the throat; almost any mental effort tends to tighten these areas. Script 2 is aimed at encouraging awareness and relaxation of these areas. Similarly, one may develop other special relaxation sequences, for example, for the pelvis, the relaxation of which often alleviates dysmenorrhea (menstrual cramps) and facilitates natural childbirth.

Script 2

Sit or lie down in a comfortable position. Let your eyes be closed. Now, while breathing, press ankles together, knees together, tighten buttocks, and pull your anus to your belly button. Lift your arms slightly, bend the elbows, tighten fists. Wrinkle your face, tighten your neck. Now take a deep breath and hold. . . . Be sure your ankles are still pressing against each other. . . .

Exhale, relax and let go. Let your whole body go limp and relaxed. . . . Observe the difference between the tension and the letting go. Allow breath to go in and out. Let go to the relaxation. . . .

Repeat. Tighten all muscles. Take a deep breath and hold. . . . Relax and let go. Feel the whole body relaxing and letting go. For the next minute, allow the relaxation to deepen and recapitulate the letting go you achieved in Script 1. . . .

Direct your attention to the area of your eyes. . . . Wrinkle your forehead and hold. Be sure the rest of your body is relaxed. Continue to breathe easily. . . . Relax and let go. Observe the letting go. . . . Frown and notice the tension. . . . Relax and let go. . . . Let your forehead be smooth. . . . Close your eyes tightly and hold. . . . Relax and let go. . . .

Look up with eyes closed, without straining. Be sure jaw and tongue are loose and relaxed. Be sure you breathe easily. . . . Relax and let go. . . . Now look left with your eyes closed. Keep looking. Hold. . . . Let go. . . . Look right with your eyes closed and continue to look right. . . . Relax and let go. . . . Look at your nose. Be sure your tongue and jaw are relaxed. . . . Relax and let go. . . . Look downward with lids closed. Let your neck stay loose. Relax and let go. Look at the tip of your nose. . . . Relax and let go. . . .

Allow your eyes to soften and gently sink into their sockets. Let your whole body relax more. . . . For the next few minutes, inspect your body. If you locate any area of tension, tighten that area and let go. . . .

While staying totally relaxed, visualize the tip of a pen moving across paper and observe sensations around and in the eyes. Hold the image while breathing easily. . . . Relax and let go. . . . For the next few minutes continue to visualize different scenes, such as birds flying, a car race, etc. After visualizing each scene, allow the eyes to relax. . . .

Finally allow your eyes to be soft and cool, and to gently sink into their sockets.

Direct your attention to the area of your throat. Close your jaws firmly. Observe the tension. . . . Let go and relax. . . . Open your jaw. Hold it open.

Remember to keep breathing. . . . Relax and let go. . . .

Smile so that your teeth show. Hold. Be sure your neck stays relaxed. . . . Relax and let go. . . .

Pout. Hold. . . . Relax and let go. . . . Push your tongue against your teeth. Be sure your eyes and the rest of your face stay relaxed. . . . Relax and let go. . . .

Pull your tongue backwards. . . . Relax and let go. . . . Start swallowing. Hold. Keep breathing. . . . Relax and let go. . . .

Now count out loud from one to ten. Observe tightening in neck and throat. Relax and let go. . . . Count very softly, one to ten. Observe any tension in the body. Relax and let go. . . . Whisper one to ten. Relax and let go. Count so softly no one can hear you, one to ten. Relax and let go. . . . Observe how the throat feels different between the relaxed and tensed state. Let your throat go more and more limp and soft. Notice a gentle soothing softness as you relax. . . .

Now imagine you are counting. Observe any tension in your throat. . . . Relax and let go. Let your lips part. . . .

Now imagine you are saying your first name. . . . Relax and let go. . . .

Now think of different verbal tasks where you see yourself talking. Imagine for a moment. Observe the tension. Then relax and let go. Repeat for different activities for the next few minutes. . . .

Now tighten all the muscles of your body. Take a deep breath and hold. . . . Let go and relax and observe the sensation of letting go. . . . Say to yourself on the inhalation *I am* . . ., and on the exhalation, . . . *relaxed.*

Repeat and allow the sensation of relaxation to occur. . . . After a few minutes, stop, relax, and stretch the body. Take a deep breath. Exhale and gently open your eyes. Do you notice a difference in how you feel? Can you keep the relaxed feeling while you stand up and move about? Do you notice a difference in brightness, clarity, vividness, aliveness, and depth in vision, and in the ease, resonance, deepening, and softness of your voice as you speak?

Each day, after you have gone through the script, complete the Log Sheet—Week 2. At the end of the week, answer Questions—Week 2. Then meet with your group and complete Discussion and Conclusions—Week 2.

Trainee ______________________

Date ____________

INSTRUCTION SET A LOG SHEET—WEEK 2

After each practice, describe (a) the practice situation (your mood, the place, your physical position, etc.) and (b) experiences (both physical and subjective) both during and directly following MPR.

Day 1 a. ______________________

Date______ ______________________

b. ______________________

____

____

Day 2 a. ______________________

Date______ ______________________

b. ______________________

____

____

Day 3 a. ______________________

Date______ ______________________

b. ______________________

____

____

Day 4 a. ______________________

Date______ ______________________

b. ______________________

____

____

Day 5 a. ______________________________

Date______ ______________________________

b. ______________________________

____

____

Day 6 a. ______________________________

Date______ ______________________________

b. ______________________________

____

____

Day 7 a. ______________________________

Date______ ______________________________

b. ______________________________

____

____

Trainee ____________________

Date __________

INSTRUCTION SET A QUESTIONS—WEEK 2

1. What, if any, were the problems that occurred during your practice?

2. How did your experiences with MPR affect your vision or speech?

3. In what ways did your practice of MPR affect other aspects of your life? What were the benefits?

4. Comments:

Trainee ______________________

Date ____________

INSTRUCTION SET A DISCUSSION AND CONCLUSIONS—WEEK 2

1. Among group members, how did this week's practice of MPR affect speech, vision, or other aspects of life?

2. Among group members, was there a relationship between the subjective experience of vision and speech and habitual problems in these areas, e.g., wearing glasses?

Instruction Set—Week 3

Learning awareness and recognition of the slightest amount of tension and then relaxing and letting it go, as well as using cue words or images to encourage the relaxation, is the purpose of Script 3. During this week's practice, tighten each muscle only so tight that you begin to feel the sensation of tightening. Hold it at this level of tightness. Relax and let go. Observe the changes in sensation. With practice, one can become aware of subtle sensations of tension that previously occurred beneath the level of awareness.

Script 3

Get in a comfortable position. Minimally tighten your right fist so that you feel only the smallest amount of tension. Hold it at this level. Be sure you continue to breathe. . . . Now let go and relax. . . . Observe the difference in feelings between the right and left arm and fist. . . .

Now minimally tighten your left fist. Hold at this level so that you just feel the tightening. . . . Let go and relax. Let the relaxation spread through the arms and the rest of the body. . . .

Now tighten ever so slightly the following parts of your body. (Each time tighten only to the point at which you can observe tension, where you become conscious of or can "feel" the tension. Hold the tension at that level, and be sure you tighten only the intended muscle while the rest of the body stays quiet and relaxed. Be sure you continue to breathe. Each time you let go, let those parts relax further and further.) Tighten ever so slightly your scalp . . . let go and relax. . . . Your forehead and facial muscles . . . let go and relax. . . . The eyes . . . let go and relax. . . . The tongue, jaw, and lips . . . let go and relax. . . . Let the face become smooth and soft. . . . Let the eyes sink into their sockets. . . . Now slightly tighten the throat and neck. Hold it. . . . Let go and relax.

While continuing to breathe, minimally tighten the triceps. Be sure the neck, eyes, and tongue are relaxed. . . . Let go. . . .

Raise your shoulders to your ears minimally. Be sure the neck stays loose. Observe how the shoulders feel different from the rest of the body. . . . Let go and relax. Feel the relaxation sinking through the body. . . . Minimally tighten the stomach. Keep breathing. . . . Let go and relax. . . . Minimally tighten the buttocks. . . . Let go and relax. . . . Minimally tighten the feet, calves, and thighs. . . . Let go and relax. Let yourself reach an ever deeper level of relaxation, a calmness and serenity. . . .

Now minimally tense every muscle in your body so that you just feel the minimum tension . . . jaws . . . eyes . . . shoulders . . . arms . . . chest . . . back . . . stomach . . . legs. . . . Be sure you keep breathing. Feel the minimum tension in every part. . . . Let your whole body relax. Feel a wave of calmness as you stop tensing. . . .

Now, with your eyes closed, take a deep breath and hold it. Note all the minimum tensions. . . . Exhale and feel the relaxation and calmness developing. . . . Note the feeling of heaviness. . . .

Again take a breath and hold it. Observe the tensions. . . . Exhale and let go. Feel the relaxation developing. Breathe easily and normally so that you feel the movement in the lower abdomen. . . . As you inhale, observe how your abdomen expands. For the next minute, observe your breath. Let the abdomen move in and out while the chest stays soft and relaxed.

Each time you inhale, think, *I am* . . . and each time you exhale, think, . . . *relaxed*. Be sure your breath moves easily and smoothly in and out with a gentle movement in the abdomen. . . .

Feel the deeper relaxation. Feel calm, tranquil, and serene. . . . These feelings come with deep relaxation. . . . Notice the developing sense of inner confidence . . . a calm indifference to external events.

Now let's deepen the relaxation even further by mentally repeating the words *relax, calm,* and *serene*[9] with each exhalation for the new few minutes. . . .

[9]One can substitute any word that is meaningful, such as *peace* or *tranquility*.

Just attend to the relaxation in your body. Notice the serene, calm effect, the heavy, pleasant feelings. . . . Make sure that no tension has crept back into your head and scalp. Smooth out your forehead, eyes, face, lips, nose, tongue, and mouth. All are relaxed. Make sure that no tension has crept back into the rest of your body. Let relaxation spread through your neck, shoulders, and arms; down your sides; through your chest, stomach, lower back, knees, shins, ankles, and toes. . . . Let your entire body relax more and more deeply, as you repeat the words *relax, calm, serene,* on exhalation. . . .

Let the entire body feel more and more relaxed. Let the feeling of relaxation, calmness and serenity deepen for a few minutes. Think and feel the words *relax, calm, serene,* as you exhale. . . .

Now develop your own personal relaxing image. Take any scene which you find especially relaxing (a warm beach, sitting in front of the fire in a log cabin on a winter evening, floating on a raft on a mountain lake, sailing on a calm day . . .) and stay in your image—see it, smell it, taste it, touch it, be it. Stay focused on an image that is particularly relaxing. For the next few minutes go with the image and allow the relaxation to deepen. . . .

Maintain the sensations of relaxation. Stretch, take a deep breath. Exhale and gently open your eyes. Observe how you feel and how you experience the world.

Each day, after you have gone through the script, complete Log Sheet—Week 3, and at the end of the week, answer Questions—Week 3. Then meet with your group and complete Discussion and Conclusions—Week 3.

Trainee ____________________

Date __________

INSTRUCTION SET A LOG SHEET—WEEK 3

After each practice, describe (a) the practice situation (your mood, the place, your physical position, etc.) and (b) experiences (both physical and subjective) both during and directly following MPR. Pay attention to the effect of using cue images.

Day 1 a. ____________________

Date______ ____________________

b. ____________________

____

____

Day 2 a. ____________________

Date______ ____________________

b. ____________________

____

____

Day 3 a. ____________________

Date______ ____________________

b. ____________________

____

____

Day 4 a. ____________________

Date______ ____________________

b. ____________________

____

____

Day 5 a. ____________________

Date______ ____________________

b. ____________________

____

____

Day 6 a. ____________________

Date______ ____________________

b. ____________________

____

____

Day 7 a. ____________________

Date______ ____________________

b. ____________________

____

____

Trainee ______________________

Date __________

INSTRUCTION SET A QUESTIONS—WEEK 3

1. What, if any, were the problems that occurred during your practice?

2. In what way did your sensitivity to subtle muscular tensions change?

3. How did the cue words and images affect your relaxation experience?

4. In what ways has this week's practice of MPR affected your daily life? What were the benefits?

5. Comments:

Trainee ____________________

Date ____________

INSTRUCTION SET A DISCUSSION AND CONCLUSIONS—WEEK 3

1. Among group members, were there common problems related to this week's practice?

2. Were there common words or images that encouraged or inhibited relaxation?

3. Among group members, how were the ways by which the practices affected life experience related to ease of practice, past and present health and illness patterns, or previous exposures to relaxation or meditation techniques?

Instruction Set—Week 4

In order for relaxation training to be of most value in one's life, it is necessary to learn generalization of the skills. In other words, while it is valuable to know how to relax and let go in a quiet, private space, it is also important to be able to relax and let go during the activities of daily life. As a step toward learning generalization of relaxation skills, Script 4 encourages relaxation during simple movements. With practice, one may learn to stay relaxed while performing increasingly complex and stressful tasks, e.g., while doing dishes, or driving a car in traffic.

Script 4[10]

Get comfortable and let your body relax and rest. For the new few minutes, recapitulate the previous sensations of learned relaxation. Relax all over. Allow a pleasant leaden heaviness to develop. Allow the comfortable sensations of warmth to flow through your entire body. . . .

Feel the serenity and joyousness of being enveloped by restfulness . . . heaviness . . . and warmth, so that nothing can disturb you. . . . Feel the inner restfulness deepening, and feel that, as you relax and enjoy these sensations, you will gain a sense of strength and confidence form the inner restfulness. . . .

Feel your muscles yielding and relaxing all over. . . . Let the contractions loosen. Feel more at rest. . . .

Let your breathing come freely and easily without any effort. . . . Think of your blood vessels widening as you relax so that circulation improves without strain or effort. . . . Feel the pulsing and throbbing sensations in the fingers. Again with each inhalation think, *I am* . . . and with each exhalation feel . . . *relaxed*. Let nothing excite you or upset you. Concentrate on the feelings of relaxation and the calmness that grows out of that relaxation. Try to surrender to the good feelings all over. For the next few minutes, imagine yourself practicing the relaxation technique at home. Feel the pleasant relaxed sensation associated with the practice.

Now hear the word *calm*.[11] Think about the word *calm*, and feel it more and more. Just let the word *calm* reverberate. Feel the pleasant feelings you associate with the word *calm*.

Hear the word *serene* and go with it. Capture the feeling of serenity that comes when you relax and feel calm. Now take another word and feeling. Hear that word and go with it. Capture the feeling as you relax more. . . .

Now, sit up straight. Continue to relax as fully as you can. Raise your right arm and hold it up. The rest of your body is relaxed; you feel the tension in your right arm. Study the contrast in feeling. . . . Now let your arm fall to your side and relax it further and further, feeling the difference as the tension drains from your right arm. . . .

Now raise your left arm up and hold it, feeling the tension in your left arm as distinct from the relaxation in the rest of your body. Feel the tension . . . and let your left arm fall to your side. Relax your left arm further and further. . . . Notice the difference between relaxation and tension. . . .

Now raise both arms. Study the tension. Where do you feel it? . . . Let both arms fall and notice the tension evaporate. . . .

Now stand up, and as you are standing, relax as much as you can. Drop your shoulders, loosen your stomach, let your arms hang loosely. Relax like that for a few minutes.

Walk back and forth. Let your arms swing gently. Let go as much as you can while walking. Study your body and release any contractions you don't need.

Stand still again. Relax those parts of your body that are not in use . . . eyes closed; face, scalp, eyes, jaws—all relaxed. Tongue resting loosely in your mouth. Breathe easily. Your neck, throat, and shoulders are fully relaxed . . . stomach relaxed . . . arms and hands relaxed. Relax

[10] Adapted from A. Lazarus.
[11] Or any other cue word developed during Week 3.

your lower back, buttocks, and thighs. Feel the relaxation down your legs as best you can while standing. . . .

Again think the words *relax, calm, serene*. Just think each word and let each word enhance your overall relaxation. Develop the feeling of relaxation while standing. . . .

Now sit or lie down again. Relax comfortably and fully. . . . Rapidly go back into that heavy, comfortable feeling all over and feel the good sensations of warmth throughout your entire body. . . . Sense that nothing can disturb your feeling. Recapture the inner restfulness that deepens and gives you inner strength and confidence. Feel all the muscles yielding and relaxing as you let go of contractions everywhere. Let yourself feel completely at rest, with your breathing coming freely and easily. . . .

Slowly sit up again and relax as fully as you can. Approximate the level of relaxation you achieved while lying down. . . .

Now stand up and relax as deeply and fully as you possibly can. Feel more and more deep relaxation spreading all over. Remind yourself to stay fully and deeply relaxed. Carry this feeling with you throughout the day.

Each day after you have gone through the script, complete Log Sheet—Week 4. At the end of the week answer Questions—Week 4. Then meet with your group and complete Discussion and Conclusions—Week 4.

Trainee ______________________

Date __________

INSTRUCTION SET A LOG SHEET—WEEK 4

After each practice, note (a) your experience during and directly following the practice, and (b) the ease or difficulty of remaining relaxed during simple movements.

Day 1 a. ______________________

Date______ ______________________

b. ______________________

____

____

Day 2 a. ______________________

Date______ ______________________

b. ______________________

____

____

Day 3 a. ______________________

Date______ ______________________

b. ______________________

____

____

Day 4 a. ______________________

Date______ ______________________

b. ______________________

____

____

Day 5 a. ______________________________

Date______ ______________________________

b. ______________________________

____

____

Day 6 a. ______________________________

Date______ ______________________________

b. ______________________________

____

____

Day 7 a. ______________________________

Date______ ______________________________

b. ______________________________

____

____

Trainee ____________________

Date ____________

INSTRUCTION SET A QUESTIONS—WEEK 4

1. In which ways did your ability to stay relaxed while doing simple movement change during the week?

2. In what ways have the practices affected your daily life experience?

3. Looking back over the past four weeks, what scripts or parts of scripts were helpful to you in encouraging relaxation? Were there components that inhibited relaxation?

4. What benefits did you gain through the four weeks of practice?

Trainee ______________________

Date ___________

INSTRUCTION SET A DISCUSSION AND CONCLUSIONS—WEEK 4

1. Were there differences among group members in the ability to stay relaxed during the simple movements? How were these differences related to such variables as age, sex, individual medical history, and past experience with meditative practices?

2. Looking back over the past four weeks, were there parts of the scripts that encouraged or inhibited relaxation that were common among group members?

3. Were there benefits gained during the four weeks of practice common to group members?

SECTION 1
Electromyograph

LAB I

Understanding Biofeedback Equipment and an Introduction to the Electromyograph[1]

EQUIPMENT

Electromyograph and instruction manual, two 10-kΩ resistors, alcohol, tissue, electroconductive paste, electrode adhesive collars, tape.

ATTENTION: (1) No biofeedback equipment should be connected to the power line (AC) unless specified by the manufacturer. Whenever any equipment is connected to the power line, be sure it is *electrically isolated* from the power line—meaning that the 120-V AC current *cannot* flow to the electrodes and hurt (i.e., electrocute) the trainee. (2) Be sure equipment is *off* before inserting or removing jacks or electrodes or replacing batteries.

OBJECTIVE

Most generally, *biofeedback*[2] may be described as the monitoring of some changing physiological process and the feeding back of the generated signal to the individual being monitored. Certain of these physiological processes are accompanied by changes in bioelectric potentials that may be monitored and used as the basis of the feedback signal. Devices have been designed to record the changing electrical activity of muscles [electromyograph (EMG)], brain [electroencephalograph (EEG)], heart [electrocardiograph (EKG)], skin [electrodermograph (EDG)], and eye [electrooculograph (EOG)]. The basic principles underlying the operation of all these devices are similar; the objective of this lab is to use one of the devices, the EMG, to gain an understanding of these basic principles.

PHYSIOLOGICAL BASIS OF THE EMG SIGNAL

The functional unit of the muscle is the *motor unit,* which consists of a number of muscle cells innervated[3] by a single nerve cell (*motor neuron*) (see Figure 3). The

[1]REFERENCE: E. Peper, S. Ancoli, & M. Quinn (Eds.), *Mind/body integration: Essential readings in biofeedback,* New York: Plenum, 1978, pp. 229-274; 363-378.

[2]A helpful guide to the scientific literature on biofeedback is: F. Butler, *Biofeedback: A survey of the literature,* New York: Plenum, 1978.

[3]*Innervated by a nerve* means activated or supplied by a nerve.

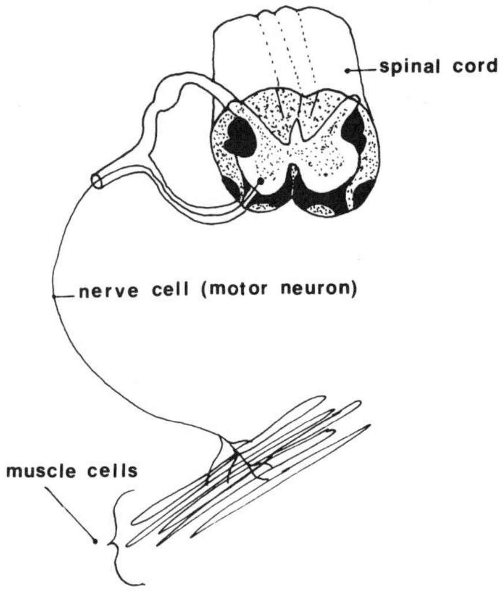

FIGURE 3. Single motor unit, consisting of a nerve cell and the muscle cells innervated by it.

activation of the single motor neuron results in contraction of all the muscle cells innervated by the neuron. This activation initiating muscle contraction is accompanied by a change in potential along both the neuron and the muscle fibers; it is this change in bioelectric potential that is the basis of the EMG signal.[4] The intensity of the signal (amplitude) is directly proportional to the number of motor units that are activated. In other words, the more muscle units activated, the larger the amplitude of the signal. Hence, the EMG signal is used as an indication of muscle activity—the greater the muscle activity the greater the amplitude of the signal.

FLOW DIAGRAM

The following flow diagram and subsequent discussion illustrate how the signal recorded from the body is processed. An understanding of this flow is important for an understanding of what the biofeedback signal actually represents and for the operation of the equipment.

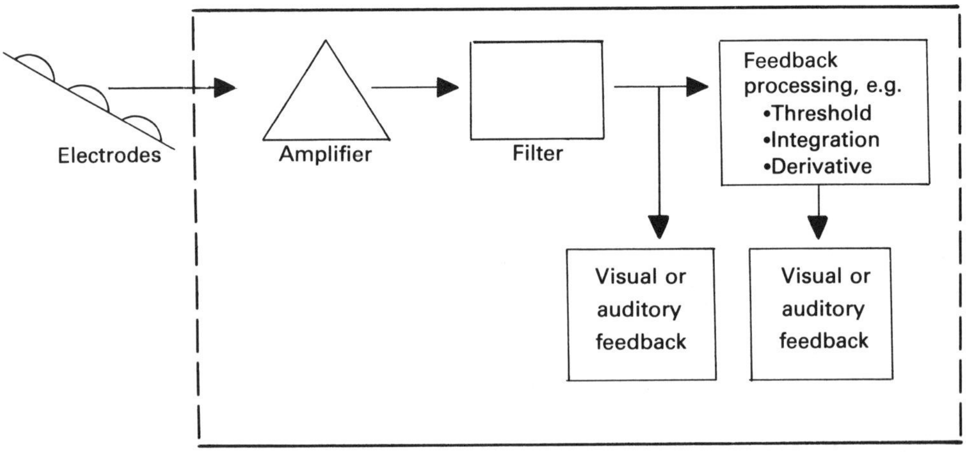

[4]See Appendix A for a review of electrical concepts.

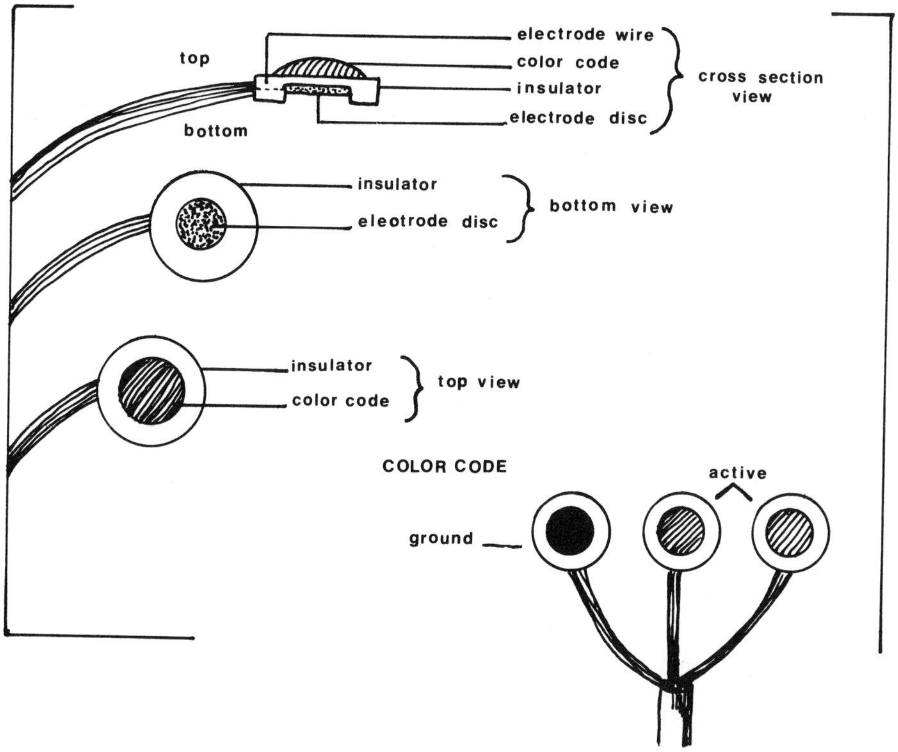

FIGURE 4. EMG electrode.

Electrodes

Electrodes are used to measure changes in electrical potential; hence they may be used for measuring muscle activity. Two different types of electrodes that are available for monitoring this activity are needle and surface electrodes. *Needle electrodes,* inserted into a muscle, are used for monitoring the activity of a single motor unit. *Surface electrodes,* placed on the skin, are used for monitoring the activity of motor units, i.e., the activity recorded by surface electrodes is the sum of motor units in proximity to the electrodes. In this lab, we will limit our discussion to surface electrodes. Figure 4 illustrates surface electrodes.

Amplification

The intensity of the EMG signal picked up by the electrodes and transmitted to the equipment is a very weak signal. It must first be amplified in order to be analyzed. Figure 5 illustrates what happens to the signal when it is amplified.

Filtering

The signal picked up by the electrodes is not only that generated by muscle activity. In fact, the signal is the sum of other bioelectric potentials (e.g., EKG), as well as environmental signals (e.g., 60 Hz) and electrical signals generated within the electrodes

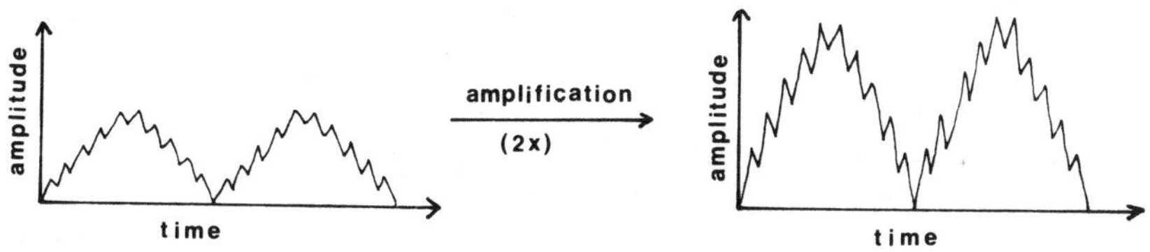

FIGURE 5. Amplification of feedback signal.

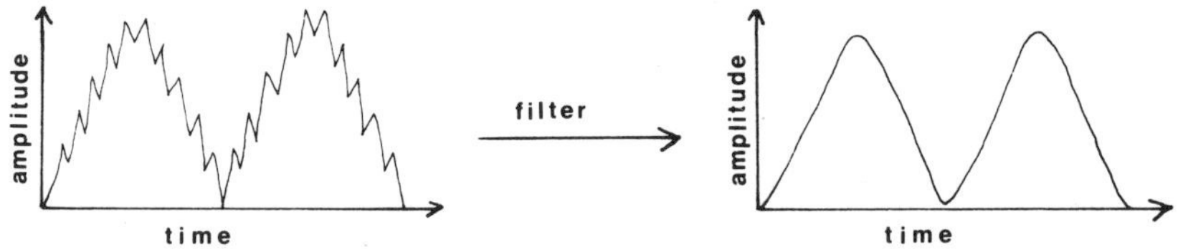

FIGURE 6. Filtering of feedback signal.

and wires themselves. All these unwanted signals unrelated to muscle activity are referred to as *artifacts*. In order to eliminate these artifacts, the incoming signal is filtered, rejecting all but certain frequencies within a certain range—this region being referred to as the *bandpass*. Bandpass characteristics vary with different manufacturers. Common ranges used are 100–200, 400–500, and 100–1000 Hz. Find the bandbass of your machine in the instruction manual. Figure 6 illustrates what happens to the signal when it is filtered. In this example, the higher frequencies are eliminated and only the lower frequencies are allowed to pass.

Processing

The signal can then be directly displayed; for example, visual or auditory feedback may be given. In this situation, any change in muscle activity would be directly shown in the signal. Or the signal may be processed

- So as to give feedback only when the signal is above or below a certain amplitude (*threshold*);
- So that the feedback represents the area under the curve of the signal over a certain time period (*integration*); or
- So that feedback is given only when there is a change in the level of activity (*derivative*).

PLACEMENT OF THE ELECTRODES

The first step in electrode placement is to identify the muscle whose activity is to be recorded. Although electrodes can be placed on almost any muscle of the body, for learning purposes start with your nondominant forearm. As you let this arm rest comfortably on your lap, have your partner place his/her hand over the forearm. Next bend your hand back at the wrist, having your partner feel where the muscle bulges most. This is where you will want to place the two active electrodes.[5] As a general rule, place the active electrodes respectively one-third and two-thirds of the way along the length of the muscle. This process of locating the muscle belly is called *palpation*. Next have your partner clean the skin in this area by rubbing with alcohol. Also clean the area over a nearby area equidistant from the two active electrodes for the ground electrode.[6] This cleaning is important in order to decrease the resistance between the electrode and the skin and to enhance conduction of the signal. Next have your partner put the electroconductive paste on the electrodes and attach the two active electrodes over the muscle belly and the ground electrode on a nearby area. Secure the electrodes either with an adhesive collar or tape. Figure 7 illustrates how to use the adhesive collar, and Figure 8, the use of tape.

OPERATION OF THE EQUIPMENT

The following is a discussion of the different functions of the EMG. It is intended to be general, and your specific machine may not have all of these functions. In order to

[5] Electrodes placed at or near the tissue under study are referred to as *active* electrodes.
[6] The *ground electrode* placed on some "neutral" tissue is connected to the earth or to the metal framework of an electrical circuit for purposes of artifact rejection.

follow this discussion, the meter and/or auditory feedback must be set in such a way as to give direct, instantaneous feedback, i.e., a change in muscle activity is directly shown in the feedback.

Battery Test

Before the electrode leads are plugged into the machine, turn on the EMG and complete a battery check if your machine has such an operation. Check your instruction manual for specific directions. You may want to see what happens to the signal when a drained battery is used. Plug electrode leads into the EMG.

Amplification

Most EMGs have an amplification switch (often referred to as *gain* or *sensitivity*) by which one can change the level of amplification of the signal. For example, for a very small signal, a large amplification may be needed in order to monitor the signal.

Relax your nondominant forearm, to which the electrodes are attached. With the machine on and with direct feedback, are you picking up a signal? If not, increase the sensitivity so that either the needle of the meter or the auditory signal is within a range where change can be observed. Always start with the least sensitive setting (lowest amplification) and increase until the signal is observable.

In order to determine the actual microvolt reading, one must account for the level of amplification. For example, if the meter reads 2 μV, and the amplification is $\times 10$, the

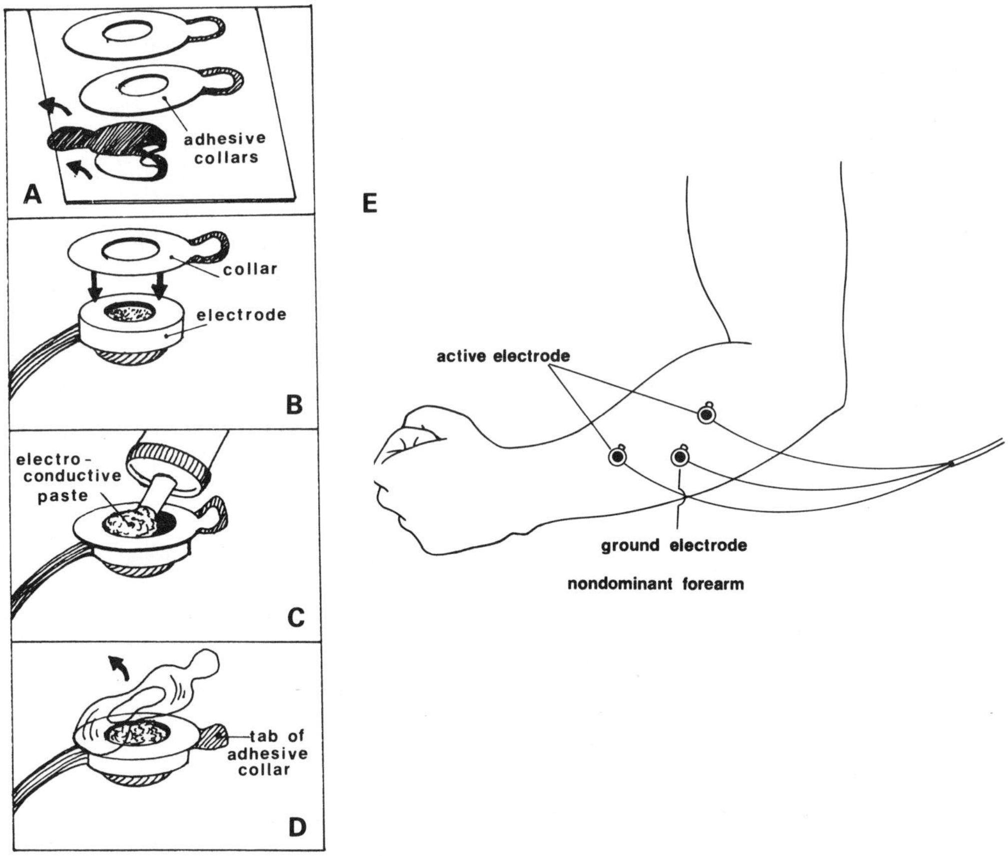

FIGURE 7. Application of EMG electrodes. (A) Collar is removed from backing. (B) Adhesive side of collar is placed onto clean electrode. (C) Hollow part of electrode is filled with electroconductive paste. (D) Top covering is removed. (E) Electrode with collar is applied onto arm.

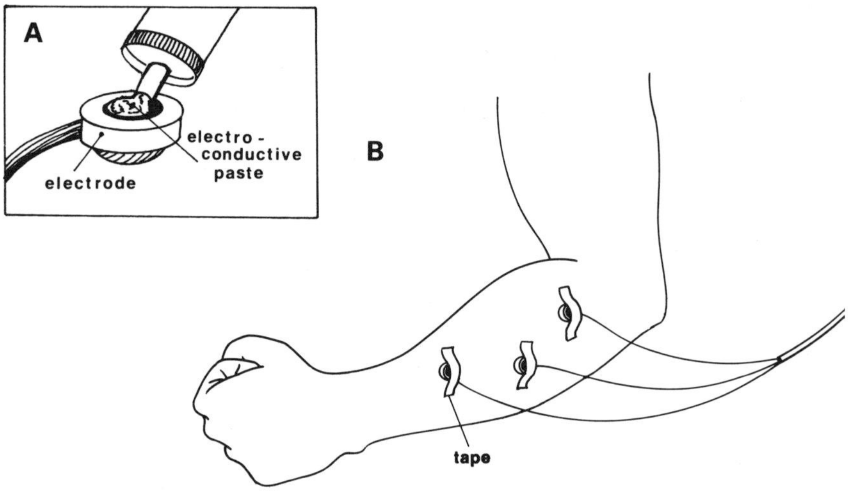

FIGURE 8. Application of EMG electrodes with tape. (A) Hollow part of electrode is filled with electroconductive paste. (B) Electrode is placed onto arm and secured with tape.

actual microvolt reading is 20 μV. What is the actual reading of your equipment with your forearm relaxed?______

Now tighten your forearm. What happens to the signal? If the signal is out of range, change the sensitivity so that you can now observe a change in the signal.

Behavioral Test

Relax your arm. Turn the sensitivity to an appropriate range, i.e., to a range in which a change can be observed. Now tighten your forearm. What happens to the signal? Now relax. Again, what happens to the signal? Were the changes in the direction you would expect? For example, when you tightened your forearm, did the signal increase? This kind of test is a *behavioral test* and is used to show that the equipment is functioning in the expected manner. It is a measure only of relative accuracy and says nothing about absolute accuracy.

Filter Setting

Some EMGs have a switch that allows one to choose the bandpass for the EMG signal. With the electrodes still on your forearm, and with your arm relaxed, change the filter settings. Note any change in the amplitude of the signal.

Filter setting (Hz)	EMG level (μV)
100–200	______
400–500	______
100–1000	______
Other:______	______

MODES OF FEEDBACK—PROCESSING THE SIGNAL

Repeat the tensing and letting go of the arm while exploring different feedback modes.

1a. Describe what happens to the auditory signal when feedback is set at "direct access" or "raw":

____

____

1b. What happens to the meter?

1c. Are they synchronous?

2a. What happens to the auditory signal when feedback is set at "tone" or "clicks"?

2b. Changes in the meter:

2c. Are they synchronous?

3a. If your machine has other modes of feedback, indicate which mode(s):

3b. Describe changes in the auditory signal:

3c. Changes in the meter:

3d. Are they synchronous?

4a. If your machine has a "threshold function," experiment with the tensing and letting go of the forearm with the switch set at different values and note the change in the auditory signal:

4b. Changes in the meter:

4c. Are they synchronous?

5a. If your machine has an "integration function," experiment with it and note the change in the auditory signal:

____

____

5b. Changes in the meter:

____

____

5c. Are they synchronous?

____

____

Have your partner remove the electrodes from your arm by gripping the electrode on the tab of the adhesive collar. Do not pull on the electrode leads. Remove the electroconductive paste with a clean tissue.

EXPLORATION OF ARTIFACTS

The following exercises are intended to acquaint one with potential sources of artifacts. It is important to know these sources in order to be able to discriminate between a signal resulting from the biological process being monitored or a signal induced by another source (i.e., an artifact). For example, say you are monitoring the frontalis and note an increase in the amplitude of the signal. Does this increase correspond to an increase in muscle tension, or is it due to the movement of the electrode leads, or to the nearby elevator going up and down? If a trainee is to learn to identify the subjective experiences associated with changes in muscle tension, the feedback signal must represent actual muscle changes; otherwise the trainee will become confused. For example, if the trainee is in fact very relaxed and the EMG is indicating an increase in muscle tension, the possibility of learning much of anything from the feedback signal is questionable.

Determination of the Noise Level of the Equipment and Electrode Artifacts

When the electrodes are attached to a trainee, the recorded signal is the result of signals picked up from the body, the noise[7] generated by the equipment and mechanical and environmental artifacts, especially those of the sensors and leads. To observe the combined noise of the equipment and the signals generated by the electrode leads, one uses a "dummy" subject: two 10-kΩ resistors, which simulate the resistance qualities of the skin but which generate no electrical signal of their own. Each of the two resistors is placed between an active and a ground electrode. The electrodes need to be firmly secured to a flat surface.

Be sure the wire leads of the resistors are clean. If necessary, use a piece of steel wool to remove any deposits on the leads.

Figure 9 illustrates the connections.

With the electrodes plugged into the EMG, turn the machine on, set the feedback for direct, instantaneous feedback, and set the sensitivity switch for the greatest sensitivity at which one can monitor the meter. Note the observed noise and electrode artifact level:______

[7]Any piece of electrical equipment generates its own internal electrical signal. These signals are referred to as *noise*. Any electrical signal weaker than those of the noise cannot be monitored unless special electrical processing techniques are used.

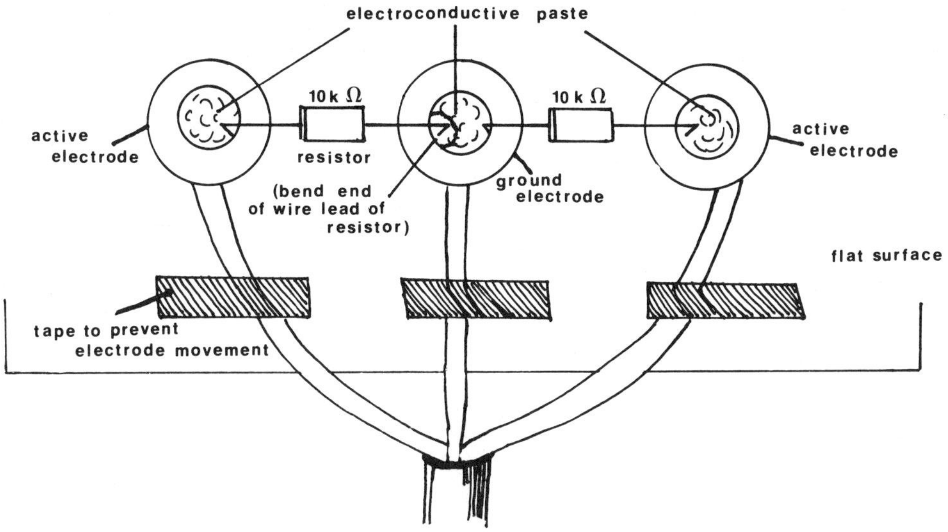

FIGURE 9. Use of "dummy" subject. Two 10,000-ohm (10-kΩ) resistors are placed between active and ground electrodes. Ends of resistor leads are embedded within electroconductive paste.

This value is important to know for each piece of equipment. It is impossible to get any signal lower than this value because this noise contributes to any reading you get.[8]

If possible, put the equipment in an electrically shielded room (Faraday cage) and repeat the determination of the combined noise and electrode artifact level. Would you expect that there would be a difference?

Exploring Mechanical and Environmental Artifacts

Explore the following activities with the electrodes still attached to the "dummy subject." Note the effect on both the auditory and visual feedback signal.

1. Touch the electrode leads.
   a. Any change in the signal?

   ____

   ____

   b. Can you explain the change?

   ____

   ____

2. Touch the electroconductive paste on one of the active electrodes.
   a. Any change in the signal?

   ____

   ____

   b. Can you explain the change?

   ____

   ____

[8]If the resistance offered by trainee's skin is less than that of the "dummy subject," the signal may in fact be lower than the value determined by this test.

3. Move the electrode leads back and forth.
   a. Any change in the signal?

   b. Can you explain the change?

4. Turn the overhead lights on and off.
   a. Any change in the signal?

   b. Can you explain the change?

5. Turn other electrical equipment (coffee pot, TV, radio, walkie-talkie, CB radio) near the EMG on and off.
   a. Any change in the signal?

   b. Can you explain the change?

6. Disconnect one of the active electrodes from the "dummy subject."
   a. Any change in the signal?

   b. Can you explain the change?

7. Touch the electroconductive paste of the loose electrode with your hand or try touching both the loose electrodes and the loose lead of the resistor.
   a. Any changes in the signal? Can you hear the 60 Hz hum?

   b. Can you explain the change?

Now have your partner reattach the electrodes on your nondominant forearm. Turn the EMG to the appropriate sensitivity and continue with direct feedback.

8. Turn the overhead lights on and off.
   a. Any change in the signal?

   b. Can you explain the change?

9. Turn other electrical equipment near the EMG on and off.
   a. Any change in the signal?

   b. Can you explain the change?

10. Were the changes in the signal the same when using a "live" participant as when using the "dummy subject"?

    If not, can you explain the difference?

Exploring Biological Artifacts—The EKG

Most of the other bioelectric signals (e.g., EEG, EDG, EOG) are eliminated by the filters of the EMG. However, frequently the EKG is present in the feedback signal, especially when the electrodes are placed over the chest or across the body. With the electrodes still on your nondominant forearm, see if you can observe the EKG signal in your feedback signal.

Now have your partner place the active electrodes on your chest muscle. Palpate this muscle by rotating the shoulders forward. Place the ground electrode on the sternum. Turn the equipment on, choose the appropriate sensitivity and use direct feedback. Do you observe any pulsing in the signal? Is this pulsing the EKG signal? (You can check by comparing with your pulse.)

Change the filter characteristics, if possible. What effect do you observe?

Roll your shoulders forward. Observe the signal. Then relax and observe the signal. Was there a difference in your ability to see the EKG artifact?

Observe what happens to the feedback signal when other modalities are used. Do you observe the EKG signal when you use "integration," "threshold," or "derivative"?

What are the best settings for your machine in order to discriminate whether an artifact is contaminating the signal?

LAB II
Location of Muscle Tension

EQUIPMENT

EMG, alcohol, tissue, electroconductive paste, electrode adhesive collars, tape.

In order to complete this lab and subsequent EMG labs successfully, one must be familiar with the material of Lab I and be able to operate the EMG equipment. It is assumed that before beginning to use the equipment one will proceed through the following steps:

1. Complete a battery check and determine that the equipment is working;
2. Place the electrodes properly;
3. Choose an appropriate sensitivity to provide meaningful feedback;
4. Complete a behavioral test; and
5. Where applicable, select appropriate settings for time integration, threshold, feedback modality, and any other function present on your EMG.

OBJECTIVE

Each of us responds to stress in different ways: some tighten in the abdominal area and breathe shallowly, some tighten their shoulders, others clench their fists and tighten their forearms. Some, in fact, do not manifest their tension in voluntary muscles, but rather in some other way such as increased acid secretion in the stomach. The objective of this lab is for you to identify a muscle group (or groups) in which you hold tension.

INSTRUCTIONS

Self-Observation Exercise

Sit comfortably and begin by imagining some situation that is stressful to you: go back to an area of unresolved conflict, or remember a time of intense anger, sadness, or fear, or a time of public performance (such as public speaking or athletic competition). Recapture the situation as clearly as possible. Now scan your body (i.e., observe your body) for the location of muscular tension. Indicate these areas on the Lab II: Worksheet as well as the intensity of muscle tension felt in each area. Describe the image you used. Have your partner complete this step at this time.

Monitoring Muscle Tension with the EMG

Since the EMG monitors muscle tension, you may use the EMG to confirm or disprove your self-observation of tension. Begin by having your partner place the electrodes on the muscle that you experienced as most tense. See Figure 10, which shows the superficial muscles and active electrode placements that may be used in biofeedback

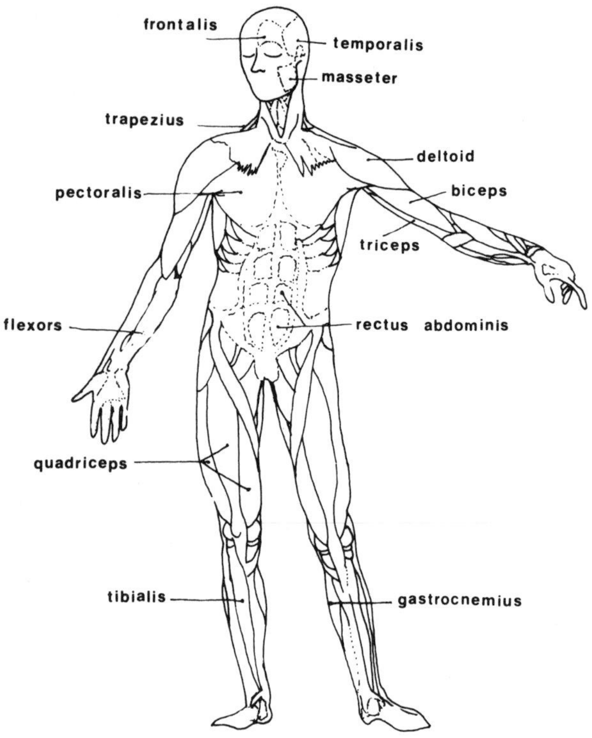

FIGURE 10A. Major muscle groups—ventral view.

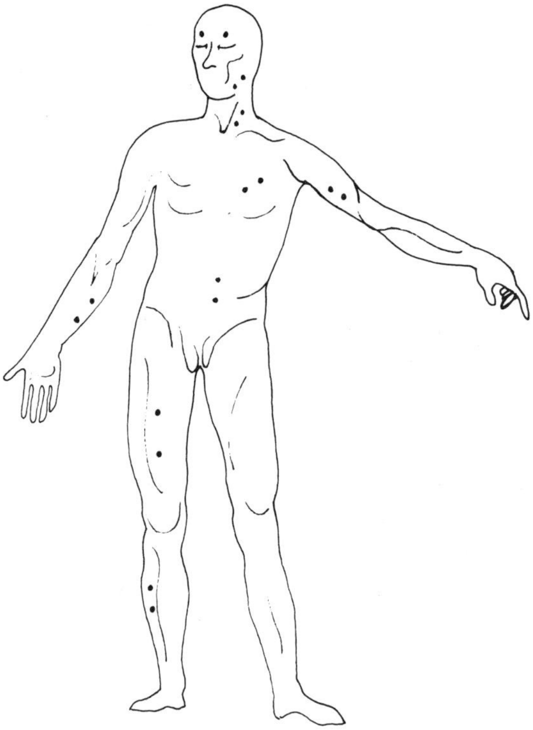

FIGURE 10B. Location for placement of active electrodes over major muscle groups—ventral view.

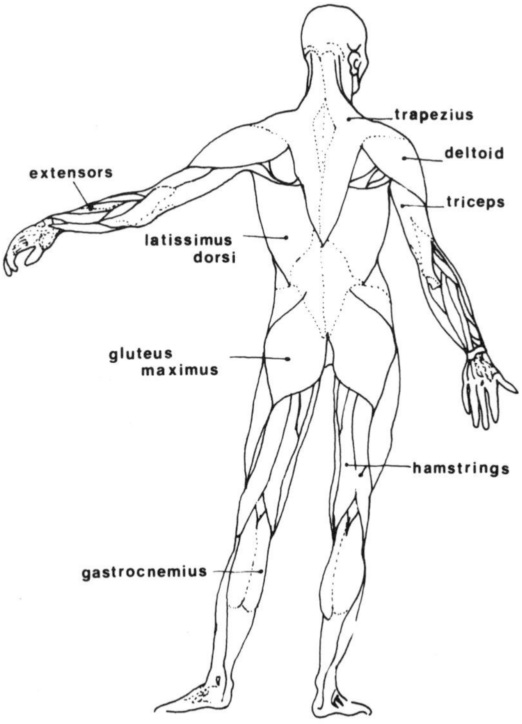

FIGURE 10C. Major muscle groups—dorsal view.

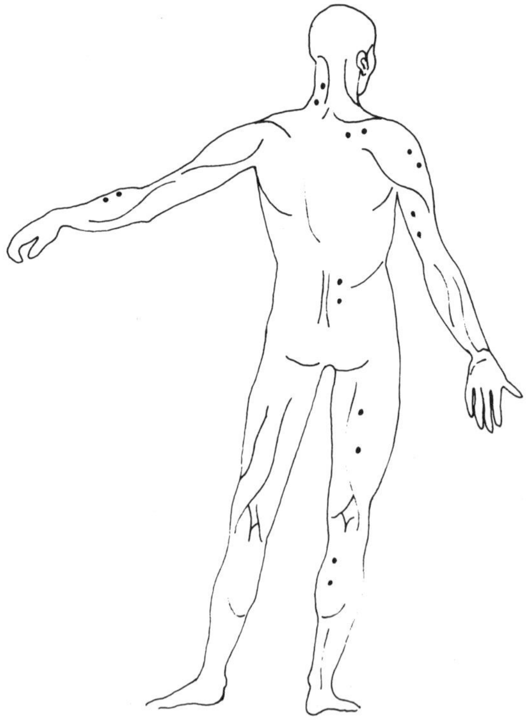

FIGURE 10D. Location for placement of active electrodes over major muscle groups—dorsal view.

training.[1] Choose a comfortable position, maintaining this position throughout the time of EMG recording. Do this lab without feedback. This means that you can neither see the visual feedback (meter, colored lights, etc.) nor hear the auditory signals (clicks, variable tone, etc.). Close your eyes and relax for a few minutes. Have your partner record your baseline measurements[2] for three minutes at intervals of ten seconds on the Lab II: Data Sheet—Muscle Group 1.

Now imagine the same stressful situation that you used in the self-observation exercise. Indicate to your partner when you are involved in the image by raising a finger. Your partner will begin to record your measurements for 2 min at 10-sec intervals, after which s/he will indicate to you that it is time to "let go of the image and relax" for a few minutes. Your partner will record your measurements for the first 2 min of this time at 10-sec intervals. Next record from another muscle group that you identified as tense during the self-observation exercise. Repeat the same procedure and record on Lab II: Data Sheet—Muscle Group 2.

Then record from a muscle group that you did not identify as holding tension (perhaps your partner may have noticed a muscle tightening that you did not), recording on Lab II: Data Sheet—Muscle Group 3.[3]

If you found that you did *not* respond in any muscle group to an imagined stressor:

1. You may not have selected a meaningful image or have allowed yourself to become involved in the image;
2. The muscles monitored may have been so tense during the baseline period that any contribution triggered by the visualization was masked; or
3. You may not be a muscle responder.

In order to determine the cause of the lack of muscle responsiveness, try the following:

1. Allow yourself to become more involved in the image by elaborating on the details of the scene and attending to the physiological responses elicited by the scene (for example, remember—and feel—your heart pounding and hands trembling when you were scared).
2. Repeat the lab at another time with another image. Attempt to do the lab as soon after some intense emotional experience as possible.
3. Do some relaxation exercise to quiet those muscles from which you are recording (like MPR or biofeedback training), and then repeat the lab.

If you still find that you do not respond to imagined stressors with muscle tension, you may be responding in another physiological system. In order to complete Labs III and

[1]As a general rule, in order to record the maximum activity of a muscle, place the active electrodes respectively approximately one-third and two-thirds of the way along the length of the muscle.

[2]In order to observe whether a given task or experience affects the physiological process being monitored, one must record the level of activity of the physiological process *before* the start of the task for comparison. The measurements taken during this pretask period are together called the *baseline*. The length of the baseline period is somewhat arbitrary, but should at least allow for the system to adapt to the environment, i.e., to stabilize. For example, in a study where one is training subjects to decrease heart rate, if a subject came in after running up the stairs and training was started immediately, a lowering of heart rate would be observed; however, the subject may not have *learned* anything, this decrease merely reflecting relaxation after strenuous exercise.

[3]For a detailed discussion of muscles, refer to a basic anatomy text, such as J. Crouch, *Functional human anatomy*, Philadelphia: Lea & Febiger, 1978. If you have access to more than one EMG, you may want to monitor several muscles simultaneously instead of sequentially.

IV, you will need to monitor another system, such as pulse rate, respiration pattern, or respiration rate.

Repeat this same procedure for your partner.

Graph your data and complete Lab II: Questions. Then meet with your group and complete Lab II: Discussion and Conclusions.

Trainee ____________________

Date ________

LAB II WORKSHEET

	Intensity of tension				
	A little tense		Tense		Extremely tense
Muscle observed as tense	1	2	3	4	5
1. ____________					
2. ____________					
3. ____________					
4. ____________					
5. ____________					

Describe image:

____

____

____

____

____

Trainee ____________________

Trainer ____________________

Date __________

LAB II DATA SHEET—MUSCLE GROUP 1

Muscle Group 1 (or where monitored): ____________________

	EMG baseline measurements (preimaging)	Measurements after trainee is "involved" in image	Measurements after "relax" instruction (postimaging)
at	0 sec ______ μV[4]	0 sec ______ μV	0 sec ______ μV
	10 sec ______ μV	10 sec ______ μV	10 sec ______ μV
	20 sec ______ μV	20 sec ______ μV	20 sec ______ μV
	30 sec ______ μV	30 sec ______ μV	30 sec ______ μV
	40 sec ______ μV	40 sec ______ μV	40 sec ______ μV
	50 sec ______ μV	50 sec ______ μV	50 sec ______ μV
	60 sec ______ μV	60 sec ______ μV	60 sec ______ μV
	70 sec ______ μV	70 sec ______ μV	70 sec ______ μV
	80 sec ______ μV	80 sec ______ μV	80 sec ______ μV
	90 sec ______ μV	90 sec ______ μV	90 sec ______ μV
	100 sec ______ μV	100 sec ______ μV	100 sec ______ μV
	110 sec ______ μV	110 sec ______ μV	110 sec ______ μV
	120 sec ______ μV	120 sec ______ μV	120 sec ______ μV
	130 sec ______ μV		
	140 sec ______ μV		
	150 sec ______ μV		
	160 sec ______ μV		
	170 sec ______ μV		
	180 sec ______ μV		

[4]If your equipment uses a scale that does not read in microvolts, use the numerical values on the scale without the units.

Trainee ____________________

Trainer ____________________

Date ____________

LAB II GRAPH—MUSCLE GROUP 1[5]

Muscle Group 1: ________________________________

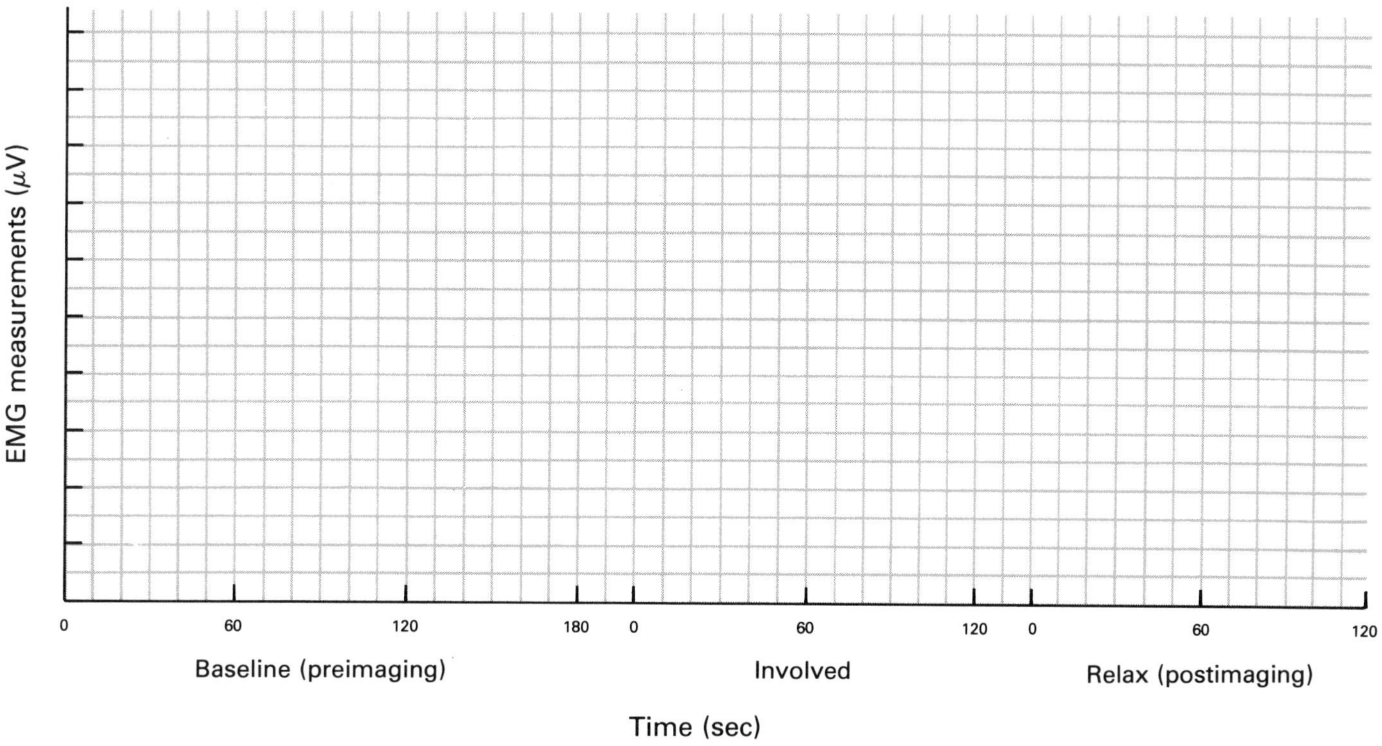

[5]See Appendix B for graphing instructions.

Trainee ____________________

Trainer ____________________

Date __________

LAB II DATA SHEET—MUSCLE GROUP 2

Muscle Group 2 (or where monitored): ____________________

	EMG baseline measurements (preimaging)	Measurements after trainee is "involved" in image	Measurements after "relax" instruction (postimaging)
at	0 sec ______ μV	0 sec ______ μV	0 sec ______ μV
	10 sec ______ μV	10 sec ______ μV	10 sec ______ μV
	20 sec ______ μV	20 sec ______ μV	20 sec ______ μV
	30 sec ______ μV	30 sec ______ μV	30 sec ______ μV
	40 sec ______ μV	40 sec ______ μV	40 sec ______ μV
	50 sec ______ μV	50 sec ______ μV	50 sec ______ μV
	60 sec ______ μV	60 sec ______ μV	60 sec ______ μV
	70 sec ______ μV	70 sec ______ μV	70 sec ______ μV
	80 sec ______ μV	80 sec ______ μV	80 sec ______ μV
	90 sec ______ μV	90 sec ______ μV	90 sec ______ μV
	100 sec ______ μV	100 sec ______ μV	100 sec ______ μV
	110 sec ______ μV	110 sec ______ μV	110 sec ______ μV
	120 sec ______ μV	120 sec ______ μV	120 sec ______ μV
	130 sec ______ μV		
	140 sec ______ μV		
	150 sec ______ μV		
	160 sec ______ μV		
	170 sec ______ μV		
	180 sec ______ μV		

Trainee ____________________

Trainer ____________________

Date __________

LAB II GRAPH—MUSCLE GROUP 2

Muscle Group 2: ______________________________

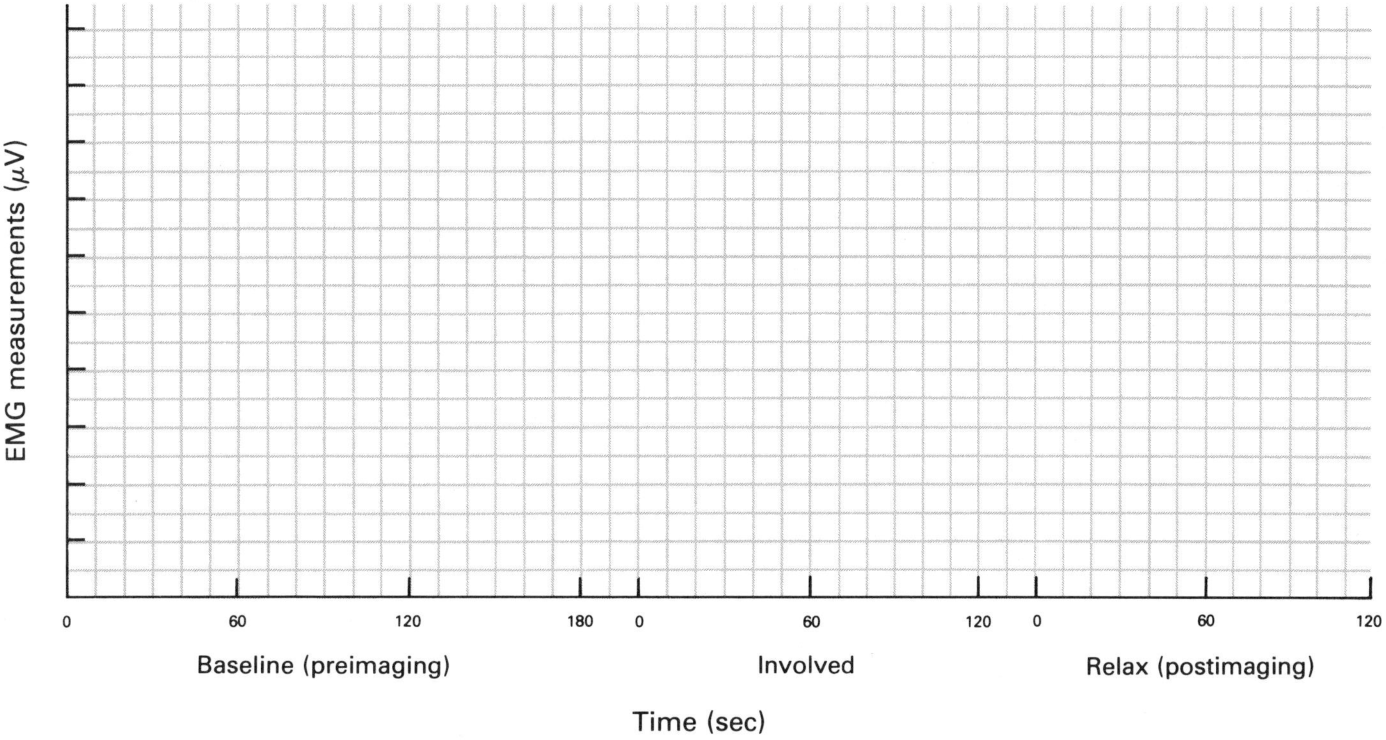

Trainee ____________________

Trainer ____________________

Date __________

LAB II DATA SHEET—MUSCLE GROUP 3

Muscle Group 3 (or where monitored): ____________________

	EMG baseline measurements (preimaging)	Measurements after trainee is "involved" in image	Measurements after "relax" instruction (postimaging)
at	0 sec _____ μV	0 sec _____ μV	0 sec _____ μV
	10 sec _____ μV	10 sec _____ μV	10 sec _____ μV
	20 sec _____ μV	20 sec _____ μV	20 sec _____ μV
	30 sec _____ μV	30 sec _____ μV	30 sec _____ μV
	40 sec _____ μV	40 sec _____ μV	40 sec _____ μV
	50 sec _____ μV	50 sec _____ μV	50 sec _____ μV
	60 sec _____ μV	60 sec _____ μV	60 sec _____ μV
	70 sec _____ μV	70 sec _____ μV	70 sec _____ μV
	80 sec _____ μV	80 sec _____ μV	80 sec _____ μV
	90 sec _____ μV	90 sec _____ μV	90 sec _____ μV
	100 sec _____ μV	100 sec _____ μV	100 sec _____ μV
	110 sec _____ μV	110 sec _____ μV	110 sec _____ μV
	120 sec _____ μV	120 sec _____ μV	120 sec _____ μV
	130 sec _____ μV		
	140 sec _____ μV		
	150 sec _____ μV		
	160 sec _____ μV		
	170 sec _____ μV		
	180 sec _____ μV		

Trainee ____________________

Trainer ____________________

Date __________

LAB II GRAPH—MUSCLE GROUP 3

Muscle Group 3: ______________________________

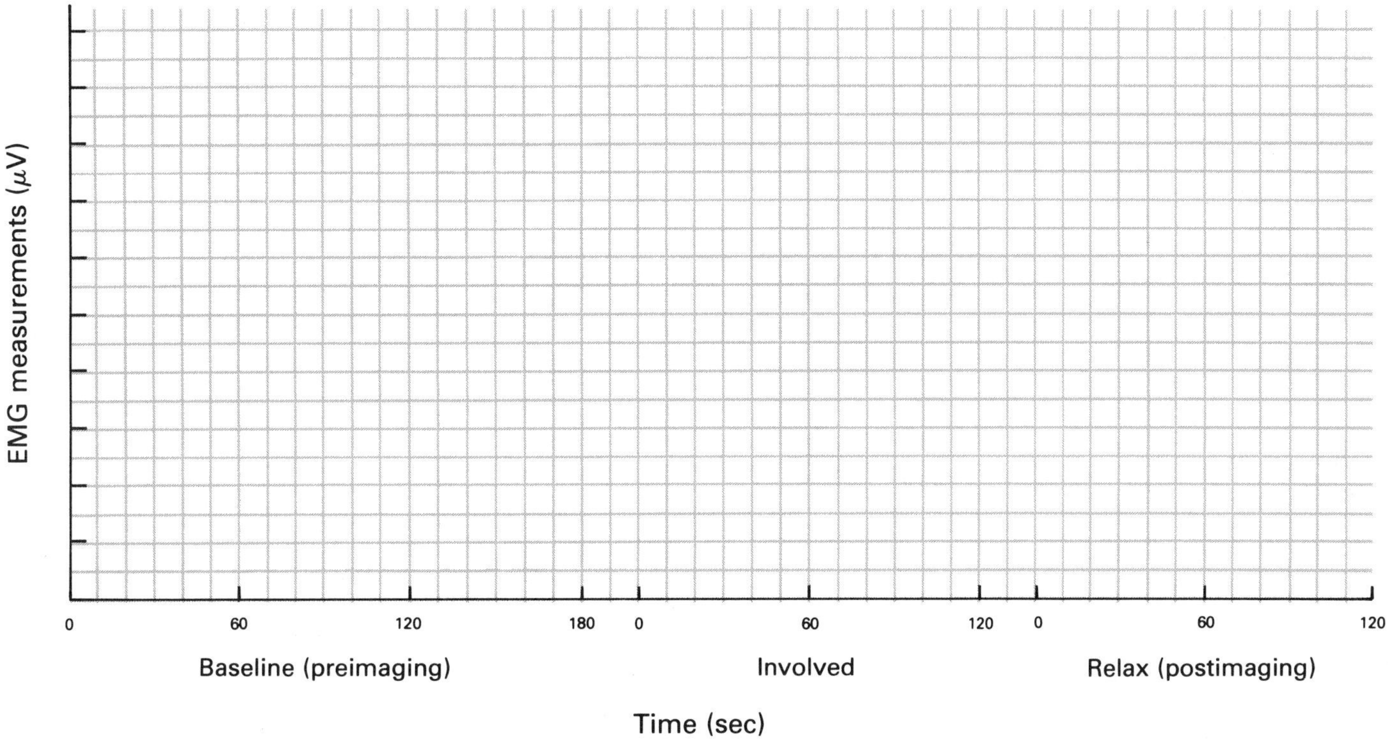

Trainee ______________________

Date __________

LAB II QUESTIONS

1. Were the muscles observed to be tense during the self-observation exercise shown to be tense with the EMG?

____

2. Was there congruence between the level of muscle tension recorded by the EMG during imaging and the intensity you noted during the self-observation exercise?

____

____

____

____

3. Were there muscles shown to be tense with the EMG that you did not indicate as holding tension during the self-observation exercise?

____

____

____

4. Looking at the postimaging recordings on your graphs, how rapidly did the tension drop to baseline values? Would you conclude that it is easy or difficult for you to let go of muscle tension?

____

____

____

5. Comments:

____

____

____

Trainee ______________________

Date __________

LAB II DISCUSSION AND CONCLUSIONS

Meet with your group and complete the following tally. Then complete the bar graph.

Muscle group identified as holding tension	Number of persons	Tally
1. Forehead (frontalis)	______	
2. Shoulders (trapezius)	______	
3. Jaw (masseter)	______	
4. Chest (pectoralis)	______	
5. Abdomen	______	
6. ______________________	______	
7. ______________________	______	
8. ______________________	______	

Bar graph

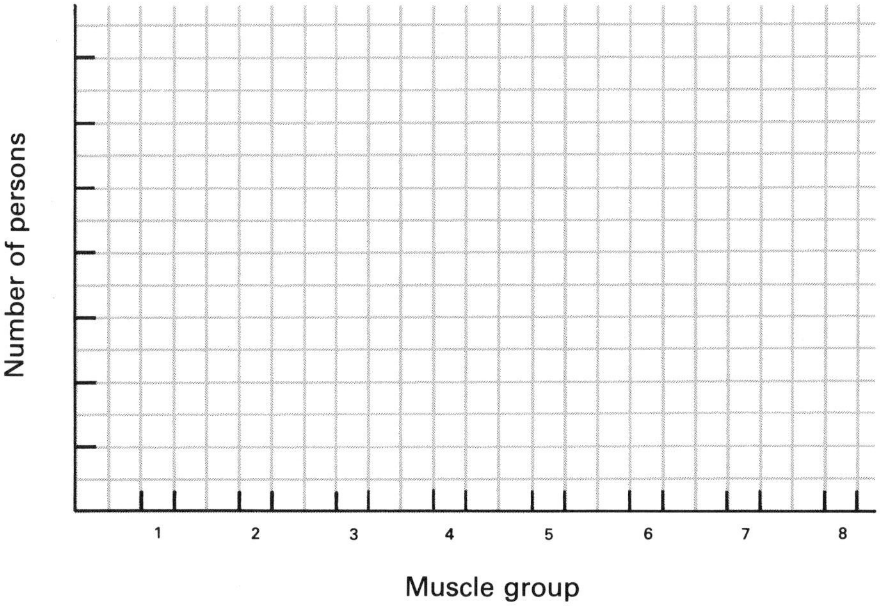

1. Looking at the group data, did you find that others hold tension in the same muscles as you do?

2. Do those persons who hold tension in the same muscle groups (e.g., neck area) report common pathologies (e.g., tension headache)? Describe the relationships.

3. Are there sex or age differences in the location of body tension?

4. Were there some persons who experienced no change in EMG levels during imaging and were similarities among these persons noted that may account for the lack of reactivity?

5. Was there variation in your group in the ability to let go of muscle tension? Does this ability relate to the potency of the image or some other factor? Discuss.

SUGGESTIONS FOR FUTURE RESEARCH

1. Explore laterality difference in muscle tensions when imaging.

LAB III

Experience of Imagined Stressor

EQUIPMENT

EMG, alcohol, tissue, electroconductive paste, electrode adhesive collars, tape.

OBJECTIVE

As people vary in the way that they manifest their tension, i.e., how they physically respond to stressors, they also vary in the manner in which they subjectively experience the stressor. In this lab you will look at how you experience an imagined stressor, the relationship between your physical response and your reported subjective experience, and which imagined stressor elicits the most intense response.[1]

INSTRUCTIONS

Have your partner place the EMG electrodes on the muscle group that you determined to be most responsive in Lab II. Use this same muscle group throughout this lab. Choose a comfortable position, maintaining this same position throughout the time of EMG recording. Do this lab without feedback. Close your eyes and relax for a few moments. Have your partner record your baseline measurements for 3 min at intervals of 10 sec on Lab III: Data Sheet—Image 1. Now imagine some situation that is stressful. Indicate to your partner when you are involved in the image by raising a finger. Then have your partner record your measurements for 2 min at 10-sec intervals, after which time s/he will indicate to you that it is time to let go of the image and "relax" for a few minutes. Your partner will record your measurements for the first 2 min of this time at 10-sec intervals. Answer Lab III: Questions—Image 1.

Now repeat this procedure holding a different stressful image, e.g., if you imagined a fearful situation, try a sad one. If time permits, try a third image. Now repeat the procedure for your partner. Graph your data and complete Lab III: Summary of Questions. Meet with your group and complete Lab III: Discussion and Conclusions.

[1]One may respond to stress in systems other than or in addition to the voluntary muscles (e.g., cardiovascular, respiratory). Hence feedback equipment that monitors these other systems (e.g., EKG, blood pressure) may also be used to monitor the physiological response to stress.

Trainee ______________________

Trainer ______________________

Date __________

LAB III DATA SHEET—IMAGE 1

Image 1: ____

	EMG baseline measurements (preimaging)	Measurements after trainee is "involved" in image	Measurements after "relax" instruction (postimaging)
at	0 sec _____ μV	0 sec _____ μV	0 sec _____ μV
	10 sec _____ μV	10 sec _____ μV	10 sec _____ μV
	20 sec _____ μV	20 sec _____ μV	20 sec _____ μV
	30 sec _____ μV	30 sec _____ μV	30 sec _____ μV
	40 sec _____ μV	40 sec _____ μV	40 sec _____ μV
	50 sec _____ μV	50 sec _____ μV	50 sec _____ μV
	60 sec _____ μV	60 sec _____ μV	60 sec _____ μV
	70 sec _____ μV	70 sec _____ μV	70 sec _____ μV
	80 sec _____ μV	80 sec _____ μV	80 sec _____ μV
	90 sec _____ μV	90 sec _____ μV	90 sec _____ μV
	100 sec _____ μV	100 sec _____ μV	100 sec _____ μV
	110 sec _____ μV	110 sec _____ μV	110 sec _____ μV
	120 sec _____ μV	120 sec _____ μV	120 sec _____ μV
	130 sec _____ μV		
	140 sec _____ μV		
	150 sec _____ μV		
	160 sec _____ μV		
	170 sec _____ μV		
	180 sec _____ μV		

Trainee ______________________

Date __________

LAB III QUESTIONS—IMAGE 1

Image 1: ____

1. When you imagined the stressful scene, where did you visualize it? (In your head? In front of you? In your stomach? etc.)

____

____

2. Did you experience yourself as a part of the scene or was it more like viewing a movie?

____

____

3. How involved in the situation were you relative to the original experience?

Less		Same		More
1	2	3	4	5

4. How intensely did you feel sensations in your body?

A little		Some		A lot
1	2	3	4	5

5. Did you notice any body changes during the time when you were imagining the stressful situation? If yes, what were they?

____

____

____

6. Did you experience the period of time from when you raised your finger indicating involvement with your image until the time you were told to let go of the image as

Less than 2 min____ About 2 min____ Longer than 2 min____

7. While imaging the stressful situation did you experience any of the following?

	Yes	No
Warmth or cold	___	___
Sound	___	___
Taste	___	___
Smell	___	___
Pressure	___	___

8. How easy was it to let go of the image and let yourself relax?

Not easy		Easy		Very easy
1	2	3	4	5

Trainee ____________________

Trainer ____________________

Date ____________

LAB III GRAPH—IMAGE 1

Image 1: ____

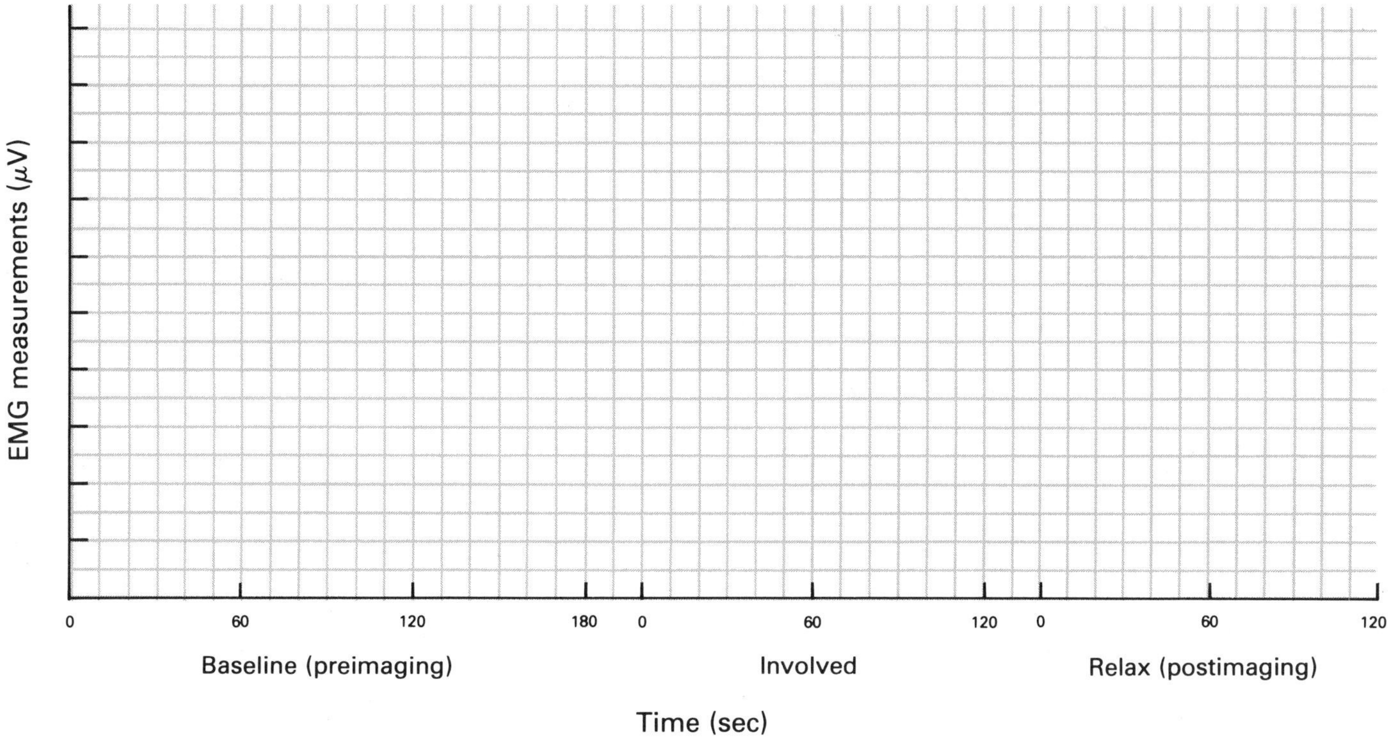

Trainee ____________________

Trainer ____________________

Date ____________

LAB III DATA SHEET—IMAGE 2

Image 2: ____

	EMG baseline measurements (preimaging)	Measurements after trainee is "involved" in image	Measurements after "relax" instruction (postimaging)
at	0 sec ______μV	0 sec ______μV	0 sec ______μV
	10 sec ______μV	10 sec ______μV	10 sec ______μV
	20 sec ______μV	20 sec ______μV	20 sec ______μV
	30 sec ______μV	30 sec ______μV	30 sec ______μV
	40 sec ______μV	40 sec ______μV	40 sec ______μV
	50 sec ______μV	50 sec ______μV	50 sec ______μV
	60 sec ______μV	60 sec ______μV	60 sec ______μV
	70 sec ______μV	70 sec ______μV	70 sec ______μV
	80 sec ______μV	80 sec ______μV	80 sec ______μV
	90 sec ______μV	90 sec ______μV	90 sec ______μV
	100 sec ______μV	100 sec ______μV	100 sec ______μV
	110 sec ______μV	110 sec ______μV	110 sec ______μV
	120 sec ______μV	120 sec ______μV	120 sec ______μV
	130 sec ______μV		
	140 sec ______μV		
	150 sec ______μV		
	160 sec ______μV		
	170 sec ______μV		
	180 sec ______μV		

Trainee ______________________

Date __________

LAB III QUESTIONS—IMAGE 2

Image 1: ____

1. When you imagined the stressful scene, where did you visualize it? (In your head? In front of you? In your stomach? etc.)

____

____

2. Did you experience yourself as a part of the scene or was it more like viewing a movie?

____

____

3. How involved in the situation were you relative to the original experience?

Less		Same		More
1	2	3	4	5

4. How intensely did you feel sensations in your body?

A little		Some		A lot
1	2	3	4	5

5. Did you notice any body changes during the time when you were imagining the stressful situation? If yes, what were they?

____

____

____

6. Did you experience the period of time from when you raised your finger indicating involvement with your image until the time you were told to let go of the image as

Less than 2 min___ About 2 min___ Longer than 2 min___

7. While imaging the stressful situation did you experience any of the following?

	Yes	No
Warmth or cold	___	___
Sound	___	___
Taste	___	___
Smell	___	___
Pressure	___	___

8. How easy was it to let go of the image and let yourself relax?

Not easy		Easy		Very easy
1	2	3	4	5

Trainee ____________________

Trainer ____________________

Date ____________

LAB III GRAPH—IMAGE 2

Image 2: ____

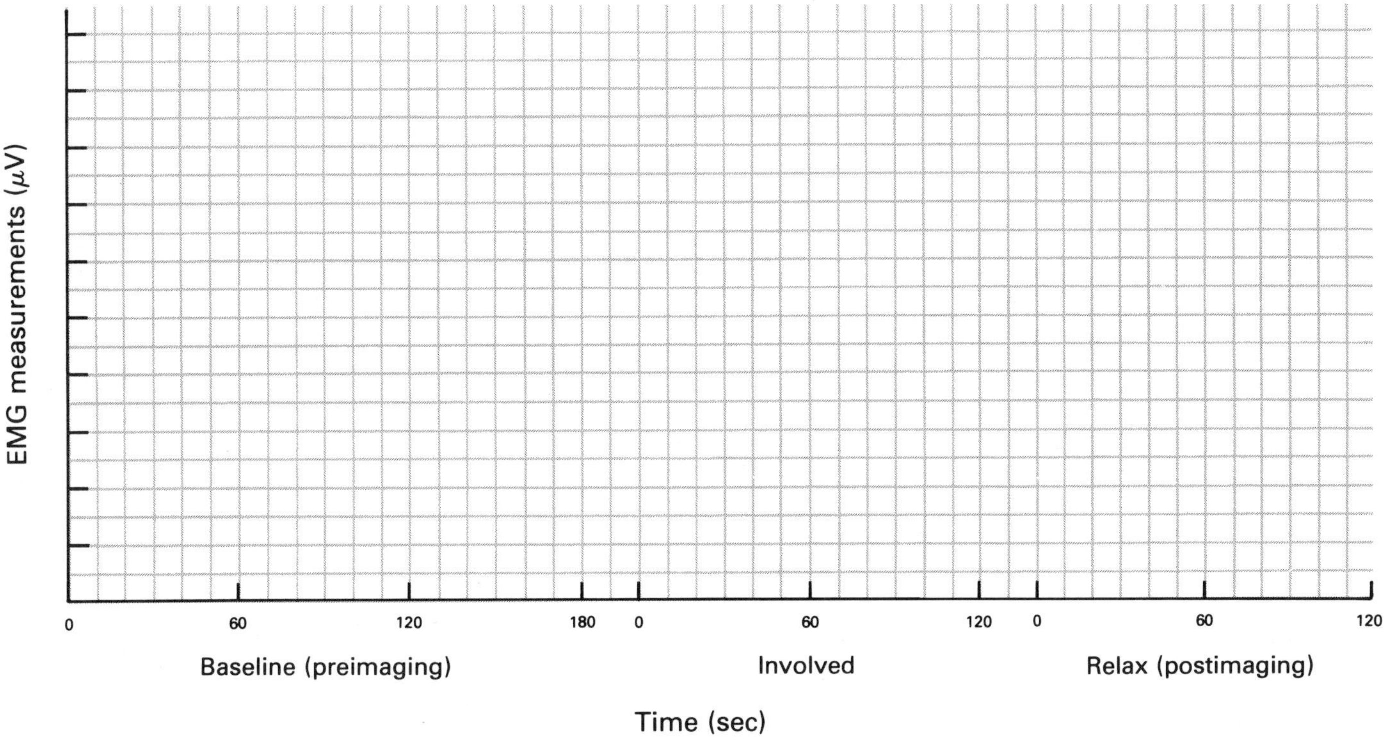

Trainee ____________________

Trainer ____________________

Date __________

LAB III DATA SHEET—IMAGE 3

Image 3: ____

	EMG baseline measurements (preimaging)	Measurements after trainee is "involved" in image	Measurements after "relax" instruction (postimaging)
at	0 sec ______ μV	0 sec ______ μV	0 sec ______ μV
	10 sec ______ μV	10 sec ______ μV	10 sec ______ μV
	20 sec ______ μV	20 sec ______ μV	20 sec ______ μV
	30 sec ______ μV	30 sec ______ μV	30 sec ______ μV
	40 sec ______ μV	40 sec ______ μV	40 sec ______ μV
	50 sec ______ μV	50 sec ______ μV	50 sec ______ μV
	60 sec ______ μV	60 sec ______ μV	60 sec ______ μV
	70 sec ______ μV	70 sec ______ μV	70 sec ______ μV
	80 sec ______ μV	80 sec ______ μV	80 sec ______ μV
	90 sec ______ μV	90 sec ______ μV	90 sec ______ μV
	100 sec ______ μV	100 sec ______ μV	100 sec ______ μV
	110 sec ______ μV	110 sec ______ μV	110 sec ______ μV
	120 sec ______ μV	120 sec ______ μV	120 sec ______ μV
	130 sec ______ μV		
	140 sec ______ μV		
	150 sec ______ μV		
	160 sec ______ μV		
	170 sec ______ μV		
	180 sec ______ μV		

Trainee ______________________

Date ____________

LAB III QUESTIONS—IMAGE 3

Image 1: ______________________________________

1. When you imagined the stressful scene, where did you visualize it? (In your head? In front of you? In your stomach? etc.)

____

____

2. Did you experience yourself as a part of the scene or was it more like viewing a movie?

____

____

3. How involved in the situation were you relative to the original experience?

Less		Same		More
1	2	3	4	5

4. How intensely did you feel sensations in your body?

A little		Some		A lot
1	2	3	4	5

5. Did you notice any body changes during the time when you were imagining the stressful situation? If yes, what were they?

____

____

____

6. Did you experience the period of time from when you raised your finger indicating involvement with your image until the time you were told to let go of the image as

Less than 2 min____ About 2 min____ Longer than 2 min____

7. While imaging the stressful situation did you experience any of the following?

	Yes	No
Warmth or cold	___	___
Sound	___	___
Taste	___	___
Smell	___	___
Pressure	___	___

8. How easy was it to let go of the image and let yourself relax?

Not easy		Easy		Very easy
1	2	3	4	5

Trainee ______________________

Trainer ______________________

Date __________

LAB III GRAPH—IMAGE 3

Image 3: ____

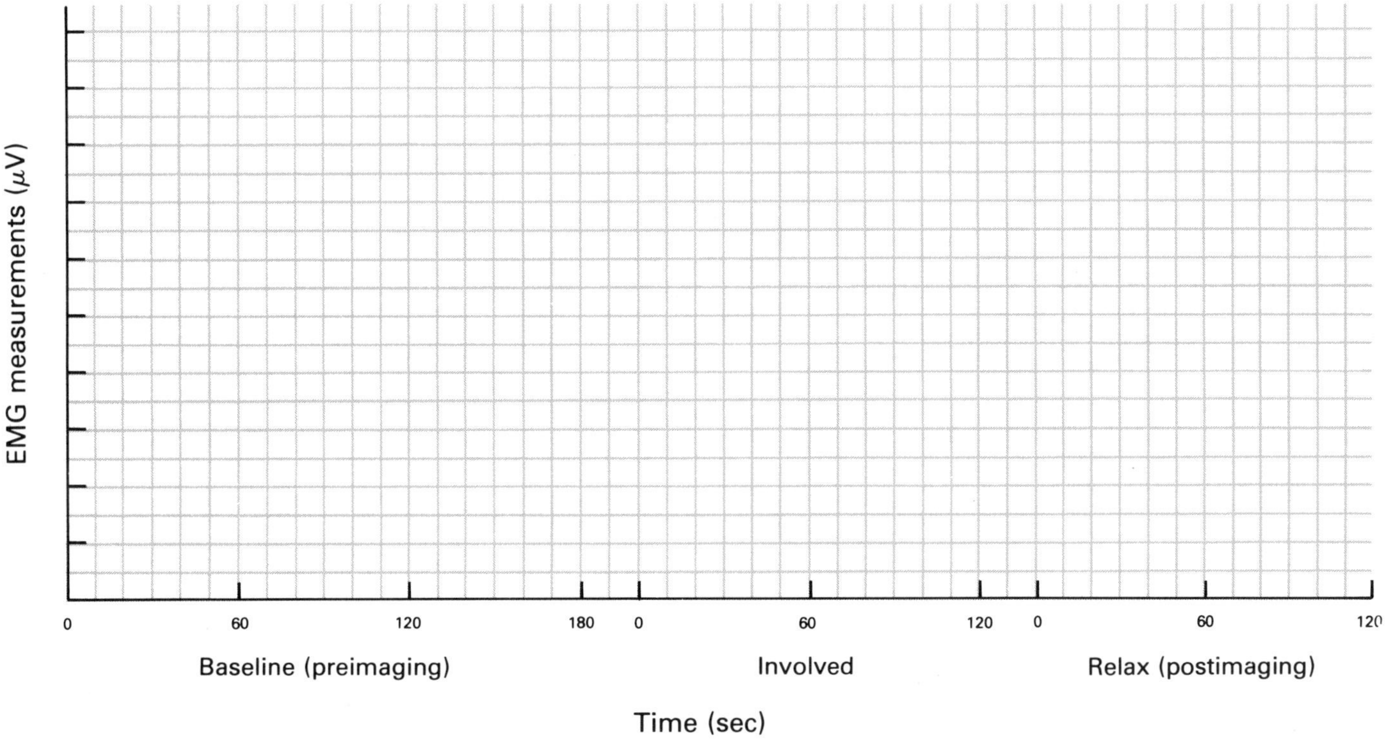

Trainee ______________________________

Date ____________

LAB III SUMMARY OF QUESTIONS

1. Comparing your responses to the Questions for the different imagined stressors, did you react differently to the different images? If so, in what way? (Where you visualized the image? Your involvement? etc.) Can you draw any conclusions about how you experience an imagined stressful situation?

2. If the intensity of body sensations varied with different images (Question 4), rank the images in order of increasing intensity of response:
   Least intense response: ______________________________

   Most intense response: ______________________________

3. Did you find a congruence between the intensity of your subjective report and the intensity of your physical response as measured by the EMG? (For example, did the image ranked as having the most intense response show the greater change in EMG recording?)

4. Comments:

Trainee ______________________

Date __________

LAB III DISCUSSION AND CONCLUSIONS

1. Did the patterns of response vary within your group? For example, did the individuals who experienced the images in the gut and themselves as a part of the image rank themselves as highly involved in the image? Discuss.

2. Were the individuals who were most involved in their images the same ones who found it difficult to let go of the images? Discuss implications.

3. Were there images that evoked intense response that were common to members of the group?

LAB IV

Experience of Imagined Stressor with Feedback[1]

EQUIPMENT

EMG, alcohol, tissue, electroconductive paste, electrode adhesive collars, tape.

OBJECTIVE

Using the EMG signal as feedback, one can learn to decrease the tension in the muscle being monitored. In learning this skill, does one's subjective experience of the imagined stressor producing the muscle tension change? In this lab, you will explore this question.

INSTRUCTIONS

Have your partner place the EMG electrodes on the muscle group that you determined to be most responsive in Lab II. Use this same muscle group throughout this lab. Choose a comfortable position, maintaining this same position throughout the time of EMG recording. Do this lab with auditory feedback *during* the time of imaging. Close your eyes and relax for a few moments. Have your partner record your baseline measurements for 3 min at intervals of 10 sec (no feedback) on Lab IV: Data Sheet. Then have your partner turn on the feedback signal.

Now imagine the situation that you found most stressful in Lab III. Indicate to your partner when you are involved in the image by raising a finger. Now, while you continue to hold the image, keep the feedback signal to a minimum. For example, if you are hearing clicks, the rapidity of which corresponds to the tension in the muscle being monitored, try to keep the rate of the clicks as low as possible. Your partner will record your measurements for 2 min at 10-sec intervals, after which time s/he will indicate to you that it is time to let go of the image and "relax" for a few minutes. The feedback signal will be turned off at this point. Your partner will record your measurements for the first 2 min of this time at 10-sec intervals. Answer Lab IV: Questions.

Now repeat this procedure for your partner. Graph your data and complete Lab IV: Summary of Questions. Meet with your group and complete Lab IV: Discussion and Conclusions.

[1]REFERENCE: *Mind/body integration,* pp. 453–464.

Trainee ____________________

Trainer ____________________

Date __________

LAB IV DATA SHEET

Image: ____

	EMG baseline measurements (preimaging)	Measurements after trainee is "involved" in image	Measurements after "relax" instruction (postimaging)
at	0 sec ______ μV	0 sec ______ μV	0 sec ______ μV
	10 sec ______ μV	10 sec ______ μV	10 sec ______ μV
	20 sec ______ μV	20 sec ______ μV	20 sec ______ μV
	30 sec ______ μV	30 sec ______ μV	30 sec ______ μV
	40 sec ______ μV	40 sec ______ μV	40 sec ______ μV
	50 sec ______ μV	50 sec ______ μV	50 sec ______ μV
	60 sec ______ μV	60 sec ______ μV	60 sec ______ μV
	70 sec ______ μV	70 sec ______ μV	70 sec ______ μV
	80 sec ______ μV	80 sec ______ μV	80 sec ______ μV
	90 sec ______ μV	90 sec ______ μV	90 sec ______ μV
	100 sec ______ μV	100 sec ______ μV	100 sec ______ μV
	110 sec ______ μV	110 sec ______ μV	110 sec ______ μV
	120 sec ______ μV	120 sec ______ μV	120 sec ______ μV
	130 sec ______ μV		
	140 sec ______ μV		
	150 sec ______ μV		
	160 sec ______ μV		
	170 sec ______ μV		
	180 sec ______ μV		

Trainee ______________________

Date __________

LAB IV QUESTIONS

Image 1: ____

1. When you imagined the stressful scene, where did you visualize it? (In your head? In front of you? In your stomach? etc.)

____

____

2. Did you experience yourself as a part of the scene or was it more like viewing a movie?

____

____

3. How involved in the situation were you relative to the original experience?

Less		Same		More
1	2	3	4	5

4. How intensely did you feel sensations in your body?

A little		Some		A lot
1	2	3	4	5

5. Did you notice any body changes during the time when you were imagining the stressful situation? If yes, what were they?

____

____

____

6. Did you experience the period of time from when you raised your finger indicating involvement with your image until the time you were told to let go of the image as

Less than 2 min___ About 2 min___ Longer than 2 min___

7. While imaging the stressful situation did you experience any of the following?

	Yes	No
Warmth or cold	___	___
Sound	___	___
Taste	___	___
Smell	___	___
Pressure	___	___

8. How easy was it to let go of the image and let yourself relax?

Not easy		Easy		Very easy
1	2	3	4	5

9. What strategy(ies) did you use to keep the EMG feedback signal low during imaging?

____

____

____

____

____

10. How did the subjective quality of the image change when you received feedback?

____

____

____

____

Trainee ______________________

Trainer ______________________

Date __________

LAB IV GRAPH

Image: ____

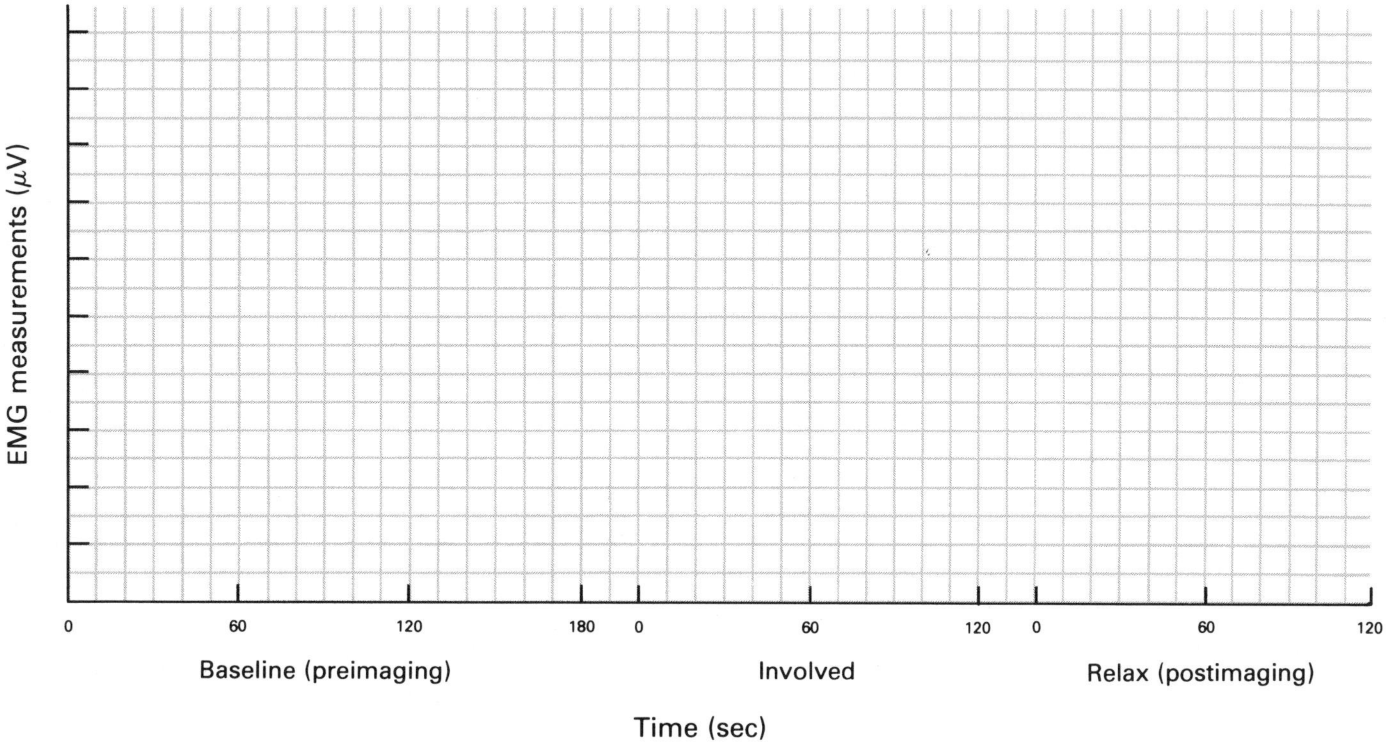

Trainee ______________________

Date __________

LAB IV SUMMARY OF QUESTIONS

1. How easy was it for you to relax during the imaging?

2. When you inhibited the muscle tensing, how did this change your experience of the stressful imagery, that is, are the answers to the Questions for this lab similar to or different from those for Lab III for the same image when you did not receive feedback?

3. Comments:

Trainee ____________________

Date __________

LAB IV DISCUSSION AND CONCLUSIONS

1. Were there differences among members of your group in the ability to inhibit the EMG signal while imaging?

2. Were the responses to the Questions in any way related to one's ability to inhibit the EMG signal while imaging (e.g., were those who had difficulty in inhibiting the signal those who were most involved?)

3. Was there variation among members of your group in the change of experience when the EMG signal was inhibited?

LAB V
Home Practice

Awareness of Thought Patterns and Muscle Tension

OBJECTIVE

One responds to certain thought patterns, such as "ruminating" and "anticipating," in a manner similar to imagined stressors, i.e., with muscle tension. The following home practice is intended to encourage self-awareness of this process and to teach ways to decrease the automatic (unconscious) response to such mental events. In becoming aware of and learning to inhibit any process one gains freedom of choice, whether to react or to act.

INSTRUCTIONS

Each day during the week on Lab V: Log Sheet:

a. Observe and record the thought pattern (rumination, anticipation, etc.) resulting in increased muscle tension. For example, while mentally rehashing a recent argument, one notes tightening of the neck and shoulders.
b. Note the areas in your body that are tense.
c. Relax and inhibit the tension while holding the thought pattern. Record the effect on your experience when you relax.

At the end of the week, complete Lab V: Questions.

Trainee ____________________

Date __________

LAB V LOG SHEET

Each day, describe (a) your thought pattern, (b) the location of tension, and (c) the effect of inhibition of tension on the experience of the thought pattern.

Day 1 a. ____________________

Date______ b. ____________________

c. ____________________

____

Day 2 a. ____________________

Date______ b. ____________________

c. ____________________

____

Day 3 a. ____________________

Date______ b. ____________________

c. ____________________

____

Day 4 a. ____________________

Date______ b. ____________________

c. ____________________

____

Day 5 a. ____________________

Date______ b. ____________________

c. ____________________

____

Day 6 a. ______

Date______ b. ______

c. ______

______

Day 7 a. ______

Date______ b. ______

c. ______

______

Trainee ______________________

Date __________

LAB V QUESTIONS

1. How and under which conditions was it easy or difficult to remind yourself to do the homework exercise? What were some of the tools you used?

2. Identify common themes that may underlie the thought patterns resulting in body tension. For example, you note tightness in your shoulders when you think of a traffic jam and when you think of being late for an appointment. The common theme could be time pressure, "hurry-up sickness."

3. Were the locations of tension the same or different for the different thought patterns? How similar or different were they to the ones observed in Lab II?

4. In what ways did inhibiting muscle tension change your experience?

5. What were the qualities of the thought patterns that made it more easy or difficult for you to inhibit body tension?

6. Comments:

LAB VI
Dysponesis[1]

EQUIPMENT

EMG, alcohol, tissue, electroconductive paste, electrode adhesive collars, tape.

OBJECTIVE

Dysponesis, from the Greek *dys,* meaning bad, and *ponesis,* meaning exertion, refers to misplaced efforts. For example, say you are giving a speech and find your arms tightened and shoulders braced. These actions of tightening and bracing are dysponetic or nonefficacious in that they do nothing to further and, in fact, may interfere with the intended activity.[2] The importance of this concept lies in the fact that dysponetic activity may be either a causative or an aggravating factor in pathological symptoms. Continuing with the above example, chronic bracing of the shoulders may lead to or aggravate tension headaches or fatigue. In this lab, you will explore this concept by learning to identify dysponetic activity, to inhibit this response (i.e., retraining of habitual patterns), and to generalize these awareness skills into other areas of your life.

Although dysponetic effort most often is used to refer to the striated muscular system, the concept can be expanded to include any nonefficacious efforts in any of the physiological systems (e.g., cardiovascular, respiratory, endocrine). By learning to reduce the dysponetic efforts in any of these physiological systems, one is encouraging the prohomeostatic processes within the body.

INSTRUCTIONS

In order to develop an understanding of dysponesis, proceed through the following exercises, all of which may involve a dysponetic component.

Observing Dysponesis with a Partner

Arm Tension while Talking

Put your hands on your lap. Sit in a comfortable chair. Have your partner gently lift your nondominant arm by holding the arm at the wrist, and move it slowly around in a nonpredictable pattern. Be sure the arm is moved very slowly and gently. Let your arm be totally supported by your partner. Inhibit any intentions of helping, hindering, or guiding the movement; just let your arm be moved passively. The more you can "give your arm" to the person who is moving your arm, the more relaxed it is. Allow this passive movement to continue for a few minutes.

After a few minutes, have your partner ask you a few questions—as s/he continues to

[1]Reference: *Mind/body integration,* pp. 379–410.

[2]For more detailed discussion of dysponesis, see G. B. Whatmore & D. R. Kohli, *The physiopathology and treatment of functional disorders,* New York: Grune & Stratton, 1974. See also M. Feldenkrais, *The case of Nora,* New York: Harper & Row, 1977.

move your arm—first about relatively insignificant issues, and then about possibly significant issues (e.g., "What did you have for breakfast?" "What did you do last night?" "Do you like your parents?"). Observe what happens to your arm. Does your arm stiffen or tighten as you anticipate the questions or as you attempt to answer the questions? Is your partner sensitive to the tightening?

After observing your reactions, go back to just having your arm moved, without questions.

Then have your partner ask you questions, saying "Stop" each time s/he observes a tightening of the arm. In response to this feedback, turn your attention from the question to your arm and allow the arm to be moved passively. Once your arm can again be moved passively, continue to answer the questions while keeping your arm relaxed. If at any time tension is observed, your partner will say, "Stop," and your focus should shift to relaxing the arm. In other words, the exercise is to learn to answer the questions while keeping the arm relaxed, not merely to answer the questions.

Arm Tension while Writing

Have your partner again move your nondominant arm. After a few minutes, while your arm is moved passively, start writing with your dominant hand, describing what you are experiencing as your partner moves your arm. What happens to the arm that is being moved as you start to write?

Each time your partner feels your arm tighten, s/he will say "Stop." Stop writing and allow your arm to relax and be moved passively. Only write when the nondominant arm is being moved passively. Generally, in any situation where one is relearning to do an activity while relaxing muscles *not* involved in the activity, it is important never to couple the activity with the nonrelaxed state. If the coupling is allowed, one reinforces the old habitual dysponetic patterns.

NOTE: If you are a person who tightens the nondominant arm when either talking or writing, be aware that this retraining takes a long time, and you should not expect it to occur in one session. Learning to reduce dysponetic activity is like learning any skill—it takes time. Would you expect to learn to play tennis in one session?

Complete Lab VI: Questions—Observing Dysponesis with a Partner. Repeat the procedures with your partner, moving his/her nondominant arm.

Trainee ______________________________

Date ____________

LAB VI QUESTIONS—OBSERVING DYSPONESIS WITH A PARTNER

1. What can you say about your ability to inhibit dysponetic activity, for example, your ability to talk and write while allowing your nondominant arm to be moved passively?

2. Comments:

Observing Dysponesis with EMG Feedback

It is important to observe that feedback may come from any of a variety of sources. In the previous exercise it was one's partner who provided the muscle tension feedback. These exercises could just as well have been done with the EMG electrodes placed on the nondominant forearm extensors, with the EMG unit providing feedback. The following exercises will be done with EMG feedback.

Dysponesis while Talking

Begin by having your partner place the EMG electrodes on your forearm or trapezius. (See Figure 10 in Lab II for placement.) Relax and sit quietly for a few moments. While remaining quiet and relaxed, without feedback, have your partner record your EMG activity every 10 sec for 1 min on Lab VI: Data Sheet—Activity 1 (A, Baseline values).

Without feedback, begin a conversation with your partner about some fairly neutral subject, such as how to prepare a favorite food or a description of a favorite hobby. Have your partner record your EMG activity every 10 sec for 1 min on Lab VI: Data Sheet—Activity 1 (B, Prelearning period) while you continue to talk.

Then have your partner turn the feedback on. While continuing to talk about some neutral issue, try to keep the feedback signal to a minimum. The task here is to learn to decrease the dysponetic activity (in this case the forearm or trapezius activity) while talking. Have your partner record your EMG activity on Lab VI: Data Sheet—Activity 1 for 1 min (C, First 60 sec with feedback). Continue the practice of inhibition of forearm or trapezius activity while talking until you have reached a plateau or are bored. Then while continuing to talk, have your partner record your EMG activity (1) for 60 sec, still with feedback (D, Last 60 sec with feedback), and then (2) for another 60 sec without feedback (E, Postlearning period). Both the length of practice time per session (anywhere up to 20 min) and the number of sessions required to learn to inhibit the dysponetic activity will vary for different individuals (anywhere up to 50 sessions).

Graph your data and then complete Lab VI: Questions—Activity 1.

Exploring Other Dysponetic Activities

Follow the outline of the previous exercise (baseline, prelearning period, etc.) using a different activity and monitoring a different muscle group. Remember that dysponesis refers to the tightening or bracing of muscles that are not necessary for the performance of the activity. Choose one activity from the following suggestions:

1. Tightening of fist without tightening trapezius (or deltoid or biceps); monitor trapezius (or deltoid or biceps).
2. Learning abdominal breathing without tightening of pectoralis; monitor pectoralis.
3. Allowing passive movement of middle finger; monitor forearm extensors.
4. Learning to keep upper leg muscles relaxed while catching a ball; monitor inner thigh muscle (gracilus) (sit in chair with legs apart).
5. Learning to touch toes without tightening upper thigh muscles (quadriceps); monitor quadriceps.
6. Learning to type without tightening shoulders (trapezius); monitor trapezius.

If time permits, complete exercise with another activity and muscle group.

Repeat procedures with your partner as trainee.

Meet with your group and complete Lab VI: Discussion and Conclusions.

Trainee ______________________

Trainer ______________________

Date ___________

LAB VI DATA SHEET—ACTIVITY 1

A Baseline values (no talking; without feedback)	B Prelearning period (without feedback)	C First 60 sec with feedback (Learning period)	Feedback learning period (_____ min) (Learning period)	D Last 60 sec with feedback (Learning period)	E Postlearning period (without feedback)
0 sec ______ μV	0 sec ______ μV	0 sec ______ μV		0 sec ______ μV	0 sec ______ μV
10 sec ______ μV	10 sec ______ μV	10 sec ______ μV		10 sec ______ μV	10 sec ______ μV
20 sec ______ μV	20 sec ______ μV	20 sec ______ μV		20 sec ______ μV	20 sec ______ μV
30 sec ______ μV	30 sec ______ μV	30 sec ______ μV		30 sec ______ μV	30 sec ______ μV
40 sec ______ μV	40 sec ______ μV	40 sec ______ μV		40 sec ______ μV	40 sec ______ μV
50 sec ______ μV	50 sec ______ μV	50 sec ______ μV		50 sec ______ μV	50 sec ______ μV
60 sec ______ μV	60 sec ______ μV	60 sec ______ μV		60 sec ______ μV	60 sec ______ μV

Describe activity:

Location of electrodes:

Trainee ____________________

Trainer ____________________

Date __________

LAB VI GRAPH—ACTIVITY 1

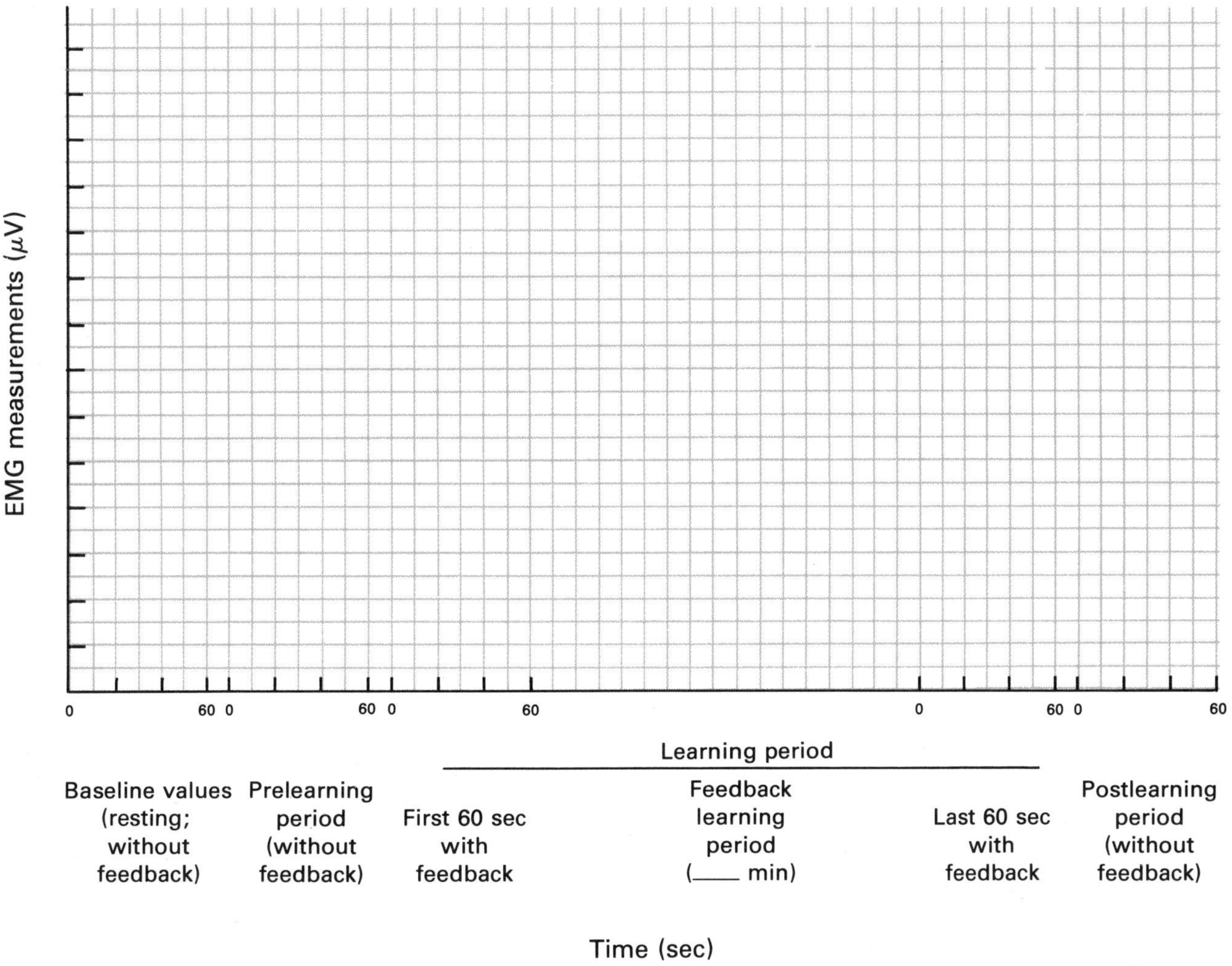

Trainee ______________________

Date ___________

LAB VI QUESTIONS—ACTIVITY 1

1a. During the prelearning period (no feedback and while talking) were you aware of any tightening in the muscle being monitored? Rate the intensity you felt.

No tensing		Some tensing		Very tense
1	2	3	4	5

1b. Compare the above subjective experience of tension with the EMG values during the prelearning period. Was there congruence between these measures? To what extent is the EMG a more sensitive measure than your internal awareness?

2. What happened to your EMG level when you started talking? (Compare baseline values with prelearning period values.) If your EMG activity increased during the activity, you exhibited dysponesis; however, it is possible that your baseline recordings already included dysponetic activity—that the muscles were never relaxed.

3. How successful were you in learning to inhibit the dysponetic activity (compare prelearning period and postlearning period values)?

4. To what extent were you able to internalize the feedback signal (compare learning period last 60 sec and postlearning period values)? If you found that the postlearning period values were greater, you have *not* yet internalized the learning and probably need more learning sessions.

5. Comments:

Trainee ____________________

Trainer ____________________

Date __________

LAB VI DATA SHEET—ACTIVITY 2

A Baseline values (resting without feedback)	B Prelearning period (without feedback)	Learning period C First 60 sec with feedback	Feedback learning period (_____ min)	D Last 60 sec with feedback	E Postlearning period (without feedback)
0 sec ______ μV	0 sec ______ μV	0 sec ______ μV		0 sec ______ μV	0 sec ______ μV
10 sec ______ μV	10 sec ______ μV	10 sec ______ μV		10 sec ______ μV	10 sec ______ μV
20 sec ______ μV	20 sec ______ μV	20 sec ______ μV		20 sec ______ μV	20 sec ______ μV
30 sec ______ μV	30 sec ______ μV	30 sec ______ μV		30 sec ______ μV	30 sec ______ μV
40 sec ______ μV	40 sec ______ μV	40 sec ______ μV		40 sec ______ μV	40 sec ______ μV
50 sec ______ μV	50 sec ______ μV	50 sec ______ μV		50 sec ______ μV	50 sec ______ μV
60 sec ______ μV	60 sec ______ μV	60 sec ______ μV		60 sec ______ μV	60 sec ______ μV

Describe activity:

Location of electrodes:

Trainee ____________________

Trainer ____________________

Date __________

LAB VI GRAPH—ACTIVITY 2

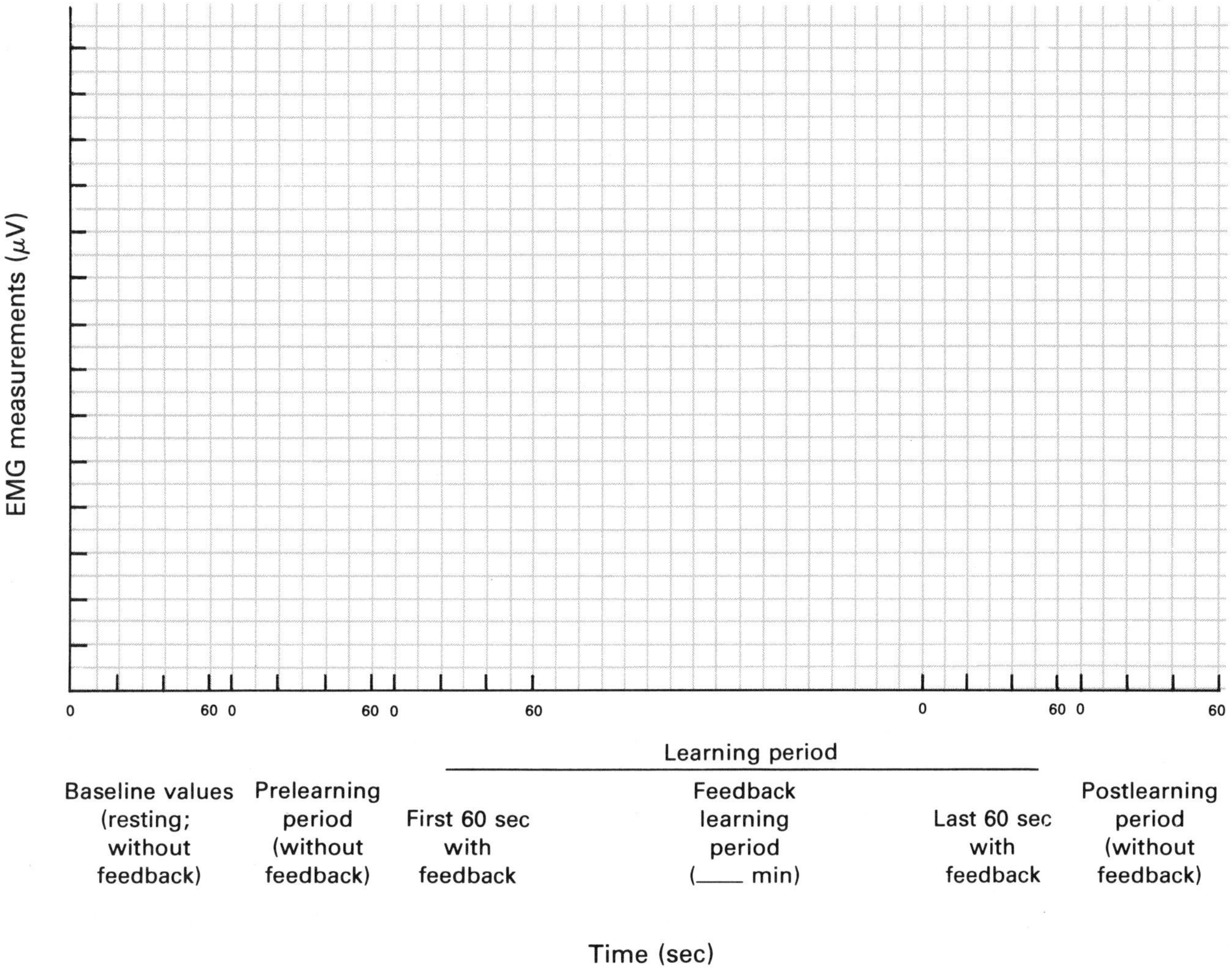

Trainee ______________________

Date ____________

LAB VI QUESTIONS—ACTIVITY 2

1a. During the prelearning period (no feedback and while performing activity) were you aware of any tightening in the muscle being monitored? Rate the intensity you felt.

No tensing		Some tensing		Very tense
1	2	3	4	5

1b. Compare the above subjective experience of tension with the EMG values during the prelearning period. Was there congruence between these measures? To what extent is the EMG a more sensitive measure than your internal awareness?

____

____

____

2. What happened to your EMG level when you started the activity? (Compare baseline values with prelearning period values.) If your EMG activity increased during the activity, you exhibited dysponesis; however, it is possible that your baseline recordings already included dysponetic activity—that the muscles were never relaxed.

____

____

____

____

____

3. How successful were you in learning to inhibit the dysponetic activity (compare prelearning period and postlearning period values)?

____

____

____

4. To what extent were you able to internalize the feedback signal (compare learning period last 60 sec and postlearning period values)? If you found that the postlearning period values were greater, you have *not* yet internalized the learning and probably need more learning sessions.

5. Comments:

Trainee ______________________

Trainer ______________________

Date __________

LAB VI DATA SHEET—ACTIVITY 3

		Learning period			
A Baseline values (resting without feedback)	B Prelearning period (without feedback)	C First 60 sec with feedback	Feedback learning period (_____ min)	D Last 60 sec with feedback	E Postlearning period (without feedback)
0 sec _____ μV	0 sec _____ μV	0 sec _____ μV		0 sec _____ μV	0 sec _____ μV
10 sec _____ μV	10 sec _____ μV	10 sec _____ μV		10 sec _____ μV	10 sec _____ μV
20 sec _____ μV	20 sec _____ μV	20 sec _____ μV		20 sec _____ μV	20 sec _____ μV
30 sec _____ μV	30 sec _____ μV	30 sec _____ μV		30 sec _____ μV	30 sec _____ μV
40 sec _____ μV	40 sec _____ μV	40 sec _____ μV		40 sec _____ μV	40 sec _____ μV
50 sec _____ μV	50 sec _____ μV	50 sec _____ μV		50 sec _____ μV	50 sec _____ μV
60 sec _____ μV	60 sec _____ μV	60 sec _____ μV		60 sec _____ μV	60 sec _____ μV

Describe activity:

Location of Electrodes:

Trainee ____________________

Trainer ____________________

Date __________

LAB VI GRAPH—ACTIVITY 3

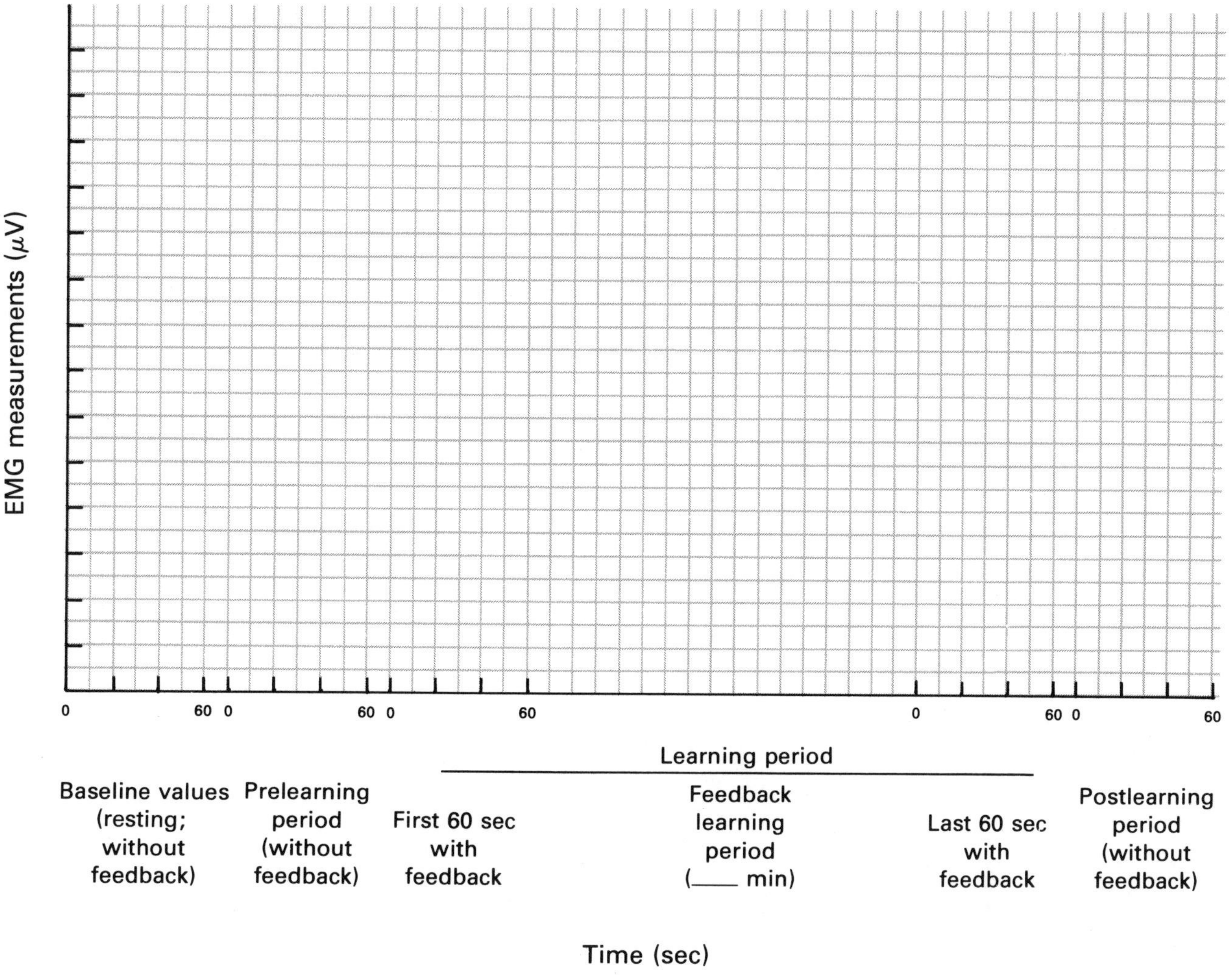

Trainee ______________________

Date ____________

LAB VI QUESTIONS—ACTIVITY 3

1a. During the prelearning period (no feedback and while performing activity) were you aware of any tightening in the muscle being monitored? Rate the intensity you felt.

No tensing		Some tensing		Very tense
1	2	3	4	5

1b. Compare the above subjective experience of tension with the EMG values during the prelearning period. Was there congruence between these measures? To what extent is the EMG a more sensitive measure than your internal awareness?

____

____

____

2. What happened to your EMG level when you started the activity? (Compare baseline values with prelearning period values.) If your EMG activity increased during the activity, you exhibited dysponesis; however, it is possible that your baseline recordings already included dysponetic activity—that the muscles were never relaxed.

____

____

____

____

____

3. How successful were you in learning to inhibit the dysponetic activity (compare prelearning period and postlearning period values)?

____

____

____

____

4. To what extent were you able to internalize the feedback signal (compare learning period last 60 sec and postlearning period values)? If you found that the postlearning period values were greater, you have *not* yet internalized the learning and probably need more learning sessions.

5. Comments:

Trainee ______________________

Date __________

LAB VI DISCUSSION AND CONCLUSIONS

1. Did others in your group vary in:
   a. The activity in which they exhibited dysponesis and the pattern of tightening?

   ____
   ____
   ____
   ____

   b. The ability to inhibit dysponesis?

   ____
   ____
   ____
   ____

2. Were age, sex, physical dexterity, past illness patterns, past experience with relaxation techniques, etc., related to:
   a. Activities in which persons exhibited dysponesis and the pattern of tightening?

   ____
   ____
   ____
   ____

   b. The ability to inhibit dysponesis?

   ____
   ____
   ____
   ____

SUGGESTIONS FOR FUTURE RESEARCH

1. Based on the observations of your dysponetic activity, choose an activity during which it was difficult for you to inhibit dysponesis. Use the EMG, as in the lab section "Observing Dysponesis with EMG Feedback," as a feedback device to enhance the learning of dysponesis inhibition.
2. Explore the effect of maintaining low EMG activity of the gluteus maximus, abdominus rectus, and muscles of the pelvic region during sexual arousal.

LAB VII
Home Practice
Dysponesis

OBJECTIVE

Many of our daily activities contain dysponetic components of which we are unaware. The objective of this home practice is to (1) identify these components and (2) inhibit them.

INSTRUCTIONS

At least once each day during the week, record on Lab VII: Log Sheet an activity during which you observe dysponesis, and then, while continuing (or repeating) the activity, reduce the dysponesis. Record:

a. The activity during which you observed dysponesis.
b. Where you observed the dysponesis (what muscles tightened).
c. The ease or difficulty with which you were able to eliminate the dysponesis and how eliminating dysponesis affected your experience of the activity.

For example, while writing a check in the supermarket, one trainee observed the raising of his shoulders and the tightening of his neck. He found that letting the neck and shoulders relax did not interfere with the check writing and in fact he felt less pressured. Another trainee noted the tightening of her abdominal muscles while driving during rush hour traffic. When she relaxed her abdomen, she felt less concern about being delayed by the traffic. Another trainee observed her shoulders tightening while she brushed her teeth. When she attempted to relax her shoulders, she found she could not continue brushing. One might deduce from this last example that the tightening of the shoulders is an integral part (i.e., *not* dysponesis) of brushing teeth. In fact, we often believe that a muscle may be involved or necessary for an activity when it is in fact not required, but rather part of a pattern. Such a pattern is illustrated in the following exercise:

1. Stand or sit comfortably.
2. Begin with your eyes straight ahead, then roll your eyes up into your head, and slowly tilt your head backward. Now bring your head forward.
3. Now move your eyes to the extreme left and slowly tilt your head backward. Now bring your head forward.

Did you note that your head tended to turn in the direction in which your eyes were turning? The habitual coupling of eye and head movement makes it difficult to separate the two movements. This kind of habitual coupling inhibits the options we have in moving our bodies. In extreme form, this kind of coupling may be seen as the source of chronic degeneration of the body and mind, common in old age.[1]

At the end of the week, complete Lab VII: Questions.

[1]For further reading see: F. M. Alexander, *Resurrection of the body,* New York: Dell, 1969; M. Feldenkrais, *Awareness through movement,* New York: Harper & Row, 1972.

Trainee ______________________

Date ________

LAB VII LOG SHEET

Each day, describe (a) the activity during which dysponesis occurred, (b) the location of muscle tightening, and (c) the ease of reducing dysponesis and the effect on the experience of the activity.

Day 1 a. ______________________

Date______ b. ______________________

c. ______________________

____

Day 2 a. ______________________

Date______ b. ______________________

c. ______________________

____

Day 3 a. ______________________

Date______ b. ______________________

c. ______________________

____

Day 4 a. ______________________

Date______ b. ______________________

c. ______________________

____

Day 5 a. ______________________

Date______ b. ______________________

c. ______________________

____

Day 6 a. ______________________________

Date______ b. ______________________________

c. ______________________________

____

Day 7 a. ______________________________

Date______ b. ______________________________

c. ______________________________

____

Trainee ______________________

Date __________

LAB VII QUESTIONS

1. What were some of the problems you encountered in doing this home practice?

____
____
____
____

2. Did you find that the location of muscle tightening varied with the activity? Explain.

____
____
____
____
____

3. In what ways did reducing dysponesis change your experience?

____
____
____
____
____

4. Comments:

____
____
____
____
____

INSTRUCTION SET B

Meditative Unstressing Techniques[1]

OBJECTIVE

In this instruction set, a number of unstressing techniques derived from meditative practices will be introduced.[2] Although frequently meditation is used as a tool for spiritual growth and development, more commonly today in the West the practices are used with a more limited goal in mind—general unstressing. It is this more practical form of meditation that will be considered here.

These meditative practices may be used as an adjunctive technique with biofeedback learning: They both encourage the attitude necessary for successful learning and provide tools for home practice. For example, Patel and North successfully used relaxation techniques derived from yoga in work with hypertensives both during feedback sessions and as homework exercises.[3] The attitude underlying both these practices and biofeedback training includes nonjudgmental acceptance (letting be whatever comes up, detachment); passive attention (absence of striving and concern for performance); and mindfulness (paying attention without being involved).

These meditative practices also share certain common assumptions with biofeedback training:

1. Mind and body are one and are interactive.
2. The trainee is responsible for his/her learning.
3. Home practice of the skills is vital.
4. Practice is required over a long period of time and one has to incorporate the learned skills into one's life pattern for significant growth to occur.

Aside from their applicability in biofeedback, we feel that these techniques by themselves are valuable both as tools for self-discovery and for fostering general mind/body unstressing. This unstressing process activates the prohomeostatic mechanisms (innate self-healing capacities) of the body. These capacities are *allowed to be,* not *directed;* neither the trainer nor the trainee has the wisdom necessary to direct the self-healing process.

[1] REFERENCE: *Mind/body integration,* pp. 119–150; 529–540.

[2] For further reading see: P. Carrington, *Freedom in meditation,* New York: Anchor/Doubleday, 1977; E. Easwaran, *Meditation,* Petaluma, California: Nilgiri Press, 1978; L. LeShan, *How to meditate,* Boston: Little Brown & Co., 1974; R. M. French (transl.), *The way of the pilgrim,* New York: Ballantine, 1974.

[3] C. Patel & W. R. S. North, Randomized controlled trial of yoga and biofeedback in management of hypertension. In *Mind/body integration,* pp. 535–540.

INSTRUCTIONS

All these practices require focus on the task at hand; if one's attention drifts away, one gently returns one's attention to the task. In this process, one neither follows thoughts or sensations nor actively tries to suppress them; rather one refocuses on the task. To illustrate this process, proceed through the following exercise:

> While sitting comfortably, observe your right thumbnail for 5 min without making any judgments. Each time your attention drifts bring your focus back to the thumbnail.
>
> Notice the plethora of thoughts and sensations that distracted you from your task.
>
> The following is illustrative of the refocusing process:
>
> Attending to nail . . . "I need to cut my nail" . . . return to attending to nail . . . "Oh, there is the phone, should I . . ." . . . return to attending to nail . . . "Better remember to buy the spinach for the lasagna . . ." . . . return to attending to nail.

With practice one learns to refocus more rapidly and the number of disruptive thoughts decreases.

This instruction set includes three different exercises, each with a different focus (either breath, mantra, or slow movement). Practice each of the techniques according to the following instructions for 1 week at least once a day for 20 min,[4] making entries on the appropriate Log Sheet. Choose a time and environment where you will not be disturbed. [See Instruction Set A (pp.3–6) for discussion of this issue.] Complete the appropriate Questions after each week of practice. After practicing all of the techniques (i.e., after 3 weeks of practice), complete Instruction Set B: Summary of Questions. Meet with your group and complete Instruction Set B: Discussion and Conclusions. Select the one technique you found most valuable and then continue practicing this selected technique for at least 6 weeks. (You may want to continue this technique; don't be limited by this time constraint.) Record your observations in a personal diary, including the information asked both on the Log Sheet and in the Questions.

Breath Awareness—Week 1

There are a number of different techniques that use breath as a focus. The following is adapted from Zen training. Sit comfortably with eyes closed and allow the breath to flow naturally. Observe the process of how the breath moves through the body. Starting with the number 1, count exhalations up to 10. Start again with the number 1 and repeat the counting of exhalations up to 10 throughout your 20 min meditation.

Mantra—Week 2

Many meditative techniques use the *mantra,* a word with spiritual significance, as the center of focus of the meditation. Select one of the mantras from the following list[5]:

Rama
Shirim
Ahnam
Allah
One

Repeat each softly out loud and then mentally to yourself. Choose the one that is most pleasant, soothing, and peaceful. Trust your intuition. Keep this same mantra at least for the 1-week mantra meditation experience.

During your 20-min meditation, sit comfortably with your eyes closed and repeat your chosen mantra mentally to yourself.

[4]To determine when 20 min have passed, one may set an alarm or set a time piece in view and glance at it when one subjectively feels 20 min have passed.

[5]If you already have a mantra for meditation, or prefer to use one not on the list, use your preferred mantra.

Slow Movement Exercise—Week 3

During your 20-min meditation, walk as *slowly* as possible, with eyes closed. Each step should be a movement of only a few centimeters. The focus of attention in this kind of meditation is the various body sensations. For example, observe the sensations in your leg, ankle, and feet. Note your sense of balance. Feel the shifting of weight from one leg to another, which muscles tighten when, and so forth.

SUGGESTIONS FOR FUTURE RESEARCH

1. In a longitudinal study observe the psychological and physiological changes that occur as people meditate.
2. Explore whether different meditative practices lead to different physiological and psychological changes.
3. Explore how the practice of meditation affects the ability to learn autonomic control with biofeedback.

Trainee ______________________

Date __________

INSTRUCTION SET B LOG SHEET—WEEK 1: Breath Awareness

After each practice, describe (a) ease of maintaining focus on breath (not being distracted), (b) subjective experience during meditation, and (c) whether you left meditation feeling different from when you entered it.

Day 1 a. ______________________
Date______ b. ______________________
Time______ c. ______________________

Day 2 a. ______________________
Date______ b. ______________________
Time______ c. ______________________

Day 3 a. ______________________
Date______ b. ______________________
Time______ c. ______________________

Day 4 a. ______________________
Date______ b. ______________________
Time______ c. ______________________

Day 5 a. ______________________
Date______ b. ______________________
Time______ c. ______________________

Day 6 a. ______________________

Date______ b. ______________________

Time______ c. ______________________

Day 7 a. ______________________

Date______ b. ______________________

Time______ c. ______________________

Trainee ____________________

Date __________

INSTRUCTION SET B QUESTIONS—WEEK 1: Breath Awareness

1. What problems did you encounter during meditation? How did you deal with them?

___

___

___

2. Did the ease of maintaining focus vary? If so, how did this relate to such variables as time of day and experiences before meditation?

___

___

___

3. Did your experience during meditation vary? If so, how did this relate to the ease of maintaining focus, and such other variables as time of day and emotional state?

___

___

___

4. In what ways did your meditative experience affect the experience following the meditation? Was there carryover of your subjective experience?

___

___

___

___

5. Comments:

___

___

___

Trainee ____________________

Date ________

INSTRUCTION SET B LOG SHEET—WEEK 2: Mantra

After each practice, describe (a) ease of maintaining focus on mantra (not being distracted), (b) subjective experience during meditation, and (c) whether you left meditation feeling different from when you entered it.

Day 1 a. ____________________
Date______ b. ____________________
Time______ c. ____________________

Day 2 a. ____________________
Date______ b. ____________________
Time______ c. ____________________

Day 3 a. ____________________
Date______ b. ____________________
Time______ c. ____________________

Day 4 a. ____________________
Date______ b. ____________________
Time______ c. ____________________

Day 5 a. ____________________
Date______ b. ____________________
Time______ c. ____________________

Day 6 a. ____

Date____ b. ____

Time____ c. ____

Day 7 a. ____

Date____ b. ____

Time____ c. ____

Trainee ______________________

Date __________

INSTRUCTION SET B QUESTIONS—WEEK 2: Mantra

1. What problems did you encounter during meditation? How did you deal with them?

____

____

____

2. Did the ease of maintaining focus vary? If so, how did this relate to such variables as time of day and experiences before meditation?

____

____

____

3. Did your experience during meditation vary? If so, how did this relate to the ease of maintaining focus, and such other variables as time of day and emotional state?

____

____

____

4. In what ways did your meditative experience affect the experience following the meditation? Was there carryover of your subjective experience?

____

____

____

____

5. Comments:

____

____

____

Trainee ______________________

Date ____________

INSTRUCTION SET B LOG SHEET—WEEK 3: Slow Movement

After each practice, describe (a) ease of maintaining focus on body sensations (not being distracted), (b) subjective experience during meditation, and (c) whether you left meditation feeling different from when you entered it.

Day 1 a. ______________________
Date______ b. ______________________
Time______ c. ______________________

Day 2 a. ______________________
Date______ b. ______________________
Time______ c. ______________________

Day 3 a. ______________________
Date______ b. ______________________
Time______ c. ______________________

Day 4 a. ______________________
Date______ b. ______________________
Time______ c. ______________________

Day 5 a. ______________________
Date______ b. ______________________
Time______ c. ______________________

Day 6 a. ______________________

Date______ b. ______________________

Time______ c. ______________________

Day 7 a. ______________________

Date______ b. ______________________

Time______ c. ______________________

Trainee ______________________

Date ____________

INSTRUCTION SET B QUESTIONS—WEEK 3: Slow Movement

1. What problems did you encounter during meditation? How did you deal with them?

2. Did the ease of maintaining focus vary? If so, how did this relate to such variables as time of day and experiences before meditation?

3. Did your experience during meditation vary? If so, how did this relate to the ease of maintaining focus, and such other variables as time of day and emotional state?

4. In what ways did your meditative experience affect the experience following the meditation? Was there carryover of your subjective experience?

5. Comments:

Trainee ____________________

Date __________

INSTRUCTION SET B SUMMARY OF QUESTIONS

1. How did your ease of maintaining focus and your subjective experience vary with the techniques?

2. Were the problems that you encountered common to all three techniques or unique to a specific technique? Explain.

3. Which technique did you select for the 6-week practice and why?

4. Comments:

Trainee ______________________________

Date ____________

INSTRUCTION SET B DISCUSSION AND CONCLUSIONS

1. For the other members of your group, did the ease of maintaining focus and the subjective experience vary with the techniques? In what way was this related to such variables as age, sex, past experience with meditation, and personality?

2. Among the group members, were there common problems encountered with the techniques? Common solutions to these problems?

SECTION 2

Temperature Unit

LAB VIII
Introduction to the Temperature Unit[1]

NOTE: This lab assumes familiarity with the basic functions of biofeedback equipment. Review Lab I.

EQUIPMENT

Temperature unit and instruction manual, laboratory thermometer, beaker, plastic bag, tape.

OBJECTIVE

Temperature feedback has been used both in dealing with vasoconstrictive disorders such as migraine and Raynaud's disease[2] and as a tool to encourage general relaxation (a general decrease in sympathetic arousal).[3] In addition, exploration has been done with the technique in facilitating childbirth and optimizing physical performance.[4]

The objective of this lab is to gain familiarity with temperature feedback equipment, to learn a technique of calibration, and to gain an understanding of the concept of thermal lag.

PHYSIOLOGICAL BASIS OF THE SIGNAL

The vessels (*arterioles*) supplying blood to the periphery of the body are surrounded by smooth muscle that is innervated by the sympathetic branch of the autonomic nervous system. Sympathetic activation results in a decrease in the diameter of the vessels (*vasoconstriction*) and a decrease in the blood flow through the vessels. Decreased sympathetic activity results in an increase in the diameter of the vessels (*vasodilation*) and an increase in blood flow. Vasoconstriction may be triggered by the "flight–fight" response (the alarm reaction) and/or in response to lowering of the core temperature (for example, in response to a cold environment).

There are multiple ways to measure changes in blood flow. For example, an increase in blood flow to a region of the body would result in a decrease in light transmission through that body part. A photoplethysmograph measures these changes in light transmis-

[1]REFERENCE: *Mind/body integration*, pp. 231–236; 241–252.

[2]C. Stroebel & E. Taub, *Task force report on vasoconstrictive syndromes*, Denver: Biofeedback Society of America, 1978; J. T. Sappington, E. M. Fiorito, & K. A. Brehony, Biofeedback as therapy in Raynaud's disease, *Biofeedback and Self-Regulation*, 1979, *4*, 155–169.

[3]E. E. Green & A. M. Green, *Beyond biofeedback*, New York: Delacorte, 1977.

[4]B. B. Brown, *Stress and the art of biofeedback*, New York: Harper & Row, 1977.

sion. An increase in blood flow to an area is also associated with an increase in skin temperature of that area. The temperature feedback unit measures these changes in skin temperature.

SENSOR

Although there are multiple ways to monitor changes in skin temperature, most electronic biofeedback units use the *thermistor*. A change in temperature results in a change in the resistance of the thermistor. These changes in resistance are then translated electronically and displayed as measurements of temperature. The thermistor is usually attached with tape to the fleshy part of the index finger, as illustrated in Figure 11C. Figures 11A and 11B show common errors in thermistor attachment.

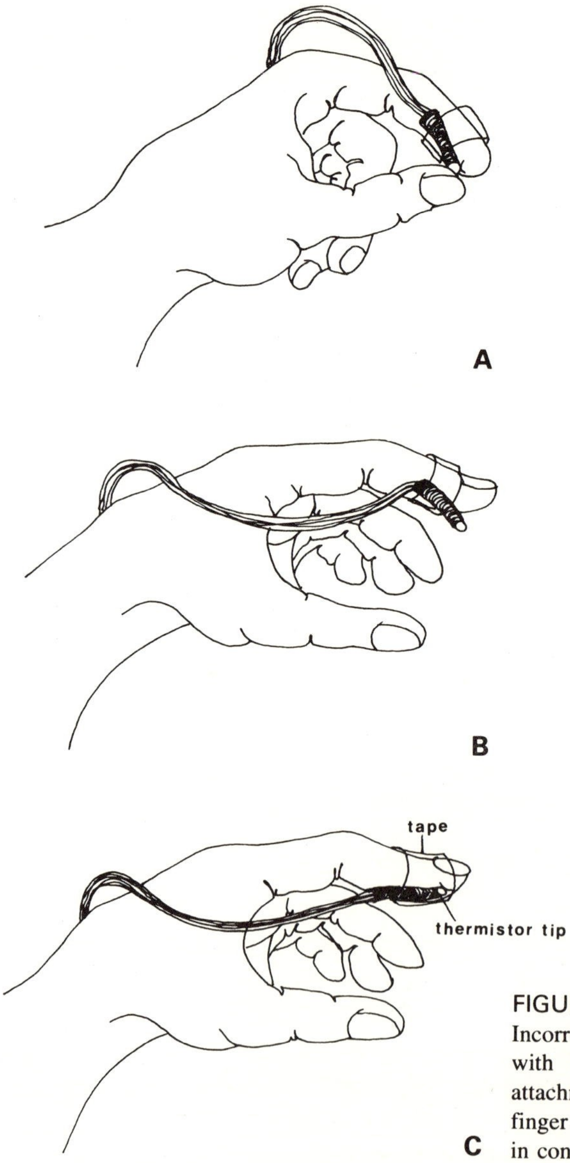

FIGURE 11. Attachment of thermistor. (A) Incorrect attachment—thermistor tip in contact with two different fingers. (B) Incorrect attachment—thermistor tip not in contact with finger. (C) Correct attachment—thermistor tip in contact with finger.

OPERATION OF THE EQUIPMENT

Battery Check, Behavioral Test, and Calibration

Plug the thermistor into the temperature unit (T unit) and turn on the machine. Place the thermistor on top of the machine. Complete a battery check if your machine has such an operation. Check your instruction manual for specific instructions. You may want to see what happens to the meter when a battery that has lost most of its charge is used. Now note the room temperature. Try exhaling your warm breath or inhaling cool air over the thermistor. Note the temperature changes. Are these changes in the direction you would expect? For example, if the room temperature was 70°F, you would expect that exhaling warm breath over the thermistor would result in an increase in the temperature of the feedback unit. This kind of test is a *behavioral test* and is used to show that the equipment is functioning in the expected manner. It is a measure of relative accuracy.

In order to determine the absolute accuracy of the T unit (that is, if the unit reads 70°, is this the true temperature?), one must compare the readings with a known standard. In order to do this, put both the thermistor and the lab thermometer (your known standard) in a plastic bag (in case your thermistor is not waterproof) and place them in a beaker with warm water (about 100°F). Make sure both the thermometer and the thermistor tip are next to each other. Wait a few minutes (at least 2 min) and read off the temperatures. Record the values on Lab VIII: Data Sheet and Graph—Calibration of T Unit. Add some cold water, wait a few minutes until the temperatures have stabilized, and then take another reading. Repeat three or four times until the thermometer reads approximately 60°F.[5] Plot your data. What is the shape of the curve? The more linear your graph, the more accurate is your T unit. Compare your results with those of others in your class. Do the results vary for different thermistors?

Sensitivity

Most T units have a sensitivity switch that allows the display of either smaller or larger temperature changes. Changing the sensitivity of a unit with a meter results in a change in the range over which the temperature is displayed. Common ranges are ± 2°, or ± 20°. Changing the sensitivity of units with digital displays results in monitoring changes either to a hundredth of a degree, to a tenth of a degree, or to the nearest degree. Check your equipment to determine its ranges. Exhale your warm breath over the thermistor with the different ranges. Note which range gives you the larger deflection and which gives you the more meaningful response. If the needle stays off the meter, then the setting is too sensitive. If the needle barely moves, the setting is too coarse.

Factors That Affect Temperature Training

The thermistor directly measures the temperature around it. Hence, when the thermistor is attached to the finger, it is affected by both the temperature of the finger and the air or other objects around it. With the thermistor attached to your finger, explore the effect of the following:

1. Have your partner fan air over the thermistor.
2. Touch your finger to your thigh so that the thermistor is between the two surfaces.
3. Touch two fingers together with the thermistor between them.

Thermal Lag

In your work so far with the T unit, have your observed that there is a time lag between a change in temperature and the registering of that change on the T unit? This is referred to as *thermal lag*. In order to better understand this phenomenon, do the following: Record the room temperature on Lab VIII: Data Sheet and Graph—Thermal Lag. Then quickly place the thermistor under your armpit and record the temperature every 10 sec for 2 min. Remove the thermistor from your armpit and expose it to the air, again re-

[5]If your lab thermometer reads in °C, convert to °F with the following formula: °F = 32° + (9/5)(°C).

cording the temperature every 10 sec for 2 min. Plot the changes in temperature over time on Lab VIII: Data Sheet and Graph—Thermal Lag. How would you describe the curves? Was the one for increasing temperature the same as that for decreasing temperature? How long did it take for the curve to level off? This is important to know, since any measurement taken before this time has elapsed may not reflect the actual temperature. Compare your results to those of other students. Is there a difference with the different thermistors?

Feedback

Feedback may be visual and/or auditory and may be either direct (a change in temperature is associated with a corresponding change in the feedback signal) or processed. Examples of processed feedback are derivative, integrated, and threshold feedback. These modes of feedback are discussed in Lab I, p. 48. Experiment with the modes of feedback on your unit. See what kind of signal you get with the different modes while warming and/or cooling or when there is no change in temperature of the thermistor.

Trainee ______________________

Date __________

LAB VIII DATA SHEET AND GRAPH—CALIBRATION OF T UNIT

Observations	Temperature of: Thermometer	Thermistor
1.	______	______
2.	______	______
3.	______	______
4.	______	______
5.	______	______
6.	______	______

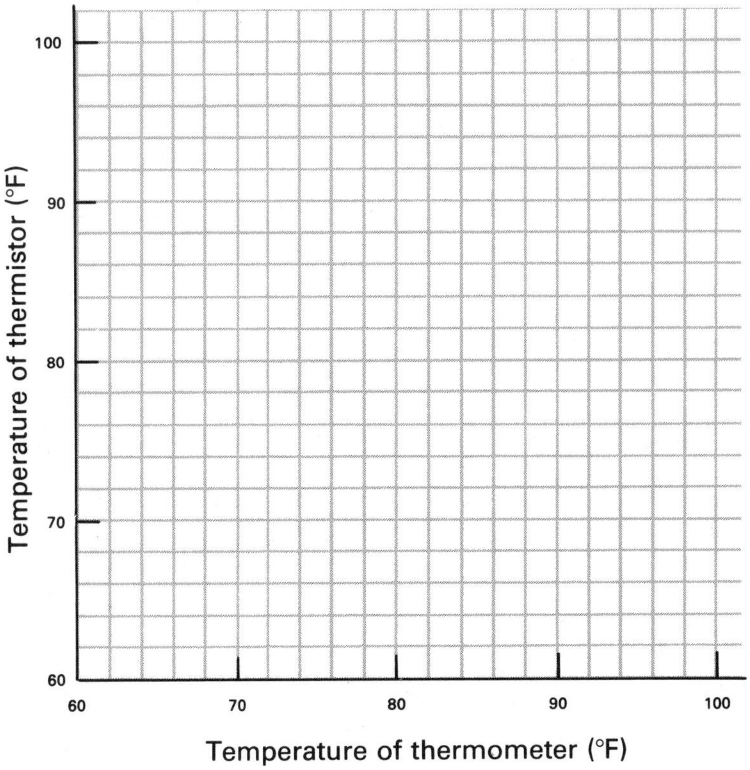

Trainee ________________________________

Date ____________

LAB VIII DATA SHEET AND GRAPH—THERMAL LAG

With thermistor under armpit

Time (sec)		Temperature of thermistor (°F)
0	(Room)	______
10		______
20		______
30		______
40		______
50		______
60		______
70		______
80		______
90		______
100		______
110		______
120		______

Thermistor taken out from armpit

Time (sec)	Temperature of thermistor (°F)
130	______
140	______
150	______
160	______
170	______
180	______
190	______
200	______
210	______
220	______
230	______
240	______

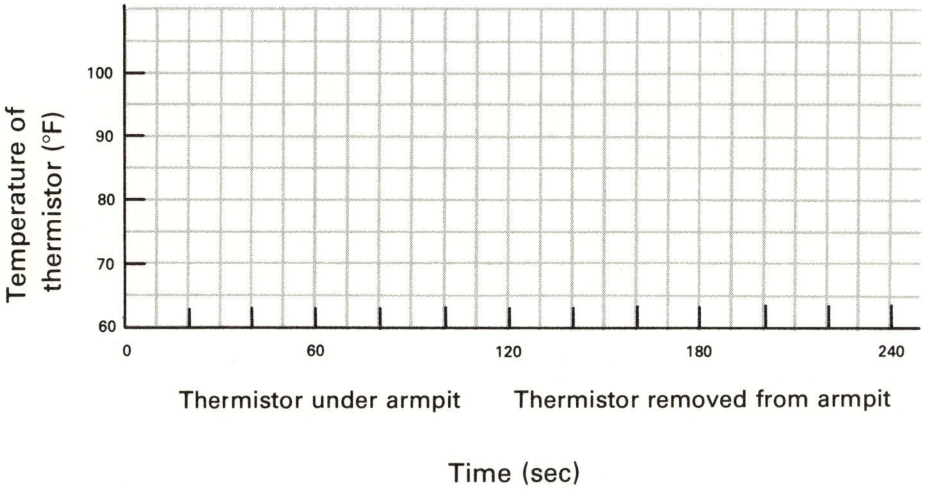

LAB IX
Techniques of Learning Temperature Change[1]

PRELAB PREPARATION

For Lab IX you will need to have prepared an image that will be used during the lab to encourage temperature learning. Proceed through the following instructions *before* your lab period.

Read the following suggestions and sample image.

Suggestions for Constructing a Meaningful Image[2]

1. Develop an image that is experienced in all five senses—tactile, visual, olfactory, auditory, and taste.
2. Use language that is very concrete and graphic; include microdetails.
3. Use a sequence of simple sentences.
4. Be sure what you describe is congruent with "reality." For example, describe a lemon as sour and not as sweet.
5. Try to reexperience the situation yourself, be aware of your senses, and then describe that experience.
6. Since you will be reading the image to your partner during the lab period, be sure that the image described is familiar to your partner. Use the descriptions your partner would use.

Sample Image

I am going to ask you to imagine an object. Remember each of us imagines in a different way. Some of us see objects in living color and great detail while others only sense it. Be comfortable with whatever you experience while reading the following sample image.

Sit comfortably. With your eyes closed, imagine a lemon. Notice the deep yellow color, the two ends, the sign "Sunkist" stamped on the side. As you put the lemon on a cutting board, notice the soft thud. Take your favorite kitchen knife in your hand, feel the coolness and pressure of the handle in your palm. Cut the lemon in half. Notice the pressure in your hand as you cut. Feel the droplets of lemon juice against your skin. Put the knife down and take one of the half lemons in your hand. Notice the droplets of lemon juice glistening in the light. Notice the half cut seeds, the outer rind, the pale yellow-white inner rind, the pulpy membranes containing the lemon juice. Now get a glass and squeeze the lemon so that the juice goes into the glass. Notice the coolness of the lemon in your hand and feel the drop-

[1]REFERENCE: *Mind/body integration,* pp. 151–162; 469–506.

[2]For additional information, see: W. S. Kroger & W. D. Felzer, *Hypnosis and behavior modification: Imagery conditioning,* Philadelphia: Lippincott, 1976; M. Samuels & N. Samuels, *Seeing with the mind's eye,* New York: Random House/Bookworks, 1975.

> lets of lemon juice against your skin. Hear the plopping of the seeds and the pulp. Smell the pungent, sharp, tart odor. Notice the tension in your arm and shoulder as you squeeze. Now take the other lemon half, squeeze it into juice also. Put that lemon half away, take the glass in your hand, feel the coldness of the glass. Bring the glass to your lips, tip the glass. Notice the pressure and coolness on the lower lip. Now taste and swallow the lemon juice. Note the pulp and seeds as you swallow.

What did you experience? Did you swallow? Did you notice an increase in saliva? Did your mouth pucker?

In creating an image, it is valuable to allow for feedback from the trainee, indicating that s/he is truly involved in the image. In this case, increased salivation would provide this feedback that the visualization has affected the autonomic nervous system.

Practice constructing an image that involves warmth, such as a sauna, a bubble bath, sitting in front of the fireplace, putting your hand in hot water, the beach, or the desert. In preparation for Lab IX, write out the visualization on the Lab IX: Guided Image. Use this image with your partner during the lab.

Trainee ____________________

Date ____________

LAB IX GUIDED IMAGE

LAB WORK

NOTE: The lab assumes familiarity with Modified Progressive Relaxation (i.e., completion of Instruction Set A).

Equipment

Temperature unit, tape.

Objective

Autonomic control is most rapidly gained through a process of passive attention; conversely, the harder you try the less you will succeed at the task (otherwise known as the Law of Reverse Effort). This is illustrated by the realization that such commands as "Be creative now!" or "Have an erection now!" have the opposite effect. Similarly, learning to relax and warm the periphery involves "allowing" the temperature to change. This "allowing" or passive attention can be fostered in many ways: (1) listening to the temperature feedback signal and identifying and optimizing the subjective experiences associated with it, (2) listening to autogenic phrases, (3) practicing progressive relaxation, and (4) listening to images that encourage autonomic changes to occur. The nonstriving attention to directed images can be a powerful trigger for autonomic changes, a fact which clarifies the 19th century label for the autonomic nervous system—the *imaginary nervous system*.

Much research with the biofeedback temperature unit has simultaneously used adjunctive techniques. When temperature changes have occurred, there has been confusion as to whether the feedback, the adjunctive techniques, or both were responsible for the change. In the following sections, you will explore four of these techniques separately, looking at which is most efficacious for you and others in your group. These techniques may be done in any order, and may be done within one lab period or completed in different lab periods. (If your group is large, it may be interesting to divide into smaller groups and explore different strategies. For example, have some proceed through the techniques in the order 1 through 4 while others proceed from 4 through 1, and still others complete the techniques over a series of different lab periods.)

Learning autonomic skills may take *many* practice sessions. In this way it is similar to learning a musical instrument. We do not expect anyone to learn to play the violin after one lesson.

It is important when guiding your partner through a technique to be cognizant of your delivery. Often the efficacy of a technique is determined by its delivery, specifically the intonation, inflection, speed of delivery and voice volume, and the correspondence between the verbal and nonverbal cues (it is hard to relax when someone is speaking in a nervous and shaky voice!).

After completion of all four techniques, complete Lab IX: Summary of Questions. Then meet with your group to complete Lab IX: Discussion and Conclusions.

TECHNIQUE I—INSTRUCTIONS FOR TEMPERATURE FEEDBACK TRAINING

After you are seated comfortably, have your partner attach the thermistor to the index finger of your dominant hand. Wait a few minutes until the temperature equilibrates (to account for the thermal lag). With your eyes closed and receiving no feedback, have your partner record baseline measurements every 15 sec for 1 min on Lab IX: Data Sheet and Graph—Temperature Feedback. Next, turn on the auditory feedback and listen to the signal, identifying which subjective experience accompanies an increase or decrease in temperature, for example, thoughts, images, emotions, or such internal body sensations as pulsing, tingling, warmth, or heaviness. Then optimize those experiences that accompany temperature increase. Do this for 5–10 min, having your partner record your temperature every minute. Turn off the feedback signal, and again have your partner record your temperature every 15 sec for 2 min, or until the temperature stabilizes. Graph your data and then answer Lab IX: Questions—Temperature Feedback. Repeat the procedure by having your partner do the feedback training.

Trainee ____________________

Trainer ____________________

Date __________

LAB IX DATA SHEET AND GRAPH—TEMPERATURE FEEDBACK

Baseline measurements (before feedback)

Time (sec)	Temperature (°F)
0	______
15	______
30	______
45	______
60	______

Measurements during training

Time (min)	Temperature (°F)
0	______
1	______
2	______
3	______
4	______
5	______
6	______
7	______
8	______
9	______
10	______

Posttraining measurements (after feedback)

Time (sec)	Temperature (°F)
0	______
15	______
30	______
45	______
60	______
75	______
90	______
105	______
120	______

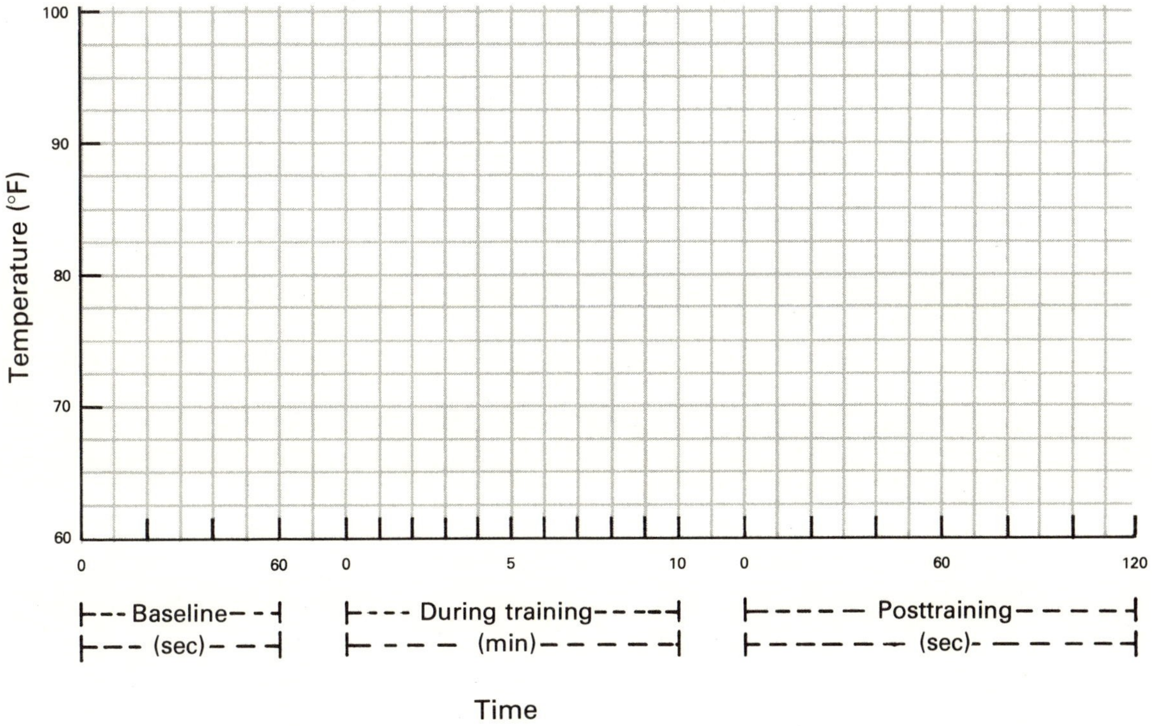

Trainee ______________________

Date __________

LAB IX QUESTIONS— TEMPERATURE FEEDBACK

1. What happened to your temperature during the training and posttraining?

____

____

2. What internal sensations, emotions, or thoughts were associated with: Increase in temperature?

____

____

Decrease in temperature?

____

____

No change in temperature?

____

____

3. Was there a congruence between the posttraining measurements and your subjective experience?

____

____

____

____

____

4. Comments:

____

____

____

____

____

TECHNIQUE II—INSTRUCTIONS FOR THE USE OF AUTOGENIC PHRASES[3]

After you are seated comfortably, have your partner attach the thermistor to the index finger of your dominant hand. With your eyes closed and receiving no feedback, have your partner record baseline measurements every 15 sec for 1 min on Lab IX: Data Sheet and Graph—Autogenic Phrases. Continue sitting quietly with your eyes closed and listen while your partner reads the following phrases slowly and in a soothing manner:

> I feel quite quiet . . . I am beginning to feel quite relaxed . . . My feet feel heavy and relaxed . . . My ankles, my knees, and my hips feel heavy, relaxed and comfortable . . . My solar plexus, and the whole central portion of my body, feel relaxed and quiet . . . My hands, my arms, and my shoulders feel heavy, relaxed and comfortable . . . My neck, my jaw, and my forehead feel relaxed . . . They feel comfortable and smooth . . . My whole body feels quiet, heavy, comfortable and relaxed. . . .
>
> I feel quite relaxed . . . My arms and hands are heavy and warm . . . I feel quite quiet . . . My whole body is relaxed and my hands are warm, relaxed and warm . . . My hands are warm . . . Warmth is flowing into my hands, they are warm . . . warm.

After the reading is completed, still without feedback, and while remaining relaxed, have your partner record your temperature every 15 sec for 2 min or until the temperature stabilizes.[4]

Graph your data and answer Lab IX: Questions—Autogenic Phrases. Then have your partner listen and relax while you read the phrases.

[3]Reference: J. Sargent, E. Green, & E. Walters, Preliminary report on the use of autogenic feedback training in the treatment of migraine and tension headaches, *Psychosomatic Medicine,* 1973, *35,* 129–135.

[4]Temperature recordings are not taken during the reading of the AT phrases, so as not to disrupt the reading; however, you may wish to glance at the visual feedback of the temperature unit and observe to which phrases your partner is responsive.

Trainee ______________________

Trainer ______________________

Date __________

LAB IX DATA SHEET AND GRAPH—AUTOGENIC PHRASES

Baseline measurements (before reading)

Time (sec)	Temperature (°F)
0	______
15	______
30	______
45	______
60	______

Posttraining measurements (after reading)

Time (sec)	Temperature (°F)
0	______
15	______
30	______
45	______
60	______
75	______
90	______
105	______
120	______

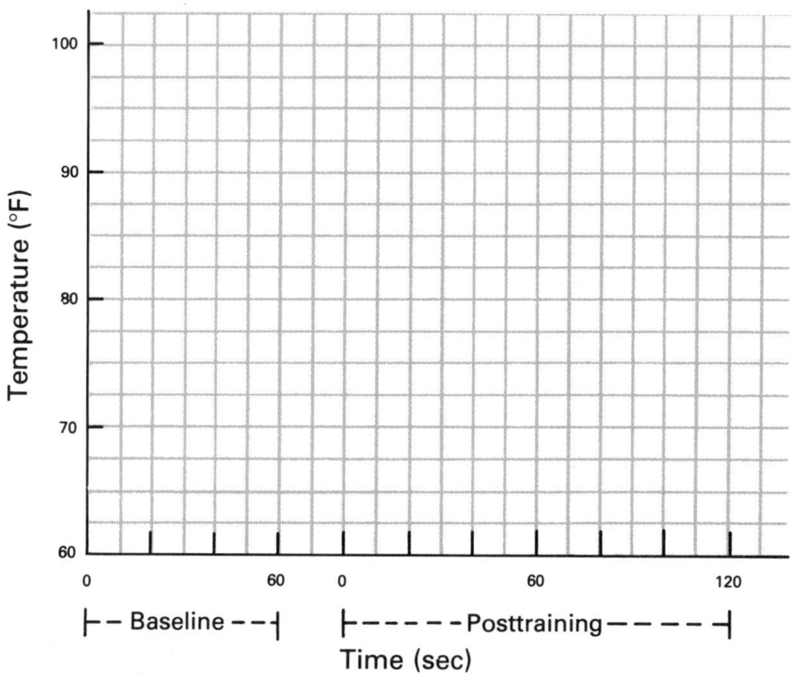

Trainee ______________________

Date ____________

LAB IX QUESTIONS—AUTOGENIC PHRASES

1. What happened to your temperature after listening to the autogenic phrases?

2. What did you experience while listening to the phrases?

3. Was there a congruence between the posttraining measurements and your subjective experience?

4. How did the delivery of the phrases affect your experience?

5. Comments:

TECHNIQUE III—INSTRUCTIONS FOR MODIFIED PROGRESSIVE RELAXATION

After you are seated comfortably, have your partner attach the thermistor to the index finger of your dominant hand. With your eyes closed and receiving no feedback, have your partner record baseline measurements every 15 sec for 1 min on Lab IX: Data Sheet and Graph—Modified Progressive Relaxation. Then, still without feedback, have your partner guide you through the relaxation that you learned in Instruction Set A—Week 1. After you are finished, still without feedback, have your partner record your temperature every 15 sec for 2 min or until your temperature stabilizes. Graph your data and answer Lab IX: Questions—Modified Progressive Relaxation. Then reverse roles and have your partner go through the MPR.

Trainee ______________________

Trainer ______________________

Date ____________

LAB IX DATA SHEET AND GRAPH—MODIFIED PROGRESSIVE RELAXATION

Baseline measurements (before reading)		Posttraining measurements (after reading)	
Time (sec)	Temperature (°F)	Time (sec)	Temperature (°F)
0	______	0	______
15	______	15	______
30	______	30	______
45	______	45	______
60	______	60	______
		75	______
		90	______
		105	______
		120	______

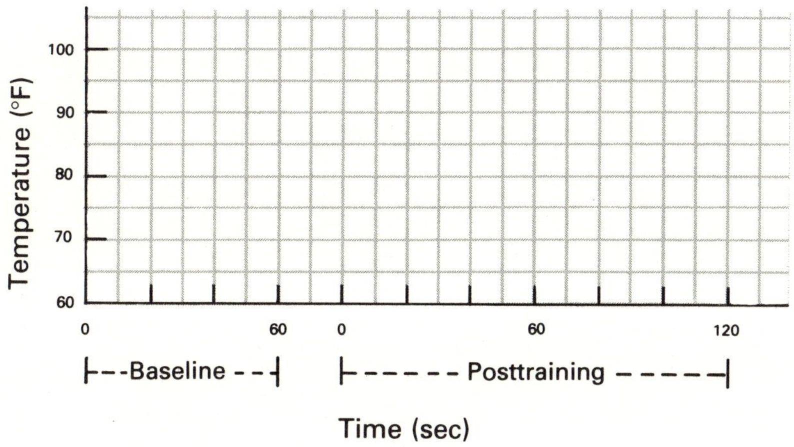

Trainee ______________________

Date __________

LAB IX QUESTIONS—MODIFIED PROGRESSIVE RELAXATION

1. What happened to your temperature after going through MPR?

2. What did you experience while listening to the phrases?

3. Was there a congruence between the posttraining measurements and your subjective experience?

4. How did the delivery of the phrases affect your experience?

5. Comments:

TECHNIQUE IV—INSTRUCTIONS FOR GUIDED IMAGE

After you are seated comfortably, have your partner attach the thermistor to the index finger of your dominant hand. With your eyes closed and receiving no feedback, have your partner record baseline measurements every 15 sec for 1 min on Lab IX: Data Sheet and Graph—Images. Now have your partner guide you through his/her scene involving warmth. After the completion of the image, have your partner record, without feedback, your temperature every 15 sec for 2 min or until your temperature stabilizes. Graph your data and answer Lab IX: Questions—Images. Then guide your partner through your scene. While reading your image to your partner, consider the following:

1. Look for feedback from your partner and use this to modify your image, if necessary. For example, if using a beach image triggers anxiety because of a past drowning experience, change to an image that elicits relaxation.
2. Never give implicit instructions or demands for the intended response, like "relax now." Rather, create an image that elicits the feeling of relaxation.
3. *Gradually* guide your partner into the image.
4. Be sure your voice is congruent with the content of the image. For example, a soothing scene should be described in a soothing, peaceful, quiet, slow voice.

Trainee ______________________

Trainer ______________________

Date ____________

LAB IX DATA SHEET AND GRAPH—IMAGES

Baseline measurements (before reading)		Posttraining measurements (after reading)	
Time (sec)	Temperature (°F)	Time (sec)	Temperature (°F)
0	______	0	______
15	______	15	______
30	______	30	______
45	______	45	______
60	______	60	______
		75	______
		90	______
		105	______
		120	______

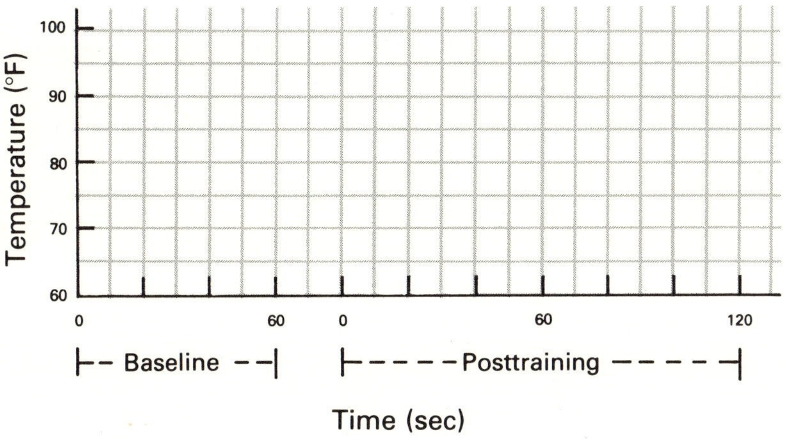

Trainee ______________________

Date __________

LAB IX QUESTIONS—IMAGES

1. What happened to your temperature after listening to your partner's image?

2. What did you experience while listening to the image?

3. Was there a congruence between the posttraining measurements and your subjective experience?

4. Did you experience the scene as real?

5. Which sense modality was most convincing for you?

6. How did the technique of delivery of the image affect your experience?

7. Comments:

Trainee ____________________

Date __________

LAB IX SUMMARY OF QUESTIONS

1. With which technique did you experience the greatest temperature change? Did the baseline measurements make a difference in the magnitude of change?[5]

2. Do you think you would have had different results if you had done the techniques in a different sequence? Explain.

3. Comments:

[5]The *Law of Initial Values* states ". . . that an ANS response to stimulation is a function of the prestimulus level. . . . The higher the prestimulus level of functioning, the smaller the response to a functioning-increasing stimulus." (R. Sternbach, *Principles of psychophysiology*, New York: Academic Press, 1966, p. 44.)

Trainee ____________________

Date __________

LAB IX DISCUSSION AND CONCLUSIONS

1. Was there variation among members of your group in the technique found to be most efficacious?

____

____

____

____

____

____

2. How is the variation related to differences in such factors as age, sex, past illness history, and past experience with a technique?

____

____

____

____

____

____

SUGGESTIONS FOR FUTURE RESEARCH

1. Combine temperature feedback with one of the adjunctive techniques.
2. Work with the thermistor on another part of the body. (A word of caution: increasing the temperature of the forehead may induce a headache.)
3. If using feedback with the autogenic phrases or MPR, when the temperature starts increasing, stop the phrases or MPR and attend gently to the sensations underneath the thermistor, such as throbbing.
4. Develop techniques to increase awareness of sensations associated with increased hand temperature, like putting the unmonitored hand in hot water or on a heating pad, and note sensations.
5. Explore the possibility of differential warming, such as warming the right hand while cooling the left hand.

LAB X
Home Practice
Learning Temperature Awareness

EQUIPMENT

Small hand thermometer.[1]

OBJECTIVE

One's peripheral skin temperature changes constantly in response to environmental changes and to any of a variety of stressors. The objective of the following home practice is to (1) develop an awareness of when your hand temperature changes, (2) begin to identify variables that may be causally related to this change (develop internal awareness), and (3) learn to warm your hands when your hand temperature has dropped.

INSTRUCTIONS

At least once each day during the week, on Lab X: Log Sheet:

a. Note your hand temperature. You may want to do this either based on subjective experience ("cool," "warm," etc.), or using a small economical hand thermometer.[1]
b. Identify variables that may be causally related to your hand temperature, i.e., where are you; whom are you with; what are you thinking about, anticipating, ruminating, feeling, doing? In other words, look at the physical, social, environmental, and personal variables involved in the situation.
c. If you observe your hands to be cool, take time out to warm your hands using one of the techniques that you found successful in the previous lab. Note any changes in your hand temperature and how the changes affect your experience.

At the end of the week, complete Lab X: Questions.

[1]See Appendix F for suggestions on where to purchase small hand thermometers.

Trainee ______________________

Date __________

LAB X LOG SHEET

Each day note the following: (a) hand temperature, (b) variables that may be causally related to the hand temperature, and (c) success at and effect of hand warming (if appropriate).

Day 1 a. ______________________
Date______ b. ______________________
c. ______________________

Day 2 a. ______________________
Date______ b. ______________________
c. ______________________

Day 3 a. ______________________
Date______ b. ______________________
c. ______________________

Day 4 a. ______________________
Date______ b. ______________________
c. ______________________

Day 5 a. ______________________
Date______ b. ______________________
c. ______________________

Day 6 a. ______________________
Date______ b. ______________________
c. ______________________

Day 7 a. ______________________
Date______ b. ______________________
c. ______________________

Trainee ______________________

Date __________

LAB X QUESTIONS

1. Identify the variables that were associated with a change in hand temperature for you.

____

____

____

2. Were there times when you were not able to warm your hands? If so, was your success related to the variables identified as associated with the hands being cool?

____

____

____

3. Identify some of the common themes that underlie the variables. For example, if you find that there is a decrease in hand temperature associated with anticipation of public speaking and associated with asking a friend out on a first date, you may discover that these events share the common underlying theme of fear of failure or rejection.

____

____

____

____

____

____

____

4. Comments:

____

____

____

LAB XI
Home Practice
Learning Intervention

OBJECTIVE

Having identified situations (the variables) to which one responds with a decrease in hand temperature, one may then learn to inhibit this automatic (unconscious) response. The objective of the following home practice is to develop this ability to keep the hands warm both in anticipation of and during a situation that previously was associated with a decrease in hand temperature.

INSTRUCTIONS

At least once each day during the week, on Lab XI: Log Sheet:

a. Note the situation previously identified (in Lab X) as causally related to a decrease in hand temperature.
b. When you anticipate confronting and in the process of confronting this situation, take time to warm your hands. Note your success or failure.
c. Note the effect of hand warming on your experience.

At the end of the week, complete Lab XI: Questions.

Trainee ______________________

Date __________

LAB XI LOG SHEET

Each day note the following: (a) situation, (b) success in hand warming, and (c) effect on experience.

Day 1 a. ______________________

Date ______ b. ______________________

c. ______________________

Day 2 a. ______________________

Date ______ b. ______________________

c. ______________________

Day 3 a. ______________________

Date ______ b. ______________________

c. ______________________

Day 4 a. ______________________

Date ______ b. ______________________

c. ______________________

Day 5 a. ______________________

Date ______ b. ______________________

c. ______________________

Day 6 a. ______________________

Date ______ b. ______________________

c. ______________________

Day 7 a. ______________________

Date ______ b. ______________________

c. ______________________

Trainee ______________________

Date __________

LAB XI QUESTIONS

1. Identify the situations during which you were successful and those in which you were unsuccessful in keeping your hands warm.

2. Generally, when you were successful in keeping your hands warm, how did this change your experience of the situation?

3. Comments:

SECTION 3

Electrodermograph

LAB XII

Introduction to the Electrodermograph[1]

NOTE: This lab assumes familiarity with the basic functions of biofeedback equipment. Review Lab I.

EQUIPMENT

Electrodermograph (EDG) and instruction manual, 10- and 50-kΩ resistors, connecting leads with alligator clips, detergent, hand cream, ski hat, and parka. *Optional:* Resistors of 15, 20, 25, 30, 35, 40, and 45 kΩ.

OBJECTIVE

The changing electrical activity of the skin has been used as the basis of the feedback signal for the various measures of electrodermal activity (EDA). Equipment monitoring EDA has been used in a variety of clinical, nonclinical, and research settings: work has been done with hypertensives,[2] phobic individuals,[3] and women in labor,[4] and the technique has also been applied to studies of the orienting response.[5]

The objective of this lab is to gain familiarity with the equipment, with the variables that affect electrodermal activity, and with your electrodermal response to various stimuli.

PHYSIOLOGICAL BASIS OF EDA

The various measures of EDA reflect changes in the electrical resistance of the skin. The resistance of the skin varies with sweat gland activity: the greater the sweat gland activity, the lower the resistance of the skin. The sweat glands themselves are under the control of the sympathetic nervous system, such that greater sympathetic arousal results in greater sweat gland activity. Hence, the various measures of EDA may be viewed as reflecting general arousal: greater arousal results in increased sweat gland activity and decreased skin resistance.[6]

[1]REFERENCE: *Mind/body integration,* pp. 231-236; 241-252; 261-268; 507-512.

[2]C. H. Patel, Yoga and biofeedback in the management of hypertension, *Lancet,* 1973, *2,* 1053-1055.

[3]G. D. Fuller, *Biofeedback: Methods and procedures in clinical practice,* San Francisco: Biofeedback Institute, 1977.

[4]R. Gregg, L. Frazier, & R. A. Nesbit, Effects of techniques of biofeedback on relaxation during childbirth, *Biofeedback and Self-Regulation,* 1976, *1,* 325-326.

[5]R. Lynn, *Attention, arousal and the orienting reflex,* New York: Pergamon, 1966.

[6]W. F. Prokasy & D. C. Raskin (Eds.), *Electrodermal activity in psychological research,* New York: Academic Press, 1973.

There are a variety of measures of EDA. In most common use is the measurement of skin resistance (SR), which is traditionally referred to as *galvanic skin response* (GSR). In this method, a small current is passed through the skin. As sweat gland activity increases, there is a decrease in skin resistance that results in either an increase in current flow or a drop in voltage.[7] These changes in current flow or voltage are detected by the EDG and translated into a feedback signal, displayed as changes in either resistance (ohms) or conductance (mhos). By convention, most psychophysiologists now use skin conductance, which is the reciprocal of SR (SC = 1/SR) as the basic measure.

Another measure of EDA, used less frequently than SR, is skin potential (SP). In this case, voltage changes in the skin are measured directly (as is the EMG signal).

BACKGROUND INFORMATION FOR EDA MEASURES

Tonic Level and Phasic Response

In looking at changes in skin activity, one may look at either of two phenomena:

1. *Tonic level:* Very slow changes that take a long period of time to observe, usually referred to as skin conductance level (SCL) or skin potential level (SPL).
2. *Phasic response:* Rapid, usually transient changes in response to some stimuli, usually referred to as skin conductance response (SCR) or skin potential response (SPR).

The major problem associated with measuring tonic level and phasic activity simultaneously is that the sensitivity needed to record the phasic response is different from that needed to record tonic levels. For example, if the equipment is set to monitor tonic levels, the phasic response will appear insignificant (see Figure 12A). Consequently, one usually uses different scales or displays for the phasic response and the tonic level.

In order to show clearly the phasic response, the signal must be amplified. Electronically, this may be accomplished by the use of a *high-pass frequency filter* (referred to as *AC-coupled*). This eliminates the direct current and the slow alternating current components that make up the tonic level. The remaining fast-frequency signal containing the phasic response is then amplified (see Figure 12B). Another technique that allows monitoring of the phasic response is called the *subtraction method* (referred to as *DC-coupled with offset*). In this case, a fixed resistance is subtracted from the signal so that the tonic level is reset to zero. Any change in the signal above and below this arbitrary zero level is then amplified (see Figure 12C).

An advantage of the high-pass filter technique is that once the equipment is set for a specific trainee, only the phasic response will be monitored; hence, the equipment does not need to be continually readjusted. However, certain information is lost: one does not see changes in the tonic level nor can one truly assess the time required for the phasic response to return to baseline. This information has been filtered out. On the other hand, the subtraction method shows both changes in the tonic level from the arbitrary zero point and the time required for the phasic response to return to baseline. Because the signal may go off scale, the equipment may need to be reset to a new arbitrary zero point.

Normal Ranges

The following is an outline of the normal ranges of the various measurements of electrodermal activity:

A. Skin conductance
   1. Tonic level: 2–100 μmhos/cm^2. (This is equivalent to 500 to 10 kΩ for the resistance measure.)
   2. Phasic level: 0.01–5 μmhos/cm^2.

[7]See Appendix A for a review of basic electrical concepts.

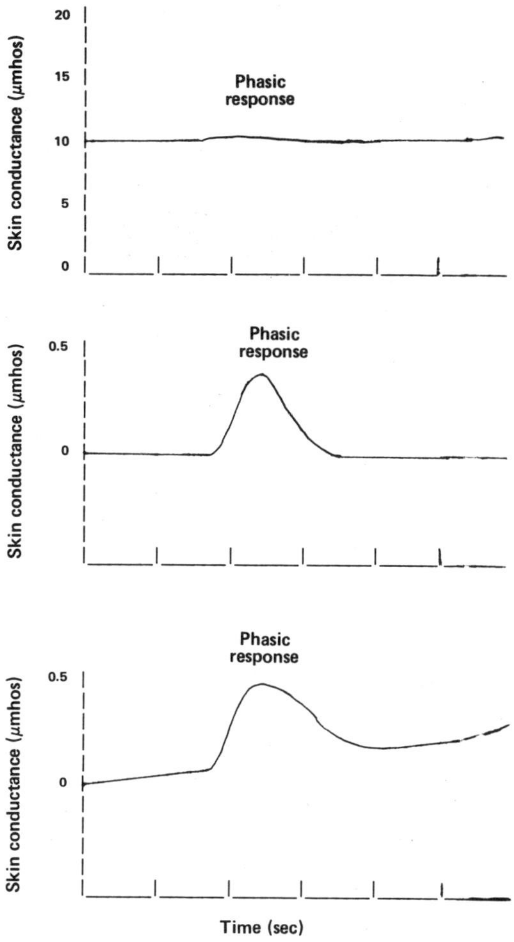

FIGURE 12. Techniques of amplification of EDA. (A) Unprocessed signal. Equipment is set to monitor tonic levels; the phasic response appears insignificant. (B) High-pass filter with signal amplification. Equipment is set to monitor phasic response. (C) Subtraction method with signal amplification. Equipment is set to monitor phasic response and changes in tonic level from arbitrary zero point.

B. Skin potential
   1. Tonic level: +10 mV to −70 mV.
   2. Phasic response: a biphasic response involving an initial negative component up to 2 mV followed by a secondary positive component up to 4 mV.

FLOW DIAGRAM

The flow diagram for the EDA signal is similar to that described in Lab I. Refer to p. 46.

PLACEMENT OF THE ELECTRODES

Most often the electrodes used for measuring EDA are metal contacts, such as silver-impregnated cloth, that do not require electrode jelly (Figure 13A). They are strapped to two fingers as shown in Figure 13B. Usually one finger is skipped to avoid the accidental shorting (touching) of the electrodes. When measuring resistance, the contact between the skin and sensor is critical; hence, care should be taken so that the electrodes fit snugly but not so tightly as to induce throbbing or occlude blood flow.

If the electrodes require electrode jelly (such as silver–silver chloride electrodes), they should be secured either with an adhesive collar or tape and placed on the palmar surface as shown in Figure 14. The palmar surface is used because the sweat glands of the palms are particularly responsive to emotional stimuli. No preparation of skin is required

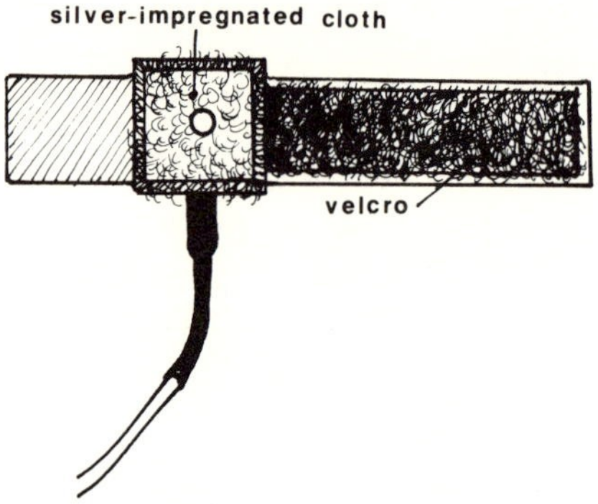

FIGURE 13A. Electrode used for electrodermal recording.

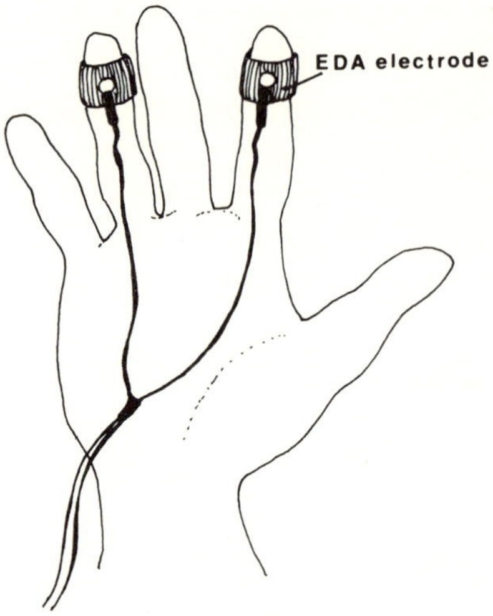

FIGURE 13B. Attachment of EDA electrode.

other than simple washing. A few researchers use grease solvents such as acetone or ether prior to electrode placement. In all studies, it is advisable to standardize such procedures.

OPERATION OF THE EQUIPMENT

The following instructions are intended to familiarize one with the use of the EDG. Some biofeedback equipment may not have a battery test, range selector, or choice of feedback display mode. In order to follow this discussion, the meter and/or auditory feedback must be set in such a way as to give direct, instantaneous feedback.

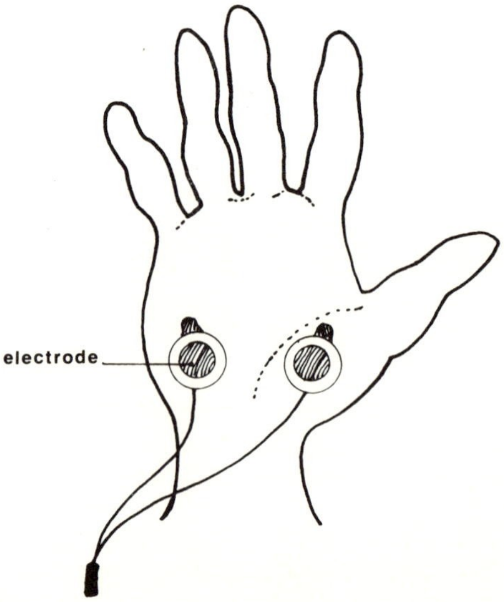

FIGURE 14. Attachment of EDA electrodes requiring adhesive collars.

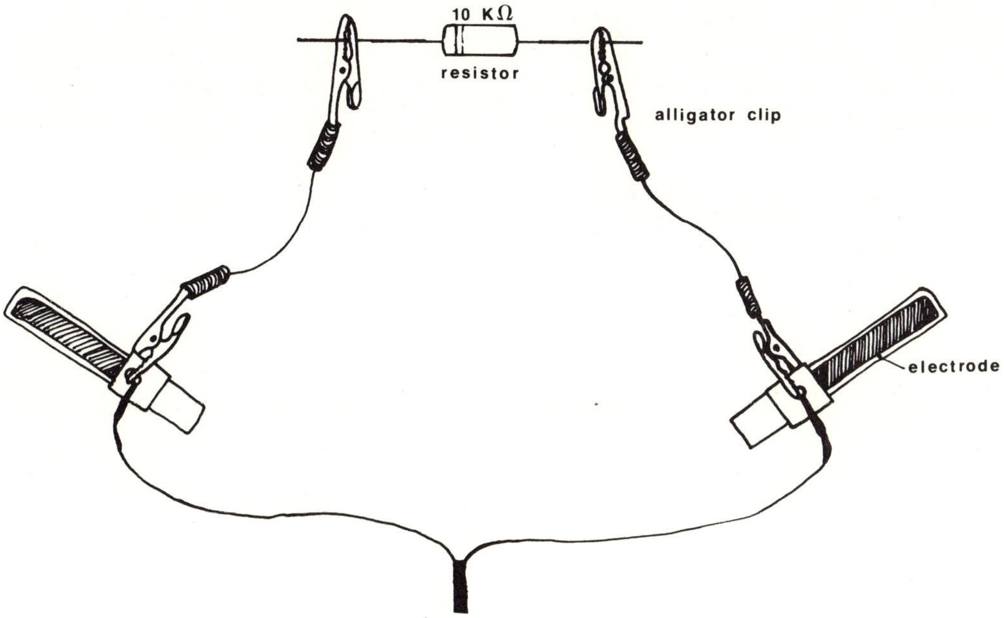

FIGURE 15. Technique of calibration for the EDG.

After the electrode leads are plugged into the machine, turn on the machine. Complete a battery check if your machine has such an operation. Check your instruction manual for specific instructions.

Battery Test

If your machine has a range selector, select the range that will allow the tonic level of skin conductance (SCL) to be observed (this is sometimes called the absolute scale).

Selection of Range

In order to determine the accuracy of the equipment (i.e., if the machine reads 30,000 Ω, is this the true resistance offered by the skin?), one must compare the readings with a known standard. Begin by placing a resistor of 10,000 Ω (10 kΩ) between the electrode leads. Figure 15 shows one method of connection.

Calibration[8]

What is the reading on the machine? ______________________

Remember that if your machine has units of μmhos, you will need to convert these values to ohms. EXAMPLE: 100 μmhos = 100×10^{-6} mhos. Since resistance = 1/conductance, resistance = $1/(100 \times 10^{-6}) = 10^4$ Ω = 10 kΩ.

Repeat using the 50,000-Ω resistor.

What is the reading on the machine? ______________________

If the EDA readings do not correspond to those of the resistors, either have the equipment calibrated by the manufacturer, or complete Lab XII: Data Sheet and Graph—Calibration of EDG. Record the observed equipment values on the calibration data sheet. Plot the equipment reading against the known resistor value. One may then use this calibration graph to determine the true value of any recording.

When beginning to work with an EDG that monitors skin conductance, one may wish to quickly determine if the machine is working. This may be done by plugging the

Behavioral Test

[8]This instruction applies only to equipment measuring SC or SR.

electrodes into the machine and holding them at a distance (say, 1 ft) from each other. The machine should read a very low conductance (near zero). Then touch the electrodes together (*for a fraction of a second only*). The machine should read a very high conductance.

As with all biofeedback equipment, it is good to begin with a behavioral test to determine if the machine is working in the expected manner. Plug the electrodes into the equipment and have your partner attach the electrodes to your hand. Turn the equipment on and set the amplification to the appropriate range, where a change in the signal can be observed (SCR or SPR). Now take a deep breath and exhale loudly. The feedback signal (meter or auditory) should increase within a few seconds (the latency period usually ranges from 1.3 to 2.5 sec) and then return shortly (recovery period usually ranges from 1 to 10 sec) to near the original value. Or have your partner unexpectedly clap his/her hands loudly near you. The signal changes should be similar to those with the deep inhalation. If you get no response, check the electrode contacts and try a more sensitive amplification.

Exploration of Feedback Modes and Signal Processing Functions

Repeat the preceding behavioral test using different feedback modes and different processing functions, such as integration or threshold, found on your piece of equipment. Note how the feedback signal changes.

Function	Effect on feedback signal or display
________	______________________________
________	______________________________

Exploration of Psychophysiological Variables That Affect the Signal

EDA is affected by a variety of factors that change both the tonic level and phasic response of the signal. The following exercises are intended as an exploration of some of these factors. If your equipment does not monitor tonic level changes, complete only the applicable portions of the exercises. Do these exercises without feedback. In recording phasic responses, you may observe less and less response to your partner's clapping. This is a common phenomenon called habituation. To address this problem, you may want other members of your group to do the exercises in a different sequence. Discuss findings with your group, and complete Lab XII: Discussion and Conclusions—Physical Variables.

1. Quality of the Skin

a. Effect of Detergent. Record electrodermal activity. Have your partner clap his/her hands suddenly and note the amplitude of your response. Then wash your hands with a strong detergent. Again record electrodermal activity. Have your partner clap his/her hands, noting your response.

	Before washing hands	After washing hands
Tonic level	______	______
Phasic response	______	______

How did washing your hands affect your tonic level and phasic response?

____

____

____

Trainee ______________________

Date __________

LAB XII DATA SHEET AND GRAPH—CALIBRATION OF EDG

Known resistor	Equipment reading (μmhos)	Equipment reading converted to kΩ
10 kΩ	______	______
15	______	______
20	______	______
25	______	______
30	______	______
35	______	______
40	______	______
45	______	______
50	______	______

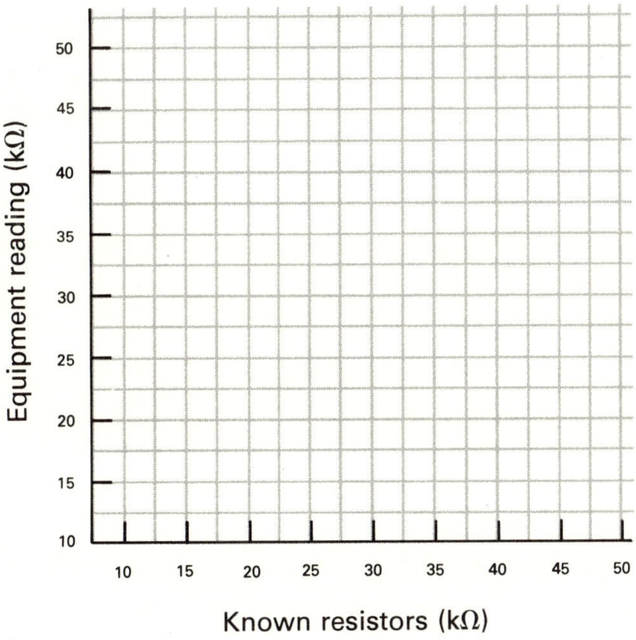

b. Effect of Hand Cream. Repeat exercise as above, applying hand cream instead of washing hands.

	Before applying hand cream	After applying hand cream
Tonic level	______	______
Phasic response	______	______

How did applying hand cream affect your tonic level and phasic response?

____

____

____

2. Electrode Contact

Record the electrodermal activity—both tonic level and phasic responses (i.e., both baseline and response to "surprise" noise)—with the electrodes (a) strapped *very* tightly, (b) strapped snugly, and (c) strapped loosely onto the finger.

	With electrodes very tight	With electrodes snug	With electrodes loose
Tonic level	______	______	______
Phasic response	______	______	______

How does the tightness affect the tonic level and phasic response?

____

____

____

3. Temperature

a. Record electrodermal activity (both tonic level and phasic response). Then put on a ski parka and hat. Wait until you feel warm. Record electrodermal activity.

	When cool	When warm
Tonic level	______	______
Phasic response	______	______

How did increasing your temperature affect the tonic level and phasic response?

____

____

____

b. Repeat exercise as above before and after holding a glass of ice water in the hand from which you are recording.

	Before holding	After holding
Tonic level	________	________
Phasic response	________	________

How did changing your hand temperature affect the tonic level and phasic response?

____

____

____

4. Dietary Intake

Record electrodermal activity before and after drinking a cup of coffee or eating a candy bar. Do this after fasting for at least 5 hr, and wait a few minutes before taking "after" measurements.

	Before eating	After eating
Tonic level	________	________
Phasic response	________	________

How did the drinking or eating affect the tonic level and phasic response?

____

____

____

NOTE: Certain medications also affect the signal. These include cholinergic blocking agents such as atropine and scopolamine.

5. Physical Position

Record electrodermal activity while sitting stiffly with legs crossed and then while sitting very relaxed with legs apart.

	Sitting stiffly	Sitting relaxed
Tonic level	________	________
Phasic response	________	________

How did changing your position affect the tonic level and phasic response?

____

____

____

6. Interpersonal Factors

Record electrodermal activity first with your partner several feet away with little eye contact between the two of you. Then take recordings with your partner sitting right next to you, almost staring at you.

	Partner distant	Partner close
Tonic level	_______	_______
Phasic response	_______	_______

How did having your partner close to you affect the tonic level and phasic response?

____

____

____

Trainee ______________________

Date __________

LAB XII DISCUSSION AND CONCLUSIONS—PSYCHOPHYSIOLOGICAL VARIABLES

1. Looking at each of these exercises, how were your results similar to or different from those of others in your group?

   Quality of skin ______________________

   Electrode contact ______________________

   Temperature ______________________

   Dietary intake ______________________

   Physical position ______________________

   Interpersonal factors ______________________

2. What are the implications of these effects for EDG training?

3. Comments:

Exploration of EDA as a Measure of Emotional Reactivity

The EDG is often used to show emotional reactivity (such is the basis for its use as a lie detector). The following exercises are intended as explorations of this relationship.

1. Response to Words (Do without Feedback)

Exchange manuals with your partner. On Lab XII: Data Sheet—Word List, you will see five words that have varying emotional valences. Add 15 more words of similarly varying emotional value (i.e., some words that you think will be neutral and some that would get an emotional reaction). You will be reading this list to your partner. Add the same words to Lab XII: Subjective Response—Word List.

Have your partner connect you to the EDG. Sit comfortably with eyes closed. Have your partner read the list of words s/he entered in your manual to you, noting on the Lab XII: Data Sheet—Word List those words to which you respond on the EDG, the maximum intensity of your response, and the time it takes for the response to return to prestimulus level. The list should be read slowly, so that if you do respond, there is time for the response to return to near baseline values before the next word is read. If it takes greater than 20 sec to return to baseline values, go on to the next word. After your partner has read the list to you, look at Lab XII: Subjective Response—Word List, and check those words to which you feel you responded during the reading. Complete Lab XII: Questions—Word List.

Now read the word list you created for your partner, repeating the same procedure as above.

2. Reviewing the Day (Do with Feedback)

Have your partner connect you to the EDG. Sit quietly and comfortably. Mentally go over the activities of the preceding day while attending to the EDG feedback signal. When there is a response, note the event you were reviewing and identify to what you were responding (e.g., psychological meaning). Note what kind of a sensation you felt and where in your body you felt it when there was a response. Complete Lab XII: Subjective Response—Events.

Complete Lab XII: Questions—Reviewing the Day. Have your partner review events.

Trainee ______________________

Trainer ______________________

Date __________

LAB XII DATA SHEET—WORD LIST

Your partner should write in the amplitude of your EDG response to each word and note the length of time before response returns to prestimulus level.

Words	Amplitude of response	Time to return to baseline
Chair		
Shoe		
Mother		
Sex		
Glasses		

Trainee ______________________

Trainer ______________________

Date ____________

LAB XII SUBJECTIVE RESPONSE—WORD LIST

Check those words to which you feel you responded.

Words	You felt a response
Chair	
Shoe	
Mother	
Sex	
Glasses	

Trainee ______________________

Date __________

LAB XII QUESTIONS—WORD LIST

1. Did you find a correspondence between the words you thought you reacted to and the actual electrodermal responses?

2. What was the relationship between the intensity of electrodermal response (amplitude) and length of time required to return to baseline?

3. Comments:

Trainee ____________________

Date __________

LAB XII SUBJECTIVE RESPONSE—EVENTS

Mentally go over the activities of the preceding day while attending to the EDG feedback signal. When there is a response, note the event you were reviewing and identify to what you were responding (e.g., psychological meaning). Note what kind of a sensation you felt and where in your body you felt it when there was a response.

Events being reviewed when change in EDA	Possible reason for response	Physical changes noted (what and where)

Trainee ______________________

Date __________

LAB XII QUESTIONS—REVIEWING THE DAY

1. Describe your electrodermal response pattern (EXAMPLE: Generally the response consisted of a large amplitude and rapid return to baseline).

2. Describe the common themes underlying the reasons for the electrodermal response.

3. What were the common physical sensations that accompanied the electrodermal response?

4. Do you feel that EDG is a good indicator for you of emotional reactivity and might be a valuable tool for identifying areas of unresolved conflict? Discuss.

5. Comments:

Learning Voluntary Control over EDA

Determine how you can both increase and inhibit your EDA. Try relaxation exercises (e.g., MPR, the autogenic phrases in Lab IX) or imagining scenes that involve joy, sadness, anger, apprehension, and anticipation.

Have your partner attach you to the EDG. Sit quietly while attending to your baseline for several minutes. Practice your relaxation exercise or imaging while you are receiving feedback. Attempt to either inhibit or increase the signal. Find the strategy that is most helpful to you. Once you feel competent, attempt to decrease (or increase) your EDA signal *without* feedback. Have your partner observe the feedback signal to confirm whether in fact you have learned control. Complete Lab XII: Questions—Learning Voluntary Control.

Switch roles with your partner. Discuss your results of this and the previous two exercises in your group and complete Lab XII: Discussion and Conclusions—EDA.

Trainee ______________________

Date __________

LAB XII QUESTIONS—LEARNING VOLUNTARY CONTROL

1. What strategy was most helpful for you in:
   Decreasing the EDA

   ____

   ____

   Increasing the EDA

   ____

   ____

2. To what extent were you successful without feedback in:
   Decreasing the EDA

   ____

   ____

   Increasing the EDA

   ____

   ____

3. Comments:

   ____

   ____

   ____

   ____

   ____

   ____

   ____

   ____

   ____

   ____

Trainee ______________________

Date __________

LAB XII DISCUSSION AND CONCLUSIONS—EDA

1. In which ways did people vary in their tonic EDA level? How was the variation related to sex, age, and pathology?

____

____

____

2. Was there a variability in the EDA phasic response pattern among the members of your group and, if so, how was this variation related to sex, age, and pathology?

____

____

____

3. Was there a relationship between the tonic level and the phasic response pattern?

____

____

____

4. What were the common psychological themes underlying the electrodermal response in the exercise Reviewing the Day?

____

____

____

____

5. What strategies were effective in increasing and decreasing EDA?

____

____

____

SUGGESTIONS FOR FUTURE RESEARCH

1. Explore other body areas to record EDA (such as the feet, the forehead) and whether people vary in the areas of response. Explore the differences in response of the two types of sweat glands: apocrine glands (armpits and genital area) and eccrine glands (over entire body).
2. Explore the right-left symmetry of electrodermal response (i.e., do the right and left-handed electrodermal responses vary depending upon stimulus?).
3. Explore the electrodermal response with different pathologies (for example, what is the effect of a unilateral sympathectomy on EDA?).
4. Monitor EDA while engaging in other pursuits, such as driving a car, watching TV, or sexual activity.
5. Explore EDA during various mental efforts (like math calculations).

LAB XIII

Systematic Desensitization[1]

PRELAB PREPARATION

During the week preceding the systematic desensitization lab, note below any stimuli (people, things, thoughts, feelings, etc.) that evoke generally distressing responses, such as anxiety, fear, or embarrassment. On a scale of 0 to 100 (no distress to extreme distress) evaluate the intensity of your response. Traditionally, the intensity is referred to as "subjective units of disturbance" (SUD).[2]

Stimulus	Response	Intensity (SUD)

[1]REFERENCE: *Mind/body integration*, pp. 513–522.
[2]See p. 271, Lab XIII, Table 1, for examples.

LAB WORK

Note: In order to complete this lab, one must have successfully learned a relaxation technique (i.e., have completed Instruction Set A), and be familiar with one of the units that monitors arousal (such as EMG or EDG).

Equipment

EDG or EMG,[3] watch with second hand.

Before beginning to use the equipment, one should proceed through the following steps:

1. Complete a battery check and determine that the equipment is working.
2. Place the electrodes properly.
3. Choose the appropriate range to provide meaningful feedback.
4. Complete a behavioral test.
5. Where applicable, select appropriate settings for time integration, threshold, feedback modality, and any other functions present on your equipment.

Objective

Systematic desensitization (SD) is a technique in which the relaxation state is paired with an anxiety-provoking stimulus (thought, image, event, object). The trainee remains relaxed while visualizing increasingly anxiety-provoking stimuli, thereby becoming desensitized to them. The basic assumption underlying this technique is that relaxation and anxiety are mutually exclusive states, i.e., that a person cannot be both relaxed and anxious at the same time.[4]

Systematic desensitization may be viewed as a systematic technique intended to bring about a change in the connection between a stimulus and one's habitual reaction to the stimulus: one learns to respond in a nonanxious way to previously anxiety-producing stimuli. There are many other techniques that implicitly involve desensitization, but which do so in an unstructured fashion. For example, in meditation one does not follow or become involved in any anxiety-producing thought, but rather returns to the focus of meditation. In so doing one becomes desensitized. This process may be described as "global desensitization" (see Instruction Set B).

The objective of this lab is to become familiar with the procedures of systematic desensitization and a clinical use of the EDG.

Instructions

The basic steps of systematic desensitization are:

1. Learning profound relaxation.
2. Developing a hierarchy of anxiety-provoking stimuli.
3. Presenting the hierarchy while continuing to remain relaxed.

1. Learning Relaxation

The basis of SD is the pairing of anxiety-producing stimuli with relaxation. Therefore, it is imperative that the trainee has mastered a relaxation technique. Traditionally, a shortened version of Jacobson's Progressive Relaxation, such as that presented in Instruction Set A, is used. Mastery of this technique is necessary before proceeding through this lab and may be facilitated by the use of biofeedback equipment, such as the EDG, EMG, and temperature unit.[5] In addition, once relaxation has been learned, physiological

[3]The EDG is preferentially used as the monitor of autonomic arousal during the desensitization process.

[4]For more detailed discussions see J. Wolpe, *The practice of behavior therapy,* New York: Pergamon Press, 1969; T. Budzynski & J. Stoyva, Biofeedback techniques in behavior therapy. In W. Birbaumer (Ed.), *Neuropsychologie der Angst,* Reihe Fortschritte der Klinischen Psychologie, Volume 3, Munich: Urban & Schwarzenberg, 1973, pp. 248–270.

[5]Obviously, the unit used should monitor a system in which the trainee is responsive. Thus, the EMG would be of limited value if s/he does not respond muscularly to stress.

TABLE 1
Example of Prelab Preparation and Grouping by Theme

Prelab preparation		
Stimulus	Response	Intensity (SUD)
Dream of close person dying	Startled, terror	80
Doing aikido technique	Anxiety	60
Close friend saying "I need to talk to you"	Fear	25
Recounting attack to friend	Fear	80
While walking at night, cat jumping into path	Fear	25
Taking exam	Anxiety	25
Injection	Fear	60
Speaking in front of large group	Terror	80

Grouping by theme	
Theme 1: Fear of being judged	
Stimulus: Taking exam	SUD: 25
Speaking in front of large group	80
Theme 2: Fear of losing a loved one	
Stimulus: Dream of close person dying	SUD: 80
Close friend saying "I need to talk to you"	25
Theme 3: Fear of being physically hurt	
Stimulus: Doing aikido technique[a]	SUD: 60
Cat jumping into path	25
Recounting attack to friend	80
Concrete fears	
Stimulus: Fear of injection	SUD: 75

[a]Originally this stimulus was grouped under the fear of being judged (performance in aikido class). However, in discussion it became clear that it really belonged under the fear of being physically hurt.

monitoring may be used to confirm whether in fact the trainee is relaxed, such as prior to the desensitization process. It is very important that the trainee be in a relaxed state lest the anxiety-producing stimulus be coupled with the anxiety state. Here, biofeedback is used to verify the trainee's subjective evaluation of his/her level of relaxation. This eliminates the incorrect reporting of relaxation by the trainee, a problem that may arise when no feedback is used.

2. Development of a Hierarchy of Anxiety-Producing Stimuli

a. Grouping by Theme. Start with the list of anxiety-producing stimuli on the prelab preparation sheet. With your partner's assistance, look for themes that underlie a number of the stimuli, and then group the stimuli under common themes on Lab XIII: Data Sheet 1. Some stimuli may be concrete fears and may not be grouped under a theme, such as the fear of an injection. Table 1 illustrates the process of grouping by theme.

Often it is difficult to identify a theme or the obvious theme may not in fact be the real cause of the anxiety. For example. Wolpe[6] reports the case of a married woman for whom the theme of claustrophobia had been identified, yet the issue really was being shut in by her husband.

b. Selection of Theme. Select one of the themes (or stimuli) you would like to work on in this lab. Keep in mind that your lab time is limited—do not choose something too complex. It is important to work on a theme or stimulus that is "unreasonable" or gets in the way of your life. From the example of stimuli and themes (Table 1), the fear of injection and the fear of being judged were considered because of the obvious interference in the trainee's life. The fear of injection was finally selected because of its concrete and relatively less complex nature.

c. Development of Hierarchy. In order to proceed through the SD, one must have a hierarchy of anxiety-producing stimuli related to the same theme. In order to develop your hierarchy, you may want to use the stimuli from your selected theme on Lab XIII: Data Sheet 1; in addition, you will have to develop others based on past experience. Start by imagining the worst (most fearful) stimulus with the same theme as selected from Lab XIII: Data Sheet 1. Rank this stimulus at 100 SUD on Lab XIII: Data Sheet 2. Consider 0 to mean the relaxed state. Progressively fill in stimuli that are more anxiety-provoking. The spacing between SUD should not exceed 5–10 SUDs. Rank stimuli from least to most intense. Most hierarchies contain from 10 to 20 items.

It may be helpful in structuring the hierarchy to consider first situations connected only peripherally (either in time or space or degree of self-involvement) with the theme and then those more centrally connected. Table 2 illustrates the hierarchy developed for the fear of receiving an injection.

d. Biofeedback confirmation of hierarchy (without feedback).[7] Biofeedback can be used to monitor the intensity of the response to imagined stimuli. Have your partner attach EDG electrodes to your dominant hand. Sit quietly until the EDG has stabilized. Have

TABLE 2
Example of a Hierarchy: Fear of Injection

Stimulus	SUDs (0–100)
Relaxed state	0
Skin being scratched	10
Seeing small syringe	20
Seeing small needle	25
Seeing large syringe with needle	30
Watching someone get injection	40
Making appointment with doctor for injection a month in advance	50
Thinking of appointment 2 weeks prior to visit	60
Getting TB test	70
Day before going to doctor's office	80
Walking into doctor's office	90
Seeing needle against skin	95
Receiving injection	100

[6]Wolpe, op. cit., p. 141.

[7]Often when a trainee perceives his or her biofeedback signal, s/he reacts to the signal. This reaction may result in additional autonomic change, which will be reflected in the feedback signal. Hence the resultant feedback measure is the sum of the actual response to the presented stimulus and that to the feedback signal. In order to avoid this problem, no feedback signal should be given to the trainee when you are using the feedback signal to monitor the physiological response to specific stimuli (in this case to distress-evoking stimuli).

Trainee ____________________

Trainer ____________________

Date __________

LAB XIII DATA SHEET 1

Theme 1: ____________________

Stimulus	SUD

Theme 2: ____________________

Stimulus	SUD

Theme 3: ____________________

Stimulus	SUD

Concrete fears:

Stimulus	SUD

Trainee ______________________

Trainer ______________________

Date __________

LAB XIII DATA SHEET 2 Hierarchy

Selected theme (or specific stimulus): ______________________

Stimulus	SUD (0–100) in ascending order	Amplitude of EDG responses
Relaxed state	0	
	100	

How did the amplitude of the EDG response compare to the SUD ratings?

____

your partner ask you to imagine the stimulus with the lowest SUD rating (read off Lab XIII: Data Sheet 2). Be as involved as possible, and when you feel you are deeply involved, raise the index finger of your nondominant hand to signal to your partner your involvement. At this point, your partner will record the amplitude of the EDG signal on Lab XIII: Data Sheet 2.

After raising your finger, let go of the image and relax. When your partner observes that the EDG has returned to prestimulus value (do not wait longer than 60 sec), s/he will than ask you to image the second least intense stimulus on your list.

Go through the same procedure as for the first stimulus.

Continue through the stimulus list.

After completion of all the items in the hierarchy, compare the SUD and amplitude of the EDG response with your partner.

It is important to remember that either of the following problems may have influenced your results:

1. Inability or unwillingness to feel, to experience, or to be involved with the image. If this is a difficulty for you, it may be helpful for you to exaggerate the image in the sense modality that you experience most easily. For example, if you have a strong auditory sense, elaborate the auditory components of the image.
2. Nonreturn to baseline. If your partner gives you the next stimulus before your EDG response has returned to baseline, the EDG may reflect the preceding response as well as the new response. This problem may be eliminated by allowing larger intervals (greater than 60 sec) between presentation of stimuli.

If the EDG readings confirm the SUD ratings (i.e., the higher SUD rating is reflected in a larger EDG response), proceed with Section 3.

If there is a discrepancy between the EDG responses and SUD, reconstruct a hierarchy that is most meaningful to you given the EDG responses and the SUD evaluation.

3. Presentation of Hierarchy While Continuing to Maintain the Relaxed State (with Auditory Feedback)

The actual process of desensitization involves the presentation of increasingly anxiety-provoking stimuli while the trainee remains relaxed. For the purpose of this lab, all the stimuli will be self-generated imagined scenes.

If you are not still connected to the EDG at this time, have your partner attach the electrodes to your dominant hand. Be sure that you are in a comfortable position and are relaxed.

After the EDG has stabilized and you are deeply relaxed, your partner will ask you to imagine the first stimulus on your hierarchy (that which is least anxiety-provoking) and to hold the image for 10 sec. While imagining the scene, listen for the EDG feedback signal and if there is a response within the 10 sec (usually an increase in skin conductance), stop imagining and relax.[8,9] It is very important to stop imagining and relax as soon as there is a change in the EDG signal; otherwise, one pairs the image to the anxiety feeling.

After you have relaxed for 10–15 sec, and after the EDG is stabilized, your partner will again ask you to imagine the same scene.

If the EDG again responds, let go of the image, relax, and repeat the process until

[8]Traditionally, the trainee is instructed to let go of the image and relax when s/he indicates feeling anxious by raising the index finger.

[9]A minimal electrodermal response to several items on the hierarchy may indicate lack of involvement in the imagined scene. In this situation, when imaging, make sure to include as many senses as possible and to elaborate the details and *feelings* appropriate to the scene. It is also possible that you have chosen a theme that is not very anxiety-provoking and have desensitized yourself in the process of developing the hierarchy.

you can hold the imagined scene for 10 sec while remaining relaxed (i.e., with no EDG response).

Your partner will indicate to you when the 10 sec have passed. Again let go of the scene and relax.

Before moving on to the next stimulus on the hierarchy, you should have imagined the scene twice consecutively (10 sec each time) without an EDA response. Repeat this process until you have completed all the stimuli in the hierarchy. In reality, SD often takes multiple sessions. Once you are able to imagine a scene, to sense when you are reacting, and to let go of the scene and relax, answer Lab XIII: Questions and then complete the remainder of the items on your hierarchy as part of Lab XIV: Home Practice.

Make sure both you and your partner have had the opportunity to be both trainer and trainee. Meet with your group and complete Lab XIII: Discussion and Conclusions.

A common problem that may arise during this desensitization is that a scene in the series triggers a strong EDA response and you have difficulty letting the scene go and relaxing. Most likely, more images need to be inserted before the one that triggers the strong EDA response, i.e., the steps between scenes are too big or are out of order.

Trainee ______________________________

Date ____________

LAB XIII QUESTIONS

1. When the EDG feedback signal indicated you were reacting, what did you experience physiologically (butterflies in your stomach, a muscle twitch, etc.)?

____

____

____

2. What kinds of problems did you encounter in moving through the hierarchy?

____

____

____

____

____

____

____

____

____

____

____

3. Comments:

____

____

____

____

____

Trainee ______________________

Date __________

LAB XIII DISCUSSION AND CONCLUSIONS

1. Were there common themes or stimuli among members of your group? What were they?

2. Were there differences in abilities to move through the hierarchies? If so, were these differences related to some variable, such as ability to relax, ability to let go of the image, complexity of theme chosen for the hierarchy, intensity of the EDA response to the most anxiety-provoking stimulus, age, sex, or common pathologies?

SUGGESTIONS FOR FUTURE RESEARCH

1. Apply the desensitization procedures to the sensations of physical distress that accompany such problems as asthma, impotence, allergies, or stuttering.
2. Explore feedback of such other indices as heart rate, blood pressure, or EEG alpha as the measure of relaxation and indicator of subjective discomfort.
3. Explore other techniques to facilitate the pairing of the anxiety-producing image to a nonanxious state, such as shifting one's attention to a loved one or meditating (versus the use of progressive relaxation).
4. Explore the use of maintaining a relaxed state and mentally rehearsing future activities (for example, see yourself in the process of completing your goals).

LAB XIV
Home Practice
Desensitization

OBJECTIVE

This lab is intended to provide an opportunity to complete the hierarchy you generated in Lab XIII at home.

INSTRUCTIONS

Each day, set aside approximately 20 min and proceed through the following instructions by yourself. Find a comfortable quiet place. Allow yourself to become deeply relaxed. Then imagine the stimulus you last successfully completed (i.e., no discomfort or EDA response). Be aware of *any* discomfort in your body. Remember to let go of the image and relax at the first sign of any discomfort. After you are able to hold the image for approximately 10 sec twice consecutively, proceed with the next item on your hierarchy. Continue this process until you have proceeded through the hierarchy.

After completing the hierarchy, place yourself in a real-life situation where you will be exposed to the stimuli that previously triggered anxiety.

Each day complete Lab XIV: Log Sheet.

After completion of the hierarchy, answer Lab XIV: Questions.

Trainee ______________________

Date __________

LAB XIV LOG SHEET

Each day note: (a) the number of images successfully completed and (b) any problems encountered.

Day 1 a. ______________________________
Date________ b. ______________________________
____

Day 2 a. ______________________________
Date________ b. ______________________________
____

Day 3 a. ______________________________
Date________ b. ______________________________
____

Day 4 a. ______________________________
Date________ b. ______________________________
____

Day 5 a. ______________________________
Date________ b. ______________________________
____

Day 6 a. ______________________________
Date________ b. ______________________________
____

Day 7 a. ______________________________
Date________ b. ______________________________
____

Trainee ______________________

Date ____________

LAB XIV QUESTIONS

1. What differences did you observe when you did the desensitization by yourself versus when you were guided by your partner and used the biofeedback equipment?

2. Having completed the hierarchy, what happened when you experienced the real-life stimulus that previously provoked anxiety?

3. Comments:

SECTION 4

Electroencephalograph

LAB XV

Introduction to the Electroencephalograph[1]

NOTE: This lab assumes familiarity with the basic functions of biofeedback equipment. Review Lab I.

EQUIPMENT

Electroencephalograph and instruction manual, electrode paste (such as that manufactured by Grass) or saline solution (1 tablespoon of salt in a cup of water), metric tape measure, tape, grease pencil. *Optional:* styrofoam wig holder.

Note of caution: Low-frequency (less than 8 Hz) electroencephalograph training without supervision is contraindicated for epileptics.

OBJECTIVE

In the late 1920s, Hans Berger[2] used surface electrodes on the scalps of humans to record changing electrical activity. Since that time, the electroencephalograph (EEG) has intrigued professionals and laymen alike. Because the signal is seen to reflect the activity of the brain, the EEG has been used to study physiological and psychological functions as well as states of consciousness.

The objective of this lab is to gain familiarity with the EEG, factors which affect the signal, and ways to explore voluntary control of the signal.

PHYSIOLOGICAL BASIS OF THE SIGNAL

The cortex (outer layer) of the brain is composed of millions of nerve cells (neurons), which are complexly interconnected. The changing electrical potential of these nerve cells is the basis of the EEG signal. The signal represents the average change in the potentials of many cells, not the firing of any specific nerve cell.[3]

Most EEG research with humans has been of an empirical nature—observation of the EEG pattern under specific conditions. For example, characteristic patterns of EEG have been associated with different stages of sleep, various levels of arousal, meditation, epileptic seizures, and drug states, such as those induced by amphetamines.

The EEG pattern is defined in terms of its frequency [expressed in Hertz (Hz) or

[1]REFERENCE: *Mind/body integration,* pp. 141–150; 231–236; 241–252; 275–362.

[2]H. Berger, Hans Berger and the discovery of the electroencephalograph, translated and edited by P. Gloor, *Electroencephalography and Clinical Neurophysiology, Supplement,* 1969, *28,* 1–36.

[3]For additional information see K. Kooi, *Fundamentals of electroencephalography,* New York: Harper & Row, 1971.

TABLE 3
Some Common EEG Patterns[a]

EEG pattern	Name	Frequency (cps or Hz)	Physiological state
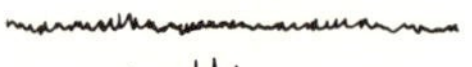	Beta	14–30	Alert
	Alpha	8–13	Usually eyes closed, relaxed wakefulness
	Theta	4–7	Hypnogogic state, early stages of sleep
	Delta	1–3	Deep sleep

[a]As a result of the limitations of early EEG equipment, the range of frequencies studied was limited to 0.5–30 Hz. This restricted focus has prevailed even though equipment and methodology exist that are not limited to this range.

cycles per second (cps)]. The patterns most often discussed and the common psychophysiological states associated with the patterns are shown in Table 3.

Although these patterns have been characterized, actual EEG recordings may be much more complex. They may be composed of many patterns with varying amplitudes. In addition, the patterns recorded will vary with the position of the electrodes (for example, alpha EEG activity is more likely to be recorded from the back of the head than from other areas).

FLOW DIAGRAM

The flow diagram of the EEG signal is similar to that of the EMG described in Lab I. Refer to p. 46. Although the filtering process is similar, the frequency range of the EEG signal (0–40 Hz) is different from that of the EMG signal (100–1000 Hz).

PLACEMENT OF THE ELECTRODES

Recording may be done with one electrode on the scalp over the brain tissue (active electrode) and one electrode over "electrically neutral" tissue such as the ear lobe (reference electrode). This method is referred to as *monopolar recording*. Another technique of recording, referred to as *bipolar recording,* is utilized by placing both electrodes on the scalp over brain tissue (two active electrodes). In both techniques (1) the electrical signal is the potential difference between these two electrodes and (2) a third electrode (ground) is placed on an "electrically neutral" site, such as the ear lobe or mastoid process. The different techniques are used with different purposes in mind. For example, bipolar recording is used preferentially in the localization of epileptic seizure, whereas monopolar recording is often used in studies of hemisphere dominance. For the purposes of this lab, only bipolar recording will be used.

The EEG signal will vary depending on the position of the electrodes from which it is recorded; consequently, the actual position of the electrodes is very important. In order to facilitate discussion among and comparison of the data from both researchers and clinicians, the international *10-20 system* has been established.[4]

The 10-20 labeling of the positions of the electrodes is based on the different brain regions over which the electrodes are placed. Figure 16 shows the major anatomical regions and their associated functions.

[4]H. H. Jasper, Report of Committee on Methods of Clinical Examination in EEG: Appendix: The ten-twenty electrode system of the International Federation, *Electroencephalography and Clinical Neurophysiology,* 1958, *10,* 371–375.

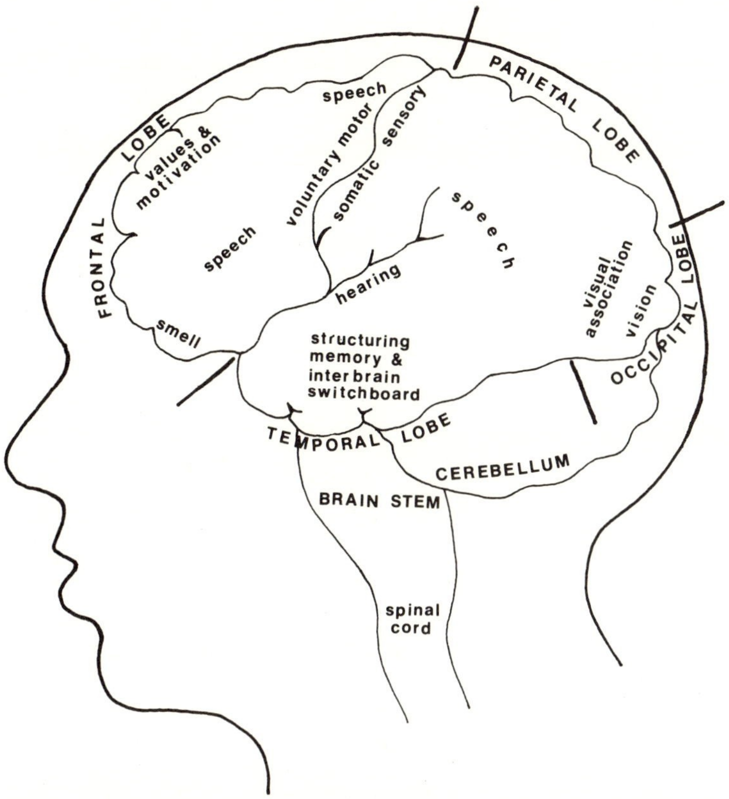

FIGURE 16. Major anatomical regions of the brain and their associated functions.

To determine the 21 electrode positions shown in Figure 17 (10-20 system), have your partner proceed through the following steps, using your head as a model. (If you have a styrofoam wig holder, practice the electrode placement on this first.)

1. Find the nasion (depression at the bridge of the nose) and the inion (the hard bone at the back of the head). To find the inion, move your hand upward along the spine until the first bony protuberance of the skull is found. Measure the distance from the nasion to the inion over the top of the head. Take 10% and 20% of this value. Mark on the scalp with a grease pencil the five (F_p, F_z, C_z, P_z, O) positions shown in Figure 18.
2. Find the preauricular depression (slight depression just in front of and above the ear lobe). See Figure 19. Measure the distance from the left to the right preauricular depression over the top of the head. Be sure the tape passes through the central point (C_z) determined in Step 1. Take 10% and 20% of this value. Mark on the scalp with a grease pencil the four (T_4, C_4, C_3, T_c) positions shown in Figure 20. Note that odd numbers are on the left side of the head, and even numbers are on the right side of the head.
3. Measure the circumference of the head, making sure the tape passes through F_p, T_4, O, and T_3 (10% positions). Take 10% of this value. Mark on the scalp with a grease pencil the positions shown in Figure 21.

Refer to Figure 22 for Steps 4–7.

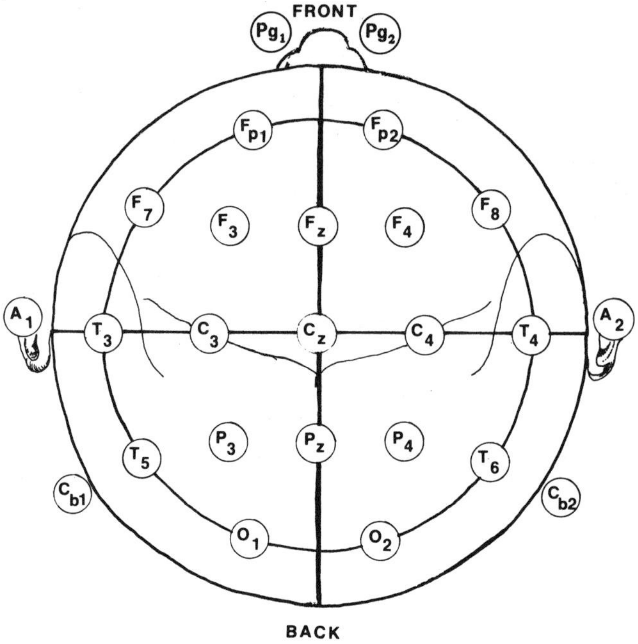

FIGURE 17. EEG electrode placement as specified by the international 10–20 system.

4. Mark position F_3 such that it is equidistant from F_{p1} and C_3 and equidistant from F_z and F_7.
5. Mark position F_4 such that it is equidistant from F_{p2} and C_4 and equidistant from F_z and F_8.
6. Mark position P_3 such that it is equidistant from O_1 and C_3 and equidistant from P_z and T_5.
7. Mark position P_4 such that it is equidistant from O_2 and C_4 and equidistant from P_z and T_6.

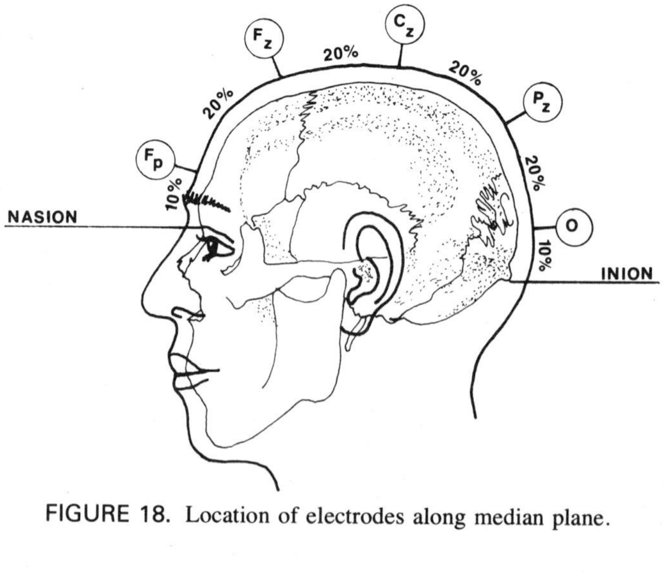

FIGURE 18. Location of electrodes along median plane.

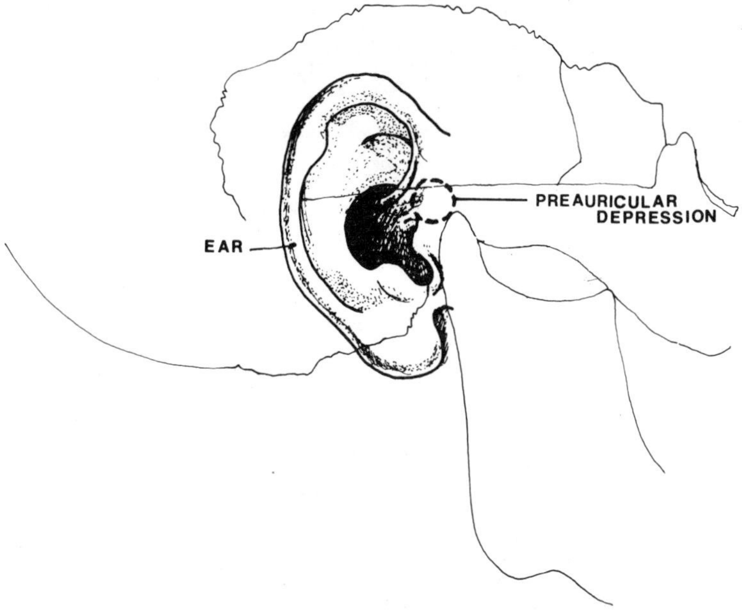

FIGURE 19. Location of preauricular depression.

A_1 and A_2 refer to electrodes placed on earlobes. Pg_1 and Pg_2 refer to nasopharyngeal electrodes (placed into the nose). C_{b1} and C_{b2} refer to electrodes placed on the cerebellum. Certain missing designations (e.g., C_1, C_2, C_5, C_6) may be used if it is desired to place electrodes between those commonly used.

ELECTRODE APPLICATION

In order to assure good contact between the scalp and the electrodes, it is necessary to part the hair and clean the scalp at those points where the electrodes are to be placed. Cleaning may be done by gently rubbing with alcohol, acetone, or an abrasive compound (such as Brasivol) so as to remove any dead cells and oil. Have your partner clean the areas of your scalp, O_1 and O_2, as well as the ear lobe or mastoid process.

There are many different kinds of electrodes and techniques of placement. Most biofeedback equipment uses either sponge electrodes with an elastic headband or precious metal electrodes. If your equipment uses sponge electrodes and a headband, begin by having your partner place the headband around your head, making sure the headband is over O_1 and O_2. Next soak the three sponge electrodes with saline solution. Have your

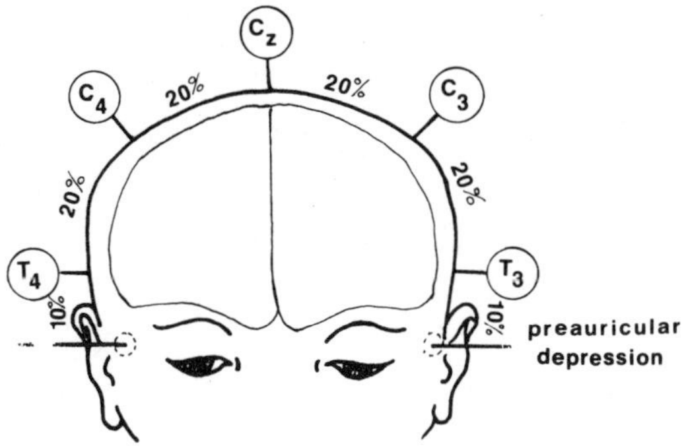

FIGURE 20. Location of electrodes along coronal plane.

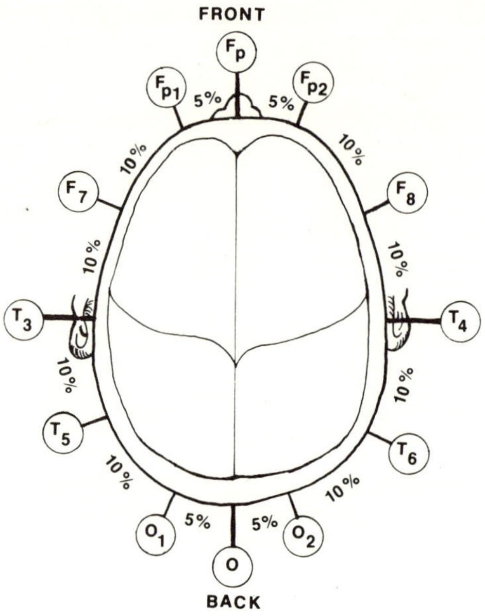

FIGURE 21. Location of electrodes around circumference of head.

partner place the two active electrodes under the headband at O_1 and O_2. You should be able to feel moisture on your scalp. Take the ground electrode (often distinguishable from the active electrodes by its color, usually black) over the mastoid process or clip it with a hair clip to the ear lobe. These positions of the ground electrode are preferable to other locations on the head as both brain and muscle artifacts are reduced. Figure 23 shows this electrode placement.

If your equipment has precious metal electrodes, begin by making sure the electrodes are clean (shining). Next have your partner rub a small amount of electrode paste onto the O_1 and O_2 positions and onto an earlobe or the mastoid process. Then your partner should

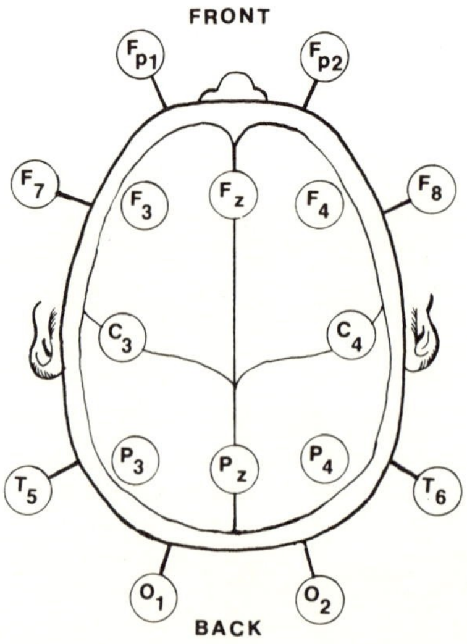

FIGURE 22. Location of midfrontal and midparietal electrodes.

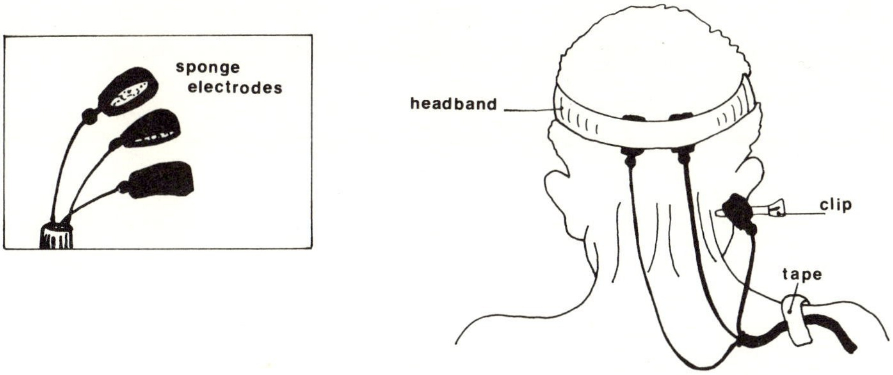

FIGURE 23. Placement of sponge electrodes.

place a blob (slightly less than 1 cc) of paste on these same positions, inserting the electrodes into the middle of the blob. The paste blob and electrode should be covered with a small piece of tissue (approximately 6 cm^2); sufficient pressure is then applied around the edges of the blob so that the electrode and paste are compressed against the scalp, earlobe, or mastoid process. (Sometimes the electrode to be placed on the earlobe has a special clip, simplifying this process, though you still need a blob of paste.) Figure 24 shows this electrode placement.

OPERATION OF EQUIPMENT

The following instructions are intended to familiarize you with the operation of the EEG. Some equipment may have fewer or more of the functions described below. The instructions are written with the assumption that the meter and/or auditory feedback is set so that feedback is direct and instantaneous.

Proceed through the following steps:

1. *Battery test.* After the electrode leads are plugged into the machine, turn on the EEG. Complete a battery check if your machine has such an operation. Check your instruction manual for specific instructions.
2. Be sure the electrodes have been appropriately applied to the scalp.
3. *Electrode test.* To test the electrode contact, wait at least 2 min after application of the electrodes. Check your instruction manual for specific instructions. An electrode contact test checks whether the resistance (impedance[5]) offered by the electrode assembly (leads and electrodes) and the interface between the electrodes and the scalp is low enough to allow for monitoring of the EEG. A resistance that is too high indicates that there is a problem at the electrode–scalp interface or that there is a break in the electrode lead assembly. Check the leads and reapply the electrodes. Be sure the scalp is cleaned and slightly abraded, that the electrodes are clean, and that there is sufficient saline solution or paste between the electrodes and the scalp.
4. *Set the frequency filter(s) (bandpass).* The frequency setting chosen depends on what frequencies of the EEG signal one wants to monitor. For the purpose of this lab, the frequency filter will be set for monitoring EEG alpha activity.

   If your equipment has independent lower and upper frequency filter settings, set the lower filter at 8 Hz and the upper at 13 Hz. With these settings, the

[5] *Impedance* is the measure employed when one is using alternating current (AC) in the test procedure.

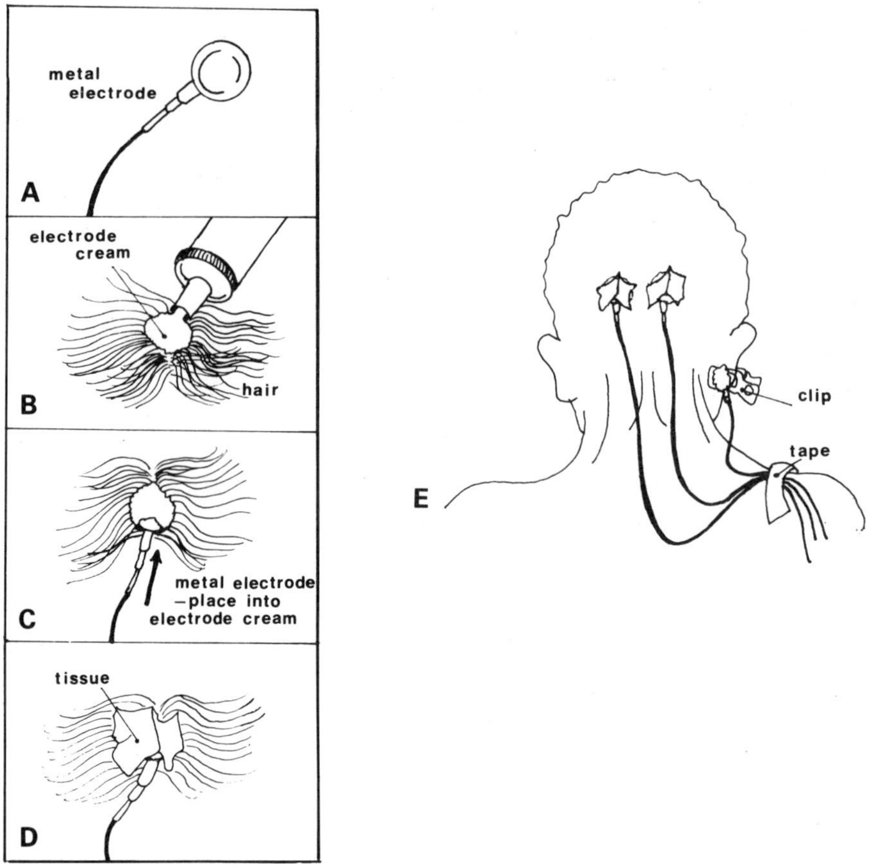

FIGURE 24. Attachment of EEG metal electrodes. (A) Clean metal electrode. (B) Place small amount of electrode cream on clean area of scalp. (C) Insert electrode into center of blob of electrode cream. (D) Place tissue over electrode with pressure applied on outer edges. (E) Location of EEG electrodes at O_1-O_2 (size of electrodes is exaggerated for illustrative purposes).

bandpass excludes all signals except those between 8 and 13 Hz. If your equipment has a single frequency setting, set this at 10 Hz, the center of the alpha frequency.

5. *Setting of amplitude threshold and behavioral test for EEG alpha activity.* The EEG signal is described by both frequency and amplitude. The lower amplitude setting is fixed so that all EEG signals below this amplitude will be filtered out; only those signals above this threshold value that are within the selected frequency range will be amplified.

   In order to establish this amplitude threshold setting, have your partner turn the control to the most sensitive (i.e., lowest μV) setting. Now focus on your thumb, which should be held 6–8 in. from your nose.[6] While tracking your thumb, gently move it back and forth. Have your partner turn the amplitude threshold toward a

[6]Alpha is most prevalent when a person closes his/her eyes and is not giving visual attention. Research by Mulholland and by Peper showed that occipital alpha always attenuates (disappears) when one gives efferent oculomotor commands (focuses externally on objects). See T. Mulholland, Feedback electroencephalography, *Activitas Nervosa Superior,* 1968, *10,* 410–438, and E. Peper, Feedback regulation of the alpha electroencephalogram activity through control of the internal and external parameters, *Kybernetik,* 1970, *7,* 107–112.

less sensitive setting (i.e., higher μV) until the equipment indicates that alpha activity is no longer present.

Now close your eyes and relax. For most trainees (about 80%) alpha activity will be indicated. If *no* alpha activity occurs for 5 min, increase the sensitivity of the amplitude (i.e., turn the control toward a lower μV setting) until some alpha activity is indicated.

Once alpha activity is indicated, open your eyes and focus again on your thumb. The feedback signal should disappear (i.e., alpha activity will no longer be present). If the feedback signal does not disappear, have your partner decrease the sensitivity of the amplitude threshold until feedback disappears.

Repeat the sequence focusing—eyes closed—focusing—eyes closed while your partner adjusts the amplitude until the feedback signal is mainly *off* when the eyes are open and focusing and sporadically *on* when the eyes are closed. How much of the time the feedback signal is on will vary for each individual.

6. Explore the different feedback functions of the equipment, such as derivative, visual, or auditory feedback.

EXPLORATION OF ARTIFACTS

For the subsequent exercises, the following conditions are assumed:

1. You are attached to the EEG electrodes at O_1-O_2 and sitting in a comfortable position.
2. You have completed the battery test, electrode check, and behavioral test.
3. Frequency is set for alpha 8–13 Hz.
4. Equipment is set for instantaneous feedback.
5. Eyes are kept open.

Mechanical and Environmental Artifacts

1. Have your partner put his/her hand on one of the active electrodes. What happens to the signal?

____

____

Explain this change.

____

____

2. Have your partner move the electrode leads back and forth. What happens to the signal?

____

____

Explain this change.

____

____

3. If you are using Grass electrode paste with the precious metal electrodes, place a large blob of paste under one active electrode and the proper amount under the other electrode. What happens to the signal?

____

Explain this change.

4. Have your partner remove one of the active electrodes. What happens to the signal?

Explain this change.

5. Have your partner remove the ground electrode. What happens to the signal?

Explain this change.

Biological Artifacts

1. Take a deep breath and exhale. What happens to the signal?

Explain this change.

2. Tighten different muscles around your face (jaw, forehead, scalp, etc.) What happens to the signal?

Explain this change.

3. Move your eyes rapidly from one side to the other or up and down. What happens to the signal?

Explain this change.

4. Swallow. What happens to the signal?

____

____

Explain this change.

____

____

This list of artifacts is not exhaustive. Other sources of artifacts include EKG and sweating. For a more detailed illustration of artifacts, see A. R. Craib and M. Perry, *EEG Handbook,* Schiller Park, Illinois: Beckman Instruments, 1973.

EEG TRAINING—ALPHA

With feedback one may learn to control any frequency or cluster of frequencies recorded from different locations on the scalp. In practice, EEG feedback training has focused primarily on alpha training.[7]

The following exercise is designed as an exploration of alpha training and its concommitant subjective states.

Preparation

Have your partner attach electrodes to O_1-O_2 and the ground electrode to the earlobe. Make sure the equipment is working (battery test, electrode test, alpha behavioral test). Set frequency at the alpha range 8–13.

Pretraining Baseline (without Feedback)

Close your eyes, sit quietly, and have your partner observe the EEG feedback signal. If the feedback signal indicates that alpha is on more than 50% of the time on the average, increase the amplitude threshold level so that the feedback is on no more than 50% of the time. On Lab XV: Data Sheet indicate the amplitude threshold level. Once the threshold is set, sit quietly with eyes closed for 2 min. At the end of this time period have your partner record on Lab XV: Data Sheet (pretraining baseline measurements) the percentage of time alpha activity was present. If your machine has a time integrator, have it set for 120 sec. If your machine does not have a time integrator, your partner will have to estimate as best s/he can the percent time alpha activity is present.

Training (with Feedback)

Set equipment so that feedback is instantaneous. For 5 min, sit quietly with eyes closed. Listen to the feedback signal. Observe the different subjective states associated with the presence and absence of alpha activity. Your partner will indicate when the 5 min are up. Then for the next 15 min, explore both with eyes open and with eyes closed strategies by which you can *increase* or *decrease* the alpha feedback signal. You might try some techniques discussed in Instruction Set B, visualize a dynamic picture, or listen to music.

Posttraining Baseline (without Feedback)

Continue to sit quietly with eyes closed.

Have your partner set the time integrator for 120 sec (or your partner will have to estimate the percent time alpha is present).

For 2 min, use the strategy that you observed kept the alpha feedback signal *on.*

[7]See T. Mulholland, op. cit.; J. Kamiya, Operant control of the EEG alpha rhythm and some of its reported effects on consciousness. In C. T. Tart (Ed.), *Altered states of consciousness,* New York: John Wiley, 1969.

Have your partner record on Lab XV: Data Sheet (alpha enhancement) the percent time alpha activity was present.

For the next 2 min use strategies that you observed kept the alpha feedback signal *off*. Have your partner record on Lab XV: Data Sheet (alpha suppression) the percent time alpha activity was present.

Answer Lab XV: Questions and repeat this procedure with your partner as the trainee. Then meet in a group and complete Lab XV: Discussion and Conclusions.

Trainee ______________________

Trainer ______________________

Date __________

LAB XV DATA SHEET

Pretraining baseline measurements

Amplitude threshold selected__________

Percent time alpha activity present__________

Posttraining baseline measurements

Alpha enhancement

Percent time alpha activity present__________

Alpha suppression

Percent time alpha activity present__________

Trainee ____________________

Date ____________

LAB XV QUESTIONS

1. What subjective experiences were associated with the presence and absence of alpha activity?

2. Comparing your posttraining to your pretraining measurement, were you successful in learning to increase and decrease alpha activity?

3. What strategies did you find were successful in increasing alpha activity?

4. What strategies did you find were successful in decreasing alpha activity?

5. Comments:

Trainee ______________________

Date ____________

LAB XV DISCUSSION AND CONCLUSIONS

1. What were the differences among group members in the subjective experiences associated with the presence of alpha activity?

____

____

____

____

____

____

2. What were the different strategies found to be successful in increasing and decreasing alpha activity?

____

____

____

____

____

____

3. To what variables were the differences in learning alpha control related (such as strategies used, past experiences with meditation or drugs, threshold selected, age, sex, or pathology)?

____

____

____

____

____

SUGGESTIONS FOR FUTURE RESEARCH

1. Look at differences in learning control of alpha activity as a function of number of training sessions.
2. Explore differences in subjective experience associated with 8 Hz alpha versus 12 Hz alpha (i.e., low- versus high-frequency alpha).
3. Explore differences in subjective experience associated with alpha activity measured on different areas of the scalp, such as frontal versus occipital, or left versus right hemisphere.
4. Explore training of other EEG frequencies, such as 18 Hz or 40 Hz.
5. Explore the effect of such variables as time of day, previous activities, and dietary intake on training.
6. Explore the effect of visualization or listening to music on the EEG pattern activity.

LAB XVI
Home Practice
Theta[1]

EQUIPMENT

Small tea bell.

OBJECTIVE

Although a great deal of the EEG biofeedback research has focused on alpha activity, there has been exploration of other EEG patterns, such as sensorimotor rhythm feedback for the treatment of epilepsy,[2] 18 Hz activity associated with healing meditation,[3] and theta activity associated with enhancement of creativity[4] and "twilight learning."[5]

Theta EEG activity (4–7 Hz) has been associated with the transition between sleep and wakefulness. During this time, one often experiences dreamlike images that appear to come from nowhere and, unlike daydreams, are not consciously generated or edited. The images associated with falling asleep are referred to as hypnogogic images and those associated with awakening as hypnopompic images. These dreamlike images have often been the source of creative insights. For example, Robert Louis Stevenson used such images as the basis of his stories and Friedrich Kekulé determined the molecular configuration of the benzene ring based on an image that came to him during a reverie state.

The fact that muscles become flaccid during the transition state between sleep and wakefulness (illustrated by a person nodding as s/he falls asleep) allows the study of theta activity associated with this transition state without sophisticated electronic equipment. For example, one may lie down and allow oneself to doze off, keeping one's forearm and hand erect. As theta activity occurs and the arm muscles become flaccid, the forearm will drop. The dropping of the arm may then be used as feedback indicating theta activity. The feedback prevents one from dropping off into sleep.[6] If one drops off into sleep, s/he loses consciousness of the images generated during this time.

[1]REFERENCE: *Mind/body integration,* pp. 125–140; 411–434.
[2]M. B. Sterman & L. R. Macdonald, Effects of central cortical EEG feedback training on incidence of poorly controlled seizures. In *Mind/body integration,* pp. 347–362.
[3]E. Peper & S. Ancoli, The two endpoints of an EEG continuum of meditation—Alpha/theta and fast beta. In *Mind/body integration,* pp. 141–150.
[4]E. Green & A. Green, *Beyond biofeedback,* New York: Dell, 1977, pp. 118–152.
[5]T. Budzynski, Tuning in on the twilight zone, *Psychology Today,* 1977, *11*(3), 39–44.
[6]Green & Green, op. cit., pp. 134–135.

INSTRUCTIONS For this home practice, proceed through the following exercise for 15–20 min at night before going to sleep or sometime during the day when you are drowsy. Lie comfortably with one forearm erect (hand pointing to ceiling). Hold a small tea bell in the hand of the erect arm (see Figure 25). Relax and allow yourself to drop off to sleep. Trying too hard will get in your way by increasing your alertness. Each time your arm drops and the bell rings, gently attend to any images and sensations previously generated. Then raise your arm again (with bell in hand). After 15–20 min of this practice, make your entries on Lab XVI: Log Sheet. Don't be discouraged if this practice is difficult for you; for some people this awareness training takes a long time.

After four days of this procedure, add the following component. While lying down comfortably, ask yourself a question of deep personal concern. Do this without demanding or expecting an answer. Continue with the procedure outlined above. Each time you lift up your arm, repeat your question. Don't use more than one question per night. Again complete Lab XVI: Log Sheet. After one week of practice, complete Lab XVI: Questions.

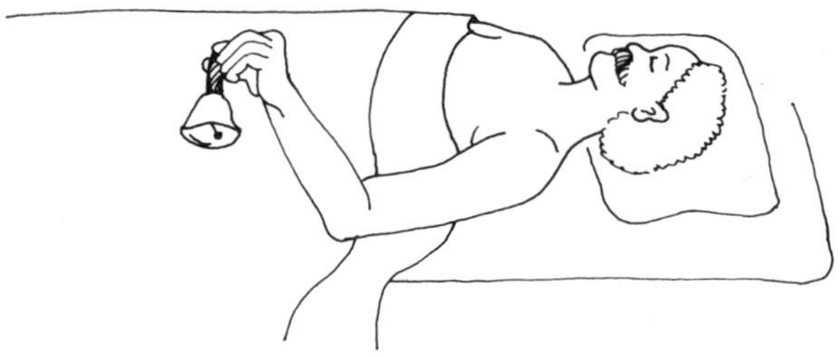

FIGURE 25. Position for theta training.

Trainee ____________________

Date __________

LAB XVI LOG SHEET

On each day note images remembered and sensations, feelings, or thoughts associated with images.

Day 1

Date ______ ____________________

Time______ ____________________

Day 2

Date ______ ____________________

Time______ ____________________

Day 3

Date ______ ____________________

Time______ ____________________

Day 4

Date ______ ____________________

Time______ ____________________

On each day note (a) images remembered (as above) and (b) questions asked.

Day 5 a. ____________________

Date______ ____________________

Time______ b. ____________________

Day 6 a. ____________________

Date______ ____________________

Time______ b. ____________________

Day 7 a. ____________________

Date______ ____________________

Time______ b. ____________________

Trainee ____________________

Date __________

LAB XVI QUESTIONS

1. What problems did you encounter during this training (Did you find yourself falling asleep? Did you react to the images so that the images disappeared or you could not remember them?)?

____

____

____

2. Did you find yourself improving in your ability to capture the images? If so, what did you do or *not* do to facilitate this process?

____

____

____

____

3. When you asked a question, did your images relate to the question asked? In what ways was the answer meaningful and how do you plan to incorporate this information into your life?

____

____

____

____

____

4. Comments:

____

____

____

____

____

INSTRUCTION SET C

Long-Term Biofeedback Training[1]

NOTE: Before proceeding through this instruction set, one must be familiar with at least one piece of biofeedback equipment. One must have completed the introduction to the EMG (Lab I), and one or more of the following labs: Introduction to the Temperature Unit (Lab VIII); Introduction to the EDG (Lab XII); and/or Introduction to the EEG (Lab XV).

Note of caution: When learning automatic control with biofeedback in a direction that is counter to normal homeostasis, one must exercise caution. A newly learned pattern may be elicited under circumstances outside training and could be pathogenic.

EQUIPMENT

Bound laboratory notebook; biofeedback device.

OBJECTIVE

The major labs of this manual provide, along with an introduction to biofeedback equipment and experiences in mind/body unity, brief experiences with learning autonomic awareness and control. However, often the learning of autonomic control requires practice over a long period of time. For example, the reversal of clinical pathology has been found to require more than fifty training sessions.[2] Biofeedback has been found to facilitate the learning of autonomic control.

The basic steps involved in learning with feedback are:

1. Monitoring the physiological system to feed back changes in that system.
2. Developing an awareness of the feedback and linking it to some internal sensation.
3. Learning to control the physiological system with the help of the feedback signal.
4. Maintaining the psychophysiological control without feedback, i.e., internalizing the learning process.

As in learning to ski, it takes time to proceed through the many steps of learning: from following the instructor's external feedback to internalizing awareness to the point where the movements of skiing proceed unconsciously. This process of learning is accompanied by subtle changes—one's perceptions of the world may change. Continuing with the above example, as one learns to ski competently, one's experience of the mountain is different.

[1]REFERENCE: *Mind/Body Integration*, pp. 5–68; 77–110; 201–228; 347–362; 435–452.

[2]T. Weiss & B. T. Engel, Operant conditioning of heart rate in patients with premature ventricular contractions, *Psychosomatic Medicine*, 1971, *33*, 301–326.

The self-experience of autonomic control is an important prerequisite for its serious use by any clinician. This experience is necessary both for an awareness of the subtle processes involved in the learning of autonomic control and for the knowledge that learning is possible. The "knowingness" is usually communicated nonverbally to trainees and is important for their successful learning of autonomic control. Dr. E. Taub, in a laboratory study, found that a trainer who did not himself believe that temperature training was possible was successful in training only one of his nine subjects to warm her hands. However, another trainer who believed that temperature training was possible was successful in training nine of his ten subjects.[3]

The objective of this instruction set is to provide an experience of long-term learning of autonomic control with the use of biofeedback. During the process of this learning one hopes to achieve the following:

1. An increased awareness of one's subtle physiological responses. Long-term learning of autonomic control provides the opportunity to increase one's sensitivity to one's body, so that, while initially one could discriminate the physiological changes accompanying, say, a change of five units on some feedback signal, at the end of training one is able to discriminate a change of two units. One gradually becomes conscious of what was previously unconscious.
2. Control of the physiological response so that one is able to maintain the response in the direction opposite that accompanying the "flight-fight" response or aroused state for at least 20 min. For example, since an increase in muscle tension often accompanies the "flight-fight" response, one then would learn to decrease muscle tension and maintain this decrease. The attainment of voluntary control of the *hypo*aroused state allows for:
   a. Operation of the body's prohomeostatic mechanisms (for example, a decrease in blood pressure has accompanied the maintenance of this state in hypertensives)[4];
   b. Access to material that is normally unconscious (for example, cancer patients in this state have been successful in querying their unconscious for healing images)[5];
   c. Reprogramming of beliefs (for example, smokers have used this state to change their dependence on cigarettes and athletes have used this state to improve their performances).[6]
3. Bidirectional voluntary control of the physiological response. The learning of bidirectional control has been identified as a significant variable in the achievement of clinical success (i.e., in reducing pathology). For example, patients with tachycardia (those having a heart rate of greater than 100 beats per minute) who learned to both increase and decrease their heart rates had greater success in controlling their pathology than did those patients who learned only to decrease their heart rate.[7] Bidirectional control clearly demonstrates competence. The patient who has experienced his/her ability to trigger the tachycardia (increase in

[3]E. Taub, Paper presented at the 10th annual meeting of the Biofeedback Society of America, San Diego, 1979.

[4]W. Luthe & S. R. Blumberger, Autogenic therapy. In E. D. Wittkower & H. Warnes (Eds.), *Psychosomatic medicine: Its clinical applications*, New York: Harper & Row, 1977, pp. 146–165.

[5]O. C. Simonton, S. Matthews-Simonton, & J. Creigton, *Getting well again*, Los Angeles: J. P. Tarcher, 1978.

[6]W. Luthe & S. R. Blumberger, op. cit.

[7]T. Weis & B. T. Engel, Operant conditioning of heart rate in patients with premature ventricular contractions, *Psychosomatic Medicine*, 1971, *33*, 301-326.

heart rate), and then decrease heart rate *knows* his/her control of and relationship to the illness.

4. Inhibition of a physiological response when challenged by a stimulus that previously triggered the response. The process of learning to maintain control of a response when challenged by a stressful stimulus is another important variable in achieving clinical success. For example, patients with Raynaud's disease (excessive vasoconstriction in the periphery when exposed to cold or stress) must learn not only to warm their hands but also to generalize this learning and keep their hands warm while holding a glass of cold water (a physiological systematic desensitization; see Lab XIII).

INSTRUCTIONS

(These steps are similar to those that one would use with clients.)

1. *Determine the goal of training*. Identify the physiological response that you would like to control, and then choose an appropriate method of feedback. For example, you may want to learn to increase alpha activity with the EEG or to warm your hands with the termperature unit.
2. *Develop a schedule for training*. You may want to work two or three times a week; a minimum would be one training session per week. Be realistic, make a commitment, and follow through. The length of the session should be such that you quit before boredom sets in. Experiment a little and find what is optimum for you. Complete Instruction Set C: Long-Term Training Protocol.
3. *Keep a detailed log*. In a separate bound lab notebook, *record your methodology and observations* for each training session. Use Instruction Set C—Sample Long-Term Training Log and Sample Long-Term Training Data and Graph Sheet as a possible format for your recordings. Be sure that the procedures are sufficiently detailed so that others could replicate your work. Make sure you include an account of what the trainer did and how s/he did it, as well as a description of the training facility and conditions (Was the room quiet? Isolated from others?, etc.). Initially, one wants to hold these variables constant; however, once competency has been achieved under these conditions, one may want to change the conditions so as to encourage generalization of the learned skill. Also include records of pre- and posttraining baseline measurements (without feedback) and recordings during the training sessions (time with feedback), and note how you would change the next session to maximize learning. Finally, include descriptions of the trainee's subjective experiences. (In this case, trainer and trainee may be the same person.)

Trainee________________________

Date__________

INSTRUCTION SET C LONG-TERM TRAINING PROTOCOL

1. Describe goal for training.

2. Physiological system to be monitored:

3. Equipment to be used:

4. Tentative training schedule (when, where, and how long):

INSTRUCTION SET C *SAMPLE* LONG-TERM TRAINING LOG

Trainee: ______________________ Date: ______________________

Trainer: ______________________ Session No.: ______________________

Equipment: ______________________ Time began: ______________________

Exact sensor location: ______________________ Time ended: ______________________

____

Description of training facility and condition:

____

____

____

Description of procedure (what exactly did you as trainer do?)

____

____

____

____

____

____

____

Suggestions for next training session:

____

____

Suggestions for home practice:

____

____

INSTRUCTION SET C *SAMPLE* LONG-TERM TRAINING DATA AND GRAPH SHEET

Pretraining baseline readings (no feedback)		Training session (with feedback)		Posttraining baseline (no feedback)	
Time	Amplitude of signal	Time	Amplitude of signal	Time	Amplitude of signal

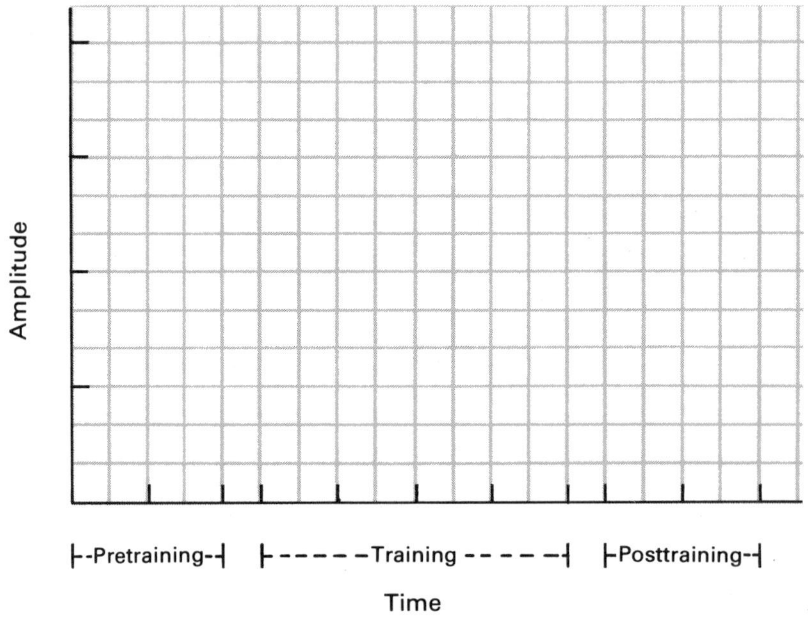

SECTION 5

Generalized Use of Biofeedback

LAB XVII
Economical Biofeedback[1]

EQUIPMENT

Two bathroom scales, stethoscope, sphygmomanometer, paper bag.

OBJECTIVE

Although biofeedback is commonly associated with electronic hardware, this equipment is not required for its use. In fact, many of the labs in this manual contain exercises that do not involve sophisticated equipment. In the dysponesis lab (Lab VI), it is your partner who provides the feedback as to when you are tensing your arm as it is being moved. In the temperature home practice (Labs X and XI) a small hand thermometer provides feedback on your peripheral hand temperature. In the theta training home practice (Lab XVI), it is a small tea bell that provides feedback as to when your muscles are going flaccid and you are entering theta. And in a variety of labs it is an enhancement of your own awareness that provides the feedback—by scanning your body carefully after imaging a stressor (Lab II: Self-Observation Exercise), or after some stressful event (Lab XXI: Prelab Preparation) or after some common activity (Lab XX: Prelab Preparation). In this lab, we will explore the use of some of these less frequently discussed modes of biofeedback.

INSTRUCTIONS

In developing biofeedback devices, keep in mind the following considerations:

1. Devices must be electrically and mechanically safe.
2. Devices are preferably noninvasive.
3. Devices must detect and feed back the specified psychophysiological process.
4. The feedback signal must occur in "real time": there should be little or no delay between the occurrence of the physiological event and the feedback signal.
5. The feedback signal must be meaningful and understandable to the trainee.

Use of Another Person for Feedback—Language Patterns

In very subtle albeit profound ways, our language patterns influence our experience of the world. For example, when a depressed insomniac changed his response to noise from, "I hate this noise," to "I look forward to the noise because it will remind me to practice the relaxation exercise," he was able to fall asleep and ignore the noise.[2]

[1] REFERENCE: *Mind/body integration*, pp. 111–118; 523–528; 541–562.
[2] E. Peper & C. Kushel, An holistic merger of biofeedback and family therapy, *American Theosophist*, 1979, *67*(5), 158–168.

These language patterns are so automatic (unconscious) that it is difficult to change them.[3] Self-awareness (the first step toward change) of a verbal pattern is facilitated by having someone else draw attention to its use.

Here, we will explore the use of other persons to facilitate the changing of verbal patterns (behavior) and the effect of this change on one's experience.

During the discussion periods of this lab, be aware of your use and the use by others in your group of the following words and phrases:

1. "But . . ."
2. "I can't . . ."
3. "I have to . . ." or "I should . . ."
4. "I'm afraid to . . ."

When you hear these words or phrases, change them or encourage another to change them to the following:

1. "And . . ." instead of "But . . ."
2. "I won't . . ." instead of "I can't . . ."
3. "I want to . . ." instead of "I have to . . ." or "I should . . ."
4. "I would like to . . ." instead of "I'm afraid to . . ."

After a period of time, feedback will no longer be necessary; awareness will have internalized and verbal patterns will have changed.

At the end of this lab (after having done the next two exercises), complete Lab XVII: Questions—Language Patterns.

[3]For further reading, see A. Ellis & R. Grieger, *Handbook of rational-emotive therapy,* New York: Springer, 1977; W. Ellerbroek, Unified field theory of human behavior, *Perspectives in Biology and Medicine,* 1973 (Winter), 240–262.

Trainee ______________________________

Date ____________

LAB XVII QUESTIONS—LANGUAGE PATTERNS

1. How easy was it for you (a) to be aware of your automated use of the selected phrases and (b) to receive feedback from others regarding these phrases? Explain.

2. How easy was it for you (a) to be aware of others using the selected phrases and (b) to provide verbal feedback to them? Explain.

3. When you changed these phrases, how did your experience of the situation and yourself change?

4. Comments:

Use of Common Devices for Feedback

There are many common devices that have a potential for feedback use. Do these exercises by yourself.

Bathroom Scale

Many activities, such as walking and skiing, require gradual shifting of weight from one leg to the other. Bathroom scales may be used to monitor and feed back this process of shifting weight, and, in so doing, to facilitate the learning of skiing and relearning of walking by stroke patients.[4]

Start by standing with each foot on a bathroom scale so that your feet are 30 cm apart. Without looking at the scales, stand so that you feel your weight is equally distributed. Now look at the scales. If the scales do not read the same weight, shift your weight while using the scales as feedback, until your weight is equally distributed. Observe any changes in how your body feels as you make the shift. Get off the scales, and then step back on. When you step back on the scale, recapture the feeling you had when you were balanced (do not look at the scales). Check to confirm that your weight is equally distributed. If the scales do not read the same, repeat the process of balancing until you can stand with your weight equally distributed without looking at the scales.

Next use the bathroom scales to help you learn to shift your weight gradually from one leg to the other. Practice so that the complete shift of weight takes at least 1 min and the process of shifting is smooth. Then complete Lab XVII: Questions—Bathroom Scale.

The Sphygmomanometer

Monitoring blood pressure may be helpful in identifying whether one responds to stressors with blood pressure changes. Learning awareness of and ability to inhibit this cardiovascular response may alleviate or prevent the onset of essential hypertension. Blood pressure can be measured directly and fed back with an automated device such as the constant cuff,[5] or pulse wave velocity can be measured.[6] The sphygmomanometer and stethoscope can be used both to calibrate other devices and to provide feedback of blood pressure. If you are not familiar with the procedure for taking blood pressure with the sphygmomanometer, refer to Appendix C for explicit instructions.

Sit in a comfortable position with your arm relaxed at heart level, resting on a flat surface. Take your blood pressure and record baseline measurements on Lab XVII: Data Sheet—Sphygmomanometer. Now spend a few minutes relaxing. Imagine a very relaxing scene. Take your blood pressure and record on the Data Sheet. Then for a few minutes think about something frustrating, unpleasant, or painful. Again take your blood pressure and record on the Data Sheet. Finally relax again for a few minutes. Again take your blood pressure and record on the Data Sheet. Complete Lab XVII: Questions—Sphygmomanometer.

Possible feedback applications of the sphygmomanometer and stethoscope include (1) monitoring blood pressure at various times during the day in order to identify situations that elicit blood pressure changes and (2) learning to control blood pressure with blood pressure feedback.

[4]E. Peper & J. A. Robertson, Biofeedback use of common objects: The bathroom scale in physical therapy, *Biofeedback and Self-Regulation,* 1976, *1,* 237–239.

[5]D. Shapiro, B. Tursky, E. Gershon, & M. Stern, Effect of feedback and reinforcement on the control of human systolic blood pressure, *Science,* 1979, *163,* 588–589.

[6]A. Steptoe, Blood pressure control with pulse wave velocity feedback: Methods of analysis and training. In J. Beatty and H. Legewie (Eds.), *Biofeedback and behavior,* New York: Plenum, 1977.

Trainee ______________________

Date __________

LAB XVII QUESTIONS—BATHROOM SCALE

1. How accurate was your perception of balance (i.e., did the scales read the same when you thought you were balanced)?

2. How rapidly did you learn the internal sense of balance and shifting of weight, and what were the accompanying physical sensations?

3. How could you apply this methodology in sports or physical therapy?

4. Comments:

Trainee ____________________

Date __________

LAB XVII DATA SHEET—SPHYGMOMANOMETER

Baseline

Systolic blood pressure: __________

Diastolic blood pressure: __________

Relaxing image

Systolic blood pressure: __________

Diastolic blood pressure: __________

Frustrating image

Systolic blood pressure: __________

Diastolic blood pressure: __________

Relaxing image

Systolic blood pressure: __________

Diastolic blood pressure: __________

Trainee ____________________

Date __________

LAB XVII QUESTIONS—SPHYGMOMANOMETER

1. How did your blood pressure change in response to imaging?

____

____

____

____

____

2. What were the internal sensations associated with changes in blood pressure?

____

____

____

____

3. Comments:

____

____

____

____

____

____

____

Self-Awareness of Internal Body Processes

The mind/body funtions as a single unit and its systems (e.g., cardiovascular, respiratory, nervous) are interconnected. A change in any one system may affect others. For example, a change in respiratory patterns may affect cardiac output.[7] Because of the interrelationship, one may observe one system and use these observations as an indicator of the state of the total organism.

In our daily lives, we are often not aware of the state of physiological systems. For example, rarely does one remain conscious of the depth and rate of one's respiration without training. However, one may learn to increase one's awareness of these systems. The following exercises are intended to develop cardiac and respiratory awareness.

Cardiac Awareness

In some cultures, such as that of the Hopi Indians, the heart is perceived as the seat of consciousness. This association of the heart with mental or emotional states is revealed in our language too. Such words and phrases as *heartbreak, heavyhearted, lighthearted,* and *his heart sank like a stone* reveal this association. List other phrases that link the heart and consciousness on Lab XVII: Questions—Cardiac Awareness. Cardiac awareness, then, is an important and interesting tool for learning about the whole organism—the mind/body interaction.

Begin the cardiac awareness exercise by sitting comfortably, quietly, by yourself. Place your right hand over your heart in the upper left-central quadrant of the chest. Observe your heart beat beneath your hand and inside the chest. Notice the myriad of sensations inside the chest, such as throbbing, pressure, warmth, or coolness. Observe gently for 5 min. If you have difficulty feeling your heartbeat, use a stethoscope. After this time, while still listening to the heartbeat, think of someone you deeply, unconditionally and automatically love, and about whom you do not feel a lot of conflict, such as grandparents, or niece or nephew. For the next 2 min, continue to think of the loved one and observe the sensations in the chest. At the end of this time, think of an image or time(s) when you broke an agreement. Maintain this image for 2 min. Notice any change in the sensations of the chest. Finally, again think of someone who automatically elicits feelings of love and observe the cardiac responses for 2 min. Then complete Lab XVII: Questions—Cardiac Awareness. Then meet with the other members of your group who have completed the exercise and fill in Lab XVII: Discussion and Conclusions—Cardiac Awareness.

[7]L. A. Sroufe, Effects of depth and rate of breathing on heart rate and heart rate variability, *Psychophysiology,* 1971, *8,* 648–655.

Trainee ____________________

Date __________

LAB XVII QUESTIONS—CARDIAC AWARENESS

1. List phrases linking the heart with emotions or consciousness. Indicate the emotional or mental state associated. For example, *heartbreak* implies rejection or loss of a loved one.

Phrase	Emotional or mental state implied

2. During the first observation of your heart, what sensations did you feel?

3a. How did the cardiac sensations change and what did you feel when you thought of someone you love (first time)?

3b. How "real" was your experience of these feelings?

Not real		Somewhat real		Very real
1	2	3	4	5

4a. How did the cardiac sensations change and what did you feel when you thought of a broken agreement?

4b. How "real" was your experience of the broken agreement?

Not real		Somewhat real		Very real
1	2	3	4	5

5a. How did the cardiac sensations change and what did you feel when you thought of someone you love (second time)?

____

____

5b. How "real" was your experience of these feelings?

Not real		Somewhat real		Very real
1	2	3	4	5

6. How could you use the cardiac awareness as a feedback tool for self-growth?

____

____

____

7. Comments:

____

____

____

Trainee ______________________

Date __________

LAB XVII DISCUSSION AND CONCLUSIONS—CARDIAC AWARENESS

1. What were the various emotional and mental states associated with the heart as revealed by linguistic phrases?

____

____

____

2. Were the sensations observed while listening to the heart the same among members of your group? Indicate similarities and differences.

____

____

____

____

3. Were patterns of sensations among group members related to such variables as illness patterns, sex, or meditation experiences? In what ways were they related? For example, were those with meditation experiences more able to maintain cardiac awareness and remain calm?

____

____

____

____

4. Were the changes in cardiac awareness related to the intensity of involvement in the images of love or broken agreements?

____

____

____

____

Breath Awareness

One's respiratory rate (number of breaths per minute) and pattern (whether breathing is thoracic or abdominal, rate of inhalation and exhalation, presence or absence of pausing or holding breath, gasping) are cues to the state of one's being. Specifically, breath holding and shallow breathing indicate the initiation of an orienting response or the alarm reaction (fight-flight or ergotropic response). For example, one trainee noticed how her breath became shallow as she recounted a traumatic episode. Are you aware of how your respiratory pattern changes throughout the day? Any changes that you observe may be used as cues that something is going on.

As with the heart, our language is filled with phrases that link our emotional and mental states with respiration. Such phrases as *it took his breath away* and *she is full of hot air* illustrate this association. List other phrases that link breath and consciousness on Lab XVII: Questions—Breath Awareness.

Begin the breath awareness exercise by sitting quietly for a few minutes by yourself. Observe your breath, both the rate and pattern of respiration. Now quickly stand up and observe your breath. What happened to your breath? Did you hold it? If so, repeat the activity while purposely breathing and note your observations on Lab XVII: Questions—Breath Awareness (questions 2 and 3). Share your experience with your lab partner and observe your breath pattern while talking. If you gasped between words (rapidly inhaled air into chest), continue to talk with your partner while breathing easily between the words or sentences. When you need to inhale while speaking, slow down and let the air gently come into your stomach. Allow plenty of time and then continue to speak. Again record the observations on Lab XVII: Questions—Breath Awareness (questions 4 and 5).

Again sit quietly. Place one hand on your abdomen and the other on your upper chest. For approximately 5 min, slowly breathe so that the hand on the abdomen moves out on inhalation while there is little movement of the hand on the chest (i.e., breathe abdominally or diaphragmatically). If you are having difficulty, do the exercise in front of a mirror. Be sure the chest stays relaxed and that the stomach can move freely (belt loose, upper button and zipper of pants undone). Observe the sensations in your body and record your observation of Lab XVII: Questions—Breath Awareness (question 6).

Next breathe so that the hand on the chest moves rapidly up and down while the abdomen is held contracted (i.e., breathe thoracically). Observe the sensations in your body and record your observations on Lab XVII: Questions—Breath Awareness (question 7).

WARNING: If you get dizzy and/or develop tingling and cold sweaty hands, *stop* the breathing practice. In case of excessive hyperventilation, breathe in and out of a brown paper bag for a short period of time.

Finally, breathe for 10 min very slowly and smoothly. Count to five while exhaling and again to five while inhaling. Be sure the chest stays relaxed and the abdomen moves out (protrudes) when you inhale and moves in while you exhale (slow abdominal breathing). Be sure the whole body is as relaxed as possible. Complete Lab XVII: Questions—Breath Awareness (question 8). Meet with other members of your group who have finished the breath exercise and complete Lab XVII: Discussion and Conclusions—Breath Awareness.

Trainee ______________________

Date __________

LAB XVII QUESTIONS—BREATH AWARENESS

1. List phrases linking breath with emotions or consciousness. Indicate the emotion or mental state associated. For example, *it took his breath away* implies surprise.

Phrase	Emotional or mental state implied
______________________	______________________________
______________________	______________________________
______________________	______________________________

2. What happened to your respiratory pattern when you stood up?

____

____

3. How did you feel when you continued to breathe while standing up?

____

____

4. Did you gasp while talking?

____

5. How did breathing easily while talking affect your speech and the experience of talking?

____

____

6. What did you observe during abdominal breathing? Did you relax? What images or emotions were associated with this kind of breathing?

____

____

7. What did you observe during thoracic breathing? Did you observe any tensions? Where? What emotions and images were associated with this kind of breathing?

____

____

8. What did you observe during slow abdominal breathing? What emotions, images, and body sensations were associated with this kind of breathing? How easy or difficult was it for you to do this kind of breathing?

____

____

____

____

____

9. Comments:

____

____

____

____

____

Trainee ______________________

Date __________

LAB XVII DISCUSSION AND CONCLUSIONS—BREATH AWARENESS

1. What were the various mental and emotional states associated with breathing as revealed by linguistic phrases?

____

____

____

2. Were there common experiences observed among members of your group during:
   a. Breathing while standing (holding and nonholding):

   ____

   ____

   b. Breathing while talking (gasping and nongasping):

   ____

   ____

   c. Abdominal breathing:

   ____

   ____

   d. Thoracic breathing:

   ____

   ____

   e. Slow abdominal breathing:

   ____

   ____

   ____

3. In what ways were these experiences associated with such variables as personal or family illness patterns, or ability to relax or meditate?

____

____

____

SUGGESTIONS FOR FUTURE RESEARCH

1. Explore teaching abdominal breathing with the use of EMG feedback, in which the EMG is recorded from the pectoralis, trapezius, or other accessory muscles of the chest. Use the feedback as an error signal that the person is breathing thoracically.
2. Explore the autonomic effects of breathing. For example, does thoracic breathing increase sympathetic arousal? Does abdominal breathing increase parasympathetic response?
3. Explore the use of existing biomedical instrumentation in a feedback paradigm (for example, the use of a stethoscope to monitor peristalsis).
4. Develop your own economic biofeedback device (for example, a pressure transducer using a metal contact, a spring, and a bell to monitor the pressure of fingers on a pen as a means of reducing writer's cramp).
5. Explore the use of video as a feedback device.

LAB XVIII
Home Practice
Language Use

OBJECTIVE

The objective of this home practice is to continue to:

1. Develop an awareness of one's verbal behavior.
2. Develop the ability to change this behavior.
3. Observe the effect of such change.

INSTRUCTIONS

During the week be aware of your language. Whenever you think, intend to speak, or actually speak, change the phrase:

from	*to*
But . . .	And . . .
I can't . . .	I won't . . .
I have to . . . I should . . .	I want to . . .
I'm afraid to . . .	I would like to . . .

You may want to use a family member to help you be aware of the use of these phrases (as in Lab XVII: Language Patterns).

At the end of each day, complete Lab XVIII: Log Sheet, and at the end of the week complete Lab XVIII: Questions.

Trainee ______________________

Date ____________

LAB XVIII LOG SHEET

Each day note (a) the situations (your emotional state, the presence of others, etc.) in which you used the new phrases, (b) times when it was easy or difficult to be aware of and use the new phrases, and (c) your experiences when you substituted the new phrases.

Day 1 a. ______________________

Date______ b. ______________________

____

c. ______________________

____

Day 2 a. ______________________

Date______ b. ______________________

____

c. ______________________

____

Day 3 a. ______________________

Date______ b. ______________________

____

c. ______________________

____

Day 4 a. ______________________

Date______ b. ______________________

____

c. ______________________

____

Day 5 a. ____________________

Date______ b. ____________________

____

c. ____________________

____

Day 6 a. ____________________

Date______ b. ____________________

____

c. ____________________

____

Day 7 a. ____________________

Date______ b. ____________________

____

c. ____________________

____

Trainee ____________________

Date __________

LAB XVIII QUESTIONS

1. Describe problems you encountered in this home practice.

2. Describe common situations when it was easy or difficult to be aware of and substitute the new phrases.

3. After a week's practice, did you find that changing your language changed your experience of the world? Describe.

4. Comments:

LAB XIX
Home Practice
Breath Awareness

OBJECTIVE

The objective of this home practice is to:

1. Identify situations during which you hold your breath or gasp.
2. Develop the ability to change this behavior.
3. Observe how a change in behavior affects your experience.

INSTRUCTIONS

During the week observe when you hold your breath or gasp.[1] The moment you observe breath holding, start breathing smoothly. Exhale and on the inhalation allow the air to come into the abdomen so that the stomach bubbles out. Be sure the chest stays loose and relaxed. While breathing abdominally, repeat the activity during which you noticed the breath holding or gasping.

Note your daily observations on Lab XIX: Log Sheet. At the end of the week answer questions on Lab XIX: Questions.

[1]The following steps have been found to be helpful in learning to develop awareness of a physiological system. They are implicit in this home practice: (1) Identify a pattern or movement (for example, gasping, bracing shoulders). (2) Exaggerate the pattern or movement and describe emotions and other body sensations associated with the pattern (tension in the shoulders and general apprehension associated with gasping, stiff neck and angry feelings associated with bracing of shoulders). (3) Perform an activity while consciously inhibiting the pattern or movement (talk without gasping, drive car in traffic without bracing shoulders).

Trainee ____________________

Date __________

LAB XIX LOG SHEET

Each day (a) note the conditions under which you either gasped or held your breath and (b) describe how it felt to repeat these activities while breathing smoothly and abdominally.

Day 1 a. ____________________

Date______ b. ____________________

____

Day 2 a. ____________________

Date______ b. ____________________

____

Day 3 a. ____________________

Date______ b. ____________________

____

Day 4 a. ____________________

Date______ b. ____________________

____

Day 5 a. ____________________

Date______ b. ____________________

____

Day 6 a. ____________________

Date______ b. ____________________

____

Day 7 a. ______________________________

Date______ b. ______________________________

____

Trainee ______________________

Date __________

LAB XIX QUESTIONS

1. Were there common theme(s) underlying the conditions under which you gasped or held your breath? What were they? (For example, every time you anticipate conflict, you hold your breath.)

2. Were there common ways in which your experience of the activities changed as you continued to breathe smoothly? What were they?

3. Comments:

LAB XX

Physiological Effects of Some Common Activities

PRELAB PREPARATION

Choose one of the following activities (or any other to which you would like to monitor your body's response). It may be of particular interest to choose an activity that you do habitually.

Drink a cup of coffee.
Drink a beer.
Smoke a cigarette.
Smoke a joint (marijuana).
On an empty stomach, eat a candy bar or other junk food item.
Hyperventilate.
Eat a huge meal.
Run a few laps around the track or up and down some stairs.
Take medication (e.g., aspirin, bronchial dilator, diuretic).

After having selected an activity, determine in which physiological systems you respond. Do this by completing the activity and carefully observing your body. For example, if you chose to drink a cup of coffee, carefully note any changes in such indicators as muscle tension, heart rate, rate and pattern of respiration, skin moisture, and hand temperature during and following the drinking of the coffee. In order to observe the effect of the activity, it is extremely important that one begin one's observations from a *resting state*. Continuing with the above example, in order to observe the effect of drinking a cup of coffee, one should not have recently had a cup of coffee or have run up the stairs. Keep in mind that some activities have effects over long periods of time that may be subtle and go unnoticed. Some people feel the effects of a cup of coffee (for example, difficulty in falling asleep) as long as 8 hr after ingestion.

Once you have determined the physiological systems in which you respond to the activity, identify the biofeedback equipment for the lab session that would be appropriate to monitor the responsive system(s). Don't limit yourself to electronic devices: one may take one's pulse to determine heart rate, observe the number of breaths, monitor pupil size or skin color, and so on. Complete Lab XX: Worksheet.

Trainee ______________________

Date __________

LAB XX WORKSHEET

1. Describe activity:

____

____

____

____

2. Physiological effects observed during and following activity:

____

____

____

____

____

3. Appropriate biofeedback equipment to be used in the lab:

____

____

LAB WORK

Equipment

Equipment to provide any of a variety of modes of biofeedback, such as EMG, EDG, EEG, temperature unit, and/or equipment to monitor blood pressure, heart rate, or rate and pattern of respiration.

Objective

Have you ever noticed your heart beating faster or your palms sweating after a cup of coffee? Have you ever felt sleepy after a large meal or short of breath after running up stairs? Certainly we do respond in a variety of ways to different activities. In this lab, we will explore the physiological effects of some of these activities.

Instructions: Monitoring with Biofeedback Equipment

Use Lab XX: Data Sheet—Activity 1, filling in the appropriate time and units of measurement. You will want to vary the time interval for taking measurements depending on the mode of biofeedback used; for example, if you are using temperature and blood pressure, you may want to record temperature every 30 sec and blood pressure every minute. In addition, the time interval is frequently lengthened as the system being monitored changes less rapidly. For example, when monitoring changes in heart rate after running, one may monitor the heart rate every 30 sec for the first 5 min after running, then every minute for another 5 min, then every 15 min for an hour, and then every half hour for 2 hr. Of course, the units of measurement will vary with the mode of biofeedback used; thus, when measuring temperature or blood pressure (cuff), the appropriate units would be degrees and mm Hg, respectively.

Begin by having your partner attach (if appropriate) the electrodes of the selected equipment. Do this lab *without* feedback.

Sitting comfortably, close your eyes, and have your partner take a baseline reading for a few minutes. Record baseline measurements from both biofeedback equipment and noninstrumented measures (e.g., pulse). Are the measures congruent with a relaxed state? Baseline values affect subsequent response amplitude. See the *Law of Initial Values* in the Glossary.

Complete the activity, sit comfortably, close your eyes, and have your partner record your measurements on Lab XX: Data Sheet—Activity 1 as soon as possible after completion of the chosen activity.

The time period following the activity during which recordings will be taken will vary both with the activity and the equipment.

Graph data on Lab XX: Graph—Activity 1. Use the same graph to plot all measures (i.e., measurements of all different physiological functions). Use a different color for each measure. Label values on the y axis for each of the measurements (see Appendix B).

Complete Lab XX: Questions—Activity 1.

Repeat similar procedures for another activity. Repeat for your partner's activity(ies). Discuss your results with others in your group. Complete Lab XX: Discussion and Conclusions.

Trainee ______________________

Trainer ______________________

Date ____________

LAB XX DATA SHEET—ACTIVITY 1

Describe activity: ____

Describe *measure* (e.g., heart rate, EMG): (1) ____________________

(2) ______________________ (3) ______________________

Describe physiological *location* of recording (e.g., brachial artery, frontalis):

(1) ______________ (2) ______________ (3) ______________

Preactivity baseline measurement (indicate units used)				Postactivity measurements			
Time[1]	Measure 1	Measure 2	Measure 3	Time	Measure 1	Measure 2	Measure 3
____	____	____	____	____	____	____	____
____	____	____	____	____	____	____	____
____	____	____	____	____	____	____	____
____	____	____	____	____	____	____	____
____	____	____	____	____	____	____	____
____	____	____	____	____	____	____	____
____	____	____	____	____	____	____	____
____	____	____	____	____	____	____	____
____	____	____	____	____	____	____	____
____	____	____	____	____	____	____	____
____	____	____	____	____	____	____	____
____	____	____	____	____	____	____	____
____	____	____	____	____	____	____	____
____	____	____	____	____	____	____	____
____	____	____	____	____	____	____	____

[1]You may need an additional data sheet for measurements over longer periods of time.

Trainee ____________________

Trainer ____________________

Date __________

LAB XX GRAPH—ACTIVITY 1

Activity: ____________________

Amplitude of signal

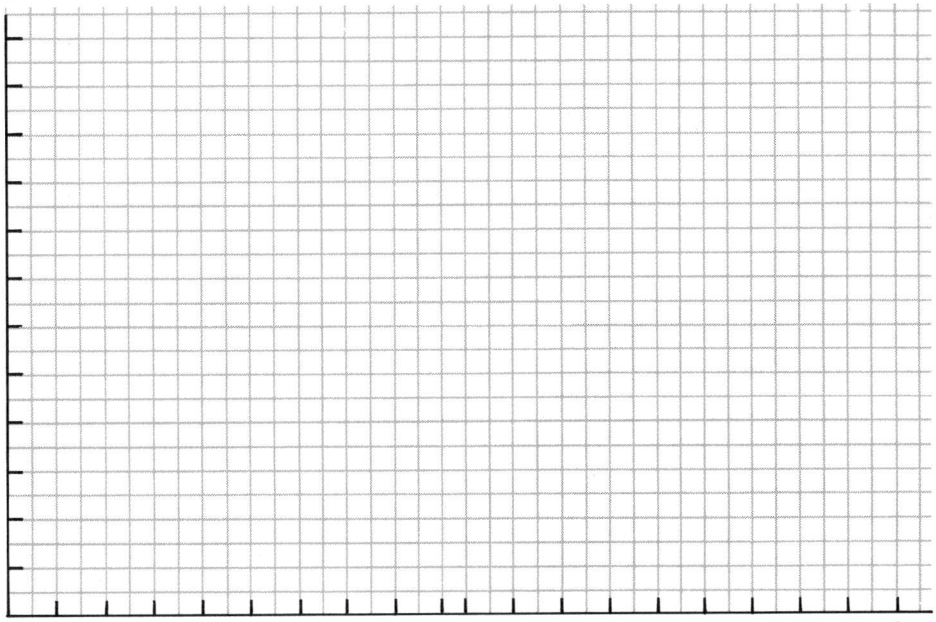

Preactivity — Postactivity

Time

Units of measurement: ____ ____ ____

Measure 1 2 3

Name of measure: (1)________ (2)________ (3)________

Color of line used for each measure: (1)________ (2)________ (3)________

Trainee ____________________

Date __________

LAB XX QUESTIONS—ACTIVITY 1

1. Looking at the graphed data, what physiological changes took place following the activity? Looking at the changes over time, when could you be sure that the physiological effects of the activity had "worn off"?

____

____

2. What physiological changes did you subjectively experience during and following the activity?

____

____

3. In what ways did the measures used reveal changes of which you were unaware?

____

____

4. What psychological and perceptual changes did you observe during and following the activity (changes in alertness, emotional responsiveness, vividness of color, flatness of visual field, etc.)?

____

____

____

5. In what ways did these psychological and perceptual experiences relate to the observed physiological changes? (For example, were colors most vivid when heart rate was rapid?)

____

____

____

6. Comments:

____

____

Trainee ______________

Trainer ______________

Date __________

LAB XX DATA SHEET—ACTIVITY 2

Describe activity: ______________

Describe *measure* (e.g., heart rate, EMG): (1) ______________

(2) ______________ (3) ______________

Describe physiological *location* of recording (e.g., brachial artery, frontalis):

(1) ______________ (2) ______________ (3) ______________

Preactivity baseline measurement (indicate units used)				Postactivity measurements			
Time	Measure 1	Measure 2	Measure 3	Time	Measure 1	Measure 2	Measure 3
____	____	____	____	____	____	____	____
____	____	____	____	____	____	____	____
____	____	____	____	____	____	____	____
____	____	____	____	____	____	____	____
____	____	____	____	____	____	____	____
____	____	____	____	____	____	____	____
____	____	____	____	____	____	____	____
____	____	____	____	____	____	____	____
____	____	____	____	____	____	____	____
____	____	____	____	____	____	____	____
____	____	____	____	____	____	____	____
____	____	____	____	____	____	____	____
____	____	____	____	____	____	____	____
____	____	____	____	____	____	____	____
____	____	____	____	____	____	____	____

Trainee ____________________

Trainer ____________________

Date __________

LAB XX GRAPH—ACTIVITY 2

Activity: ____________________

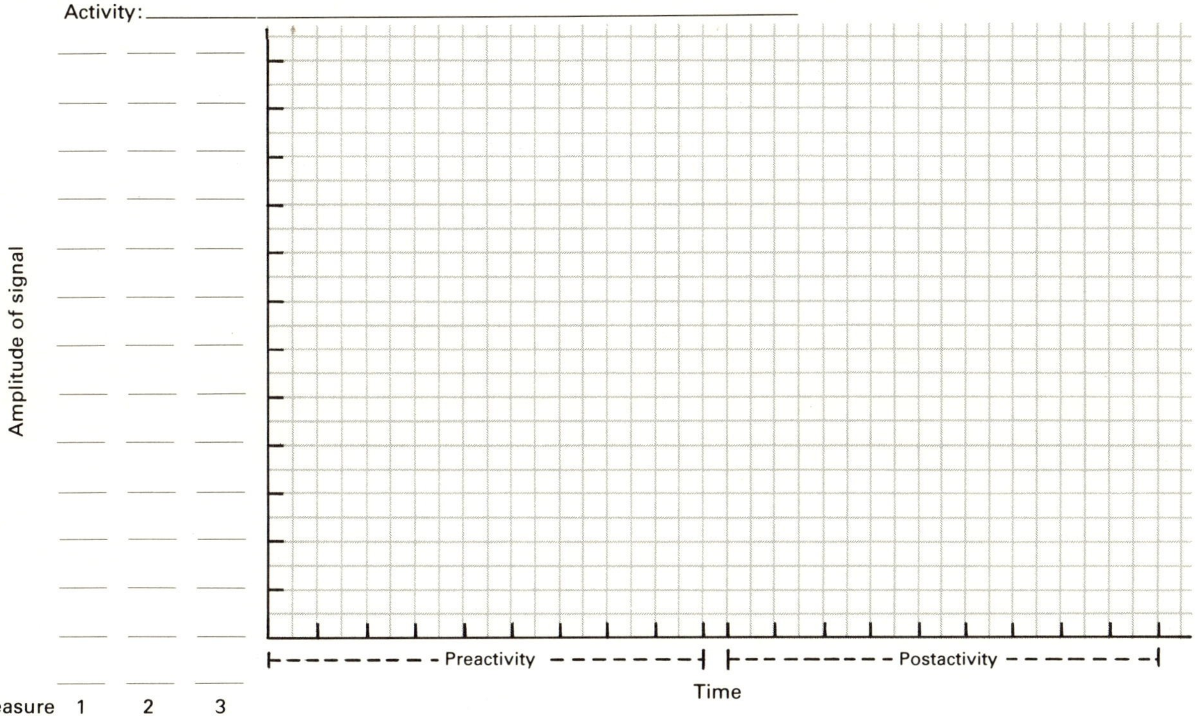

Units of measurement: ____ ____ ____

Measure 1 2 3

Name of measure: (1)________ (2)________ (3)________

Color of line used for each measure: (1)________ (2)________ (3)________

Trainee ______________________

Date ____________

LAB XX QUESTIONS—ACTIVITY 2

1. Looking at the graphed data, what physiological changes took place following this activity? Looking at the changes over time, when could you be sure that the physiological effects of the activity had "worn off"?

____

____

2. What physiological changes did you subjectively experience during and following the activity?

____

____

3. In what ways did the measures used reveal changes of which you were unaware?

____

____

4. What psychological and perceptual changes did you observe during and following the activity (changes in alertness, emotional responsiveness, vividness of color, flatness of visual field, etc.)?

____

____

____

5. In what ways did these psychological and perceptual experiences relate to the observed physiological changes? (For example, were colors most vivid when heart rate was rapid?)

____

____

____

6. Comments:

____

____

Trainee ______________________

Date __________

LAB XX DISCUSSION AND CONCLUSIONS

1. Compare your data with those of others in your group who did the same activity. In what ways did your responses vary?

____

____

____

2. Looking at the data for other activities, do you find that some activities affect specific physiological systems? Give examples.

____

____

____

____

____

3. What hypotheses can you formulate about the mechanism of your body's response to the activity and the return to preactivity baseline values?

____

____

____

____

4. In what ways did the psychological and physiological responses correlate with age, sex, or health and illness patterns?

____

____

____

5. What are the implications of this lab for biofeedback baseline measures and training?

SUGGESTIONS FOR FUTURE RESEARCH

1. Repeat the study *with* feedback, thereby learning to become more aware of physiological changes.
2. To what extent can you voluntarily reverse or inhibit the physiological changes induced by an activity?[2] (For example, how easy is it to warm the hands when a vasoconstrictive substance is ingested—as while smoking cigarettes?) Attempting to reverse normal physiological responses raises the following philosophical issue: To what extent may self-regulation be damaging to health? To what extent is one interfering with the natural homeostatic processes of the body?

[2]The physiological effects of chemicals are well documented in L. S. Goodman & A. Gilman, *The pharmacological basis of therapeutics,* New York: Macmillan, 1970.

LAB XXI
How Do You Respond to Stress?

PRELAB PREPARATION

During the week, observe how you respond to at least two different stressful events (the driver of the car in front of you slams on his brakes; you have a fight with your lover; you are taking an important exam; etc.). Observe physiological changes and record on the Lab XXI: Worksheet the system(s) (cardiovascular, gastrointestinal, etc.) in which you respond. Continue to observe the responsive system(s) and record approximately how long it takes for the system(s) to return to the pre-event levels.

LAB WORK

Equipment

All available biofeedback equipment, including EMG, temperature unit, EDG, EEG, EKG, equipment to monitor blood pressure, heart rate, respiration, etc.; ice bucket and ice.

Objective

Remember how your heart rate increased or your heart palpitated, or how you broke out in a cold sweat, or how your stomach sank when you were late for an appointment with your boss? Each of us reacts in ways like these to stressful situations, each with individual physiological specificity. In fact, we tend to respond with the same physiological system(s) time and again. Eventually pathology may manifest itself in that stressed system. Furthermore, it has been found that people who already have a specific pathology tend to respond to stressful events excessively in that system already burdened by pathology. For example, people with high blood pressure tend to respond to a stressful situation with an increase in blood pressure.

General hyperreactivity to stressful events may also contribute to the etiology of disease. Often we react to stressful events as if they were life-threatening. Wenger[1] observed that subjects who tended to respond excessively to stressors (sympathetic dominants)[2] were the same subjects who developed psychosomatic illnesses twenty years later.

The objective of this lab is to determine in which system(s) you respond to a stressor. Identification of the responsive system(s) is the first step in learning to inhibit responses. Such inhibition may then prevent the development of pathology in that system as well as optimize one's general health. An application of learning to inhibit a spontaneous re-

[1]M. A. Wenger, Studies of autonomic balance: A summary, *Psychophysiology*, 1966, *2*, 173.

[2]The response to life-threatening situations has been called the fight/flight response (alarm reaction) and is characterized by such complex physiological responses as increased heart rate, blood pressure, blood flow to muscle, and oxygen consumption. For more detailed discussion see W. B. Cannon, *The wisdom of the body*, New York: Norton, 1937; H. Selye, *The stress of life*, New York: McGraw-Hill, 1956; A. T. W. Simeons, *Man's presumptuous brain*, New York: Dutton, 1961; R. B. Malmo, *On emotions, needs and our archaic brain*, New York: Holt Rinehart & Winston, 1975.

sponse was demonstrated by Toscano and Cowings at NASA. They observed that if a subject is trained to inhibit those physiological responses (such as increased heart rate) that change with the onset of motion sickness, s/he will avoid triggering motion sickness despite being spun in a rotating chair.[3]

Instructions

In this lab you will experience two classic stressor tests. The first involves submersion of one hand in a bucket filled with ice water slush (cold stressor test) and the second involves the repeated mental subtraction of seven, starting from 1000 (serial seven test).

Cold Stressor Test

Begin by preparing the ice bucket: fill with ice and then add water to make slush.

Use Lab XXI: Data Sheet—Activity 1, filling in the appropriate time and units of measurement. You will want to vary the time interval for taking measurements depending on the mode of biofeedback used; for example, if you are using temperature and blood pressure, you may want to record temperature every 30 sec and blood pressure every minute. In addition, the time interval is frequently lengthened as the system being monitored changes less rapidly. For example, when monitoring changes in heart rate after encountering a stressor, one may monitor the heart rate every 30 sec for the first 5 min, then every minute for another 5 min, then every 15 min for an hour, and then every half hour for 2 hr. Of course, the units of measurement will vary with the mode of biofeedback used; thus, when measuring temperature or blood pressure (cuff), the appropriate units would be degrees and mm Hg, respectively.

Next have your partner attach the electrodes of the selected biofeedback equipment. Monitor as many different physiological functions as possible (at least three). Be sure to include equipment that monitors blood pressure as well as the system(s) you identified as responsive in your prelab preparation.

Sit comfortably, close your eyes, and have your partner take a baseline reading for a few minutes. Record baseline measurements from both biofeedback equipment and noninstrumented measures (e.g., pulse) on Lab XXI: Data Sheet—Activity 1. Are these measures congruent with a relaxed state? Baseline values affect subsequent response amplitude. See *Law of Initial Values* in the Glossary.

Place your hand in the ice water slush for 1 min. Your partner will tell you when the minute is up. Take your hand out of the bucket, sit quietly, and have your partner record the changes on the various measures selected. It probably will be easier if more than one person takes the measurements. The time during which recordings will be taken will vary with the equipment, i.e., some functions will stabilize more quickly than others.

Graph the data on Lab XXI: Graph Sheet—Activity 1. Use the same graph to plot all measures (i.e., measurements of all different physiological functions). Use a different color for each measure. Label values on the *y* axis for each of the measurements (see Appendix B). Complete Lab XXI: Questions—Activity 1.

Serial Seven Test

Repeat the above procedure, except instead of submerging your hand in ice water, count down mentally from 1000 by sevens as rapidly as possible for at least 1 min, calling out (to an eager audience of at least three persons) each number. Complete Lab XXI: Questions—Activity 2.

Repeat the activities with your partner as trainee. Discuss your results with others in your group. Complete Lab XXI: Discussion and Conclusions.

[3]W. B. Toscano & P. S. Cowings, Transference of learned autonomic control for symptom suppression across opposite directions of coriolis acceleration. In preprints of 1978 Annual Scientific Meeting, Aerospace Medical Association, New Orleans, May 1978, pp. 132–133.

Trainee ______________________

Date __________

LAB XXI WORKSHEET

Event 1: ____

	Systems in which response occurred	Approximate time to return to pre-event level
1.	______________________	__________
2.	______________________	__________
3.	______________________	__________

Event 2: ____

	Systems in which response occurred	Approximate time to return to pre-event level
1.	______________________	__________
2.	______________________	__________
3.	______________________	__________

Trainee ____________________

Trainer ____________________

Date ____________

LAB XXI DATA SHEET—ACTIVITY 1

Describe *measure* (e.g., heart rate, EMG): (1) ____________________

(2) ____________________ (3) ____________________

Describe physiological *location* of recording (e.g., brachial artery, frontalis):

(1) ____________ (2) ____________ (3) ____________

Preactivity baseline measurement (indicate units used)				Postactivity measurements			
Time[4]	Measure 1	Measure 2	Measure 3	Time	Measure 1	Measure 2	Measure 3

[4]You may need an additional data sheet for measurements over longer periods of time.

Trainee ____________________

Trainer ____________________

Date __________

LAB XXI GRAPH—ACTIVITY 1

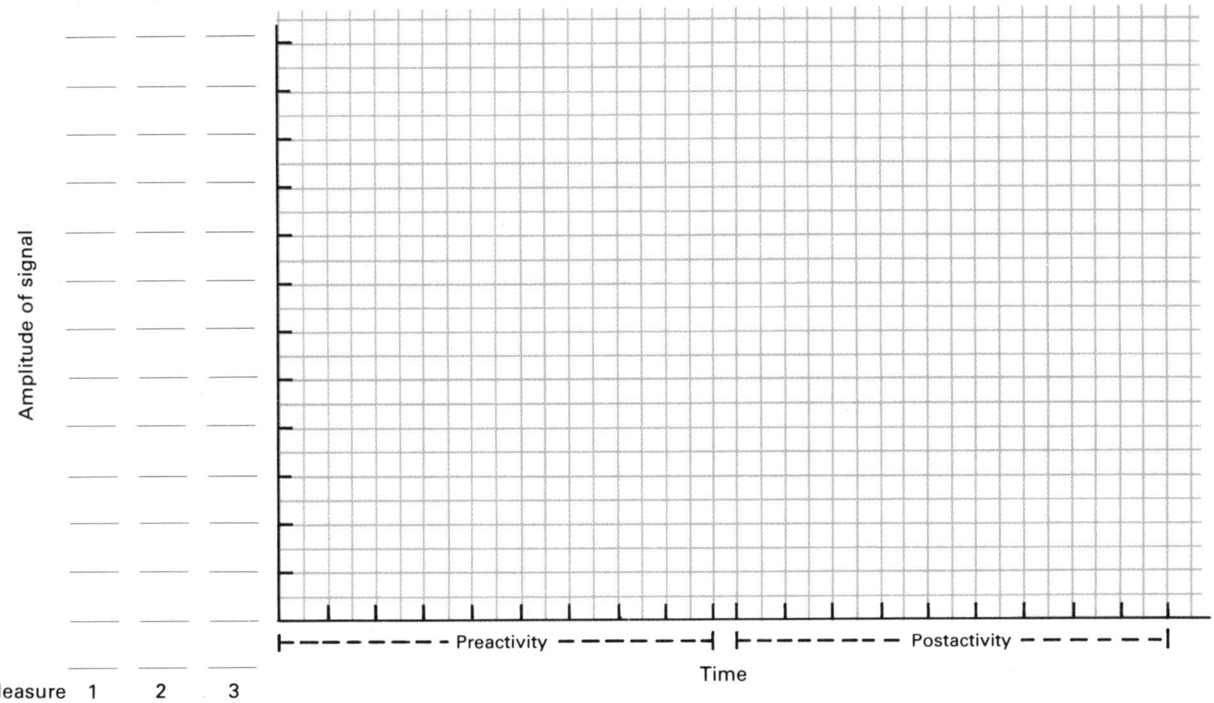

Units of measurement:

Measure 1 2 3

Name of measure: (1)__________ (2)__________ (3)__________

Color of line used for each measure: (1)__________ (2)__________ (3)__________

Trainee ______________________

Date ____________

LAB XXI QUESTIONS—ACTIVITY 1

1. How did you respond physically to the cold pressor test (with what systems, intensity of response), i.e., what is your stress profile?

2. Was there much variation among systems in the length of time required to return to preactivity levels?

3. With what attitude did you approach this activity (fear, apprehension, enthusiasm, etc.) and how did you subjectively experience this activity?

4. Comments:

Trainee ____________________

Trainer ____________________

Date __________

LAB XXI DATA SHEET—ACTIVITY 2

Describe *measure* (e.g., heart rate, EMG): (1) ____________________

(2) ____________________ (3) ____________________

Describe physiological *location* of recording (e.g., brachial artery, frontalis):

(1) ______________ (2) ______________ (3) ______________

Preactivity baseline measurement (indicate units used)				Postactivity measurements			
Time	Measure 1	Measure 2	Measure 3	Time	Measure 1	Measure 2	Measure 3
____	____	____	____	____	____	____	____
____	____	____	____	____	____	____	____
____	____	____	____	____	____	____	____
____	____	____	____	____	____	____	____
____	____	____	____	____	____	____	____
____	____	____	____	____	____	____	____
____	____	____	____	____	____	____	____
____	____	____	____	____	____	____	____
____	____	____	____	____	____	____	____
____	____	____	____	____	____	____	____
____	____	____	____	____	____	____	____
____	____	____	____	____	____	____	____
____	____	____	____	____	____	____	____
____	____	____	____	____	____	____	____
____	____	____	____	____	____	____	____

Trainee ____________________

Trainer ____________________

Date __________

LAB XXI GRAPH—ACTIVITY 2

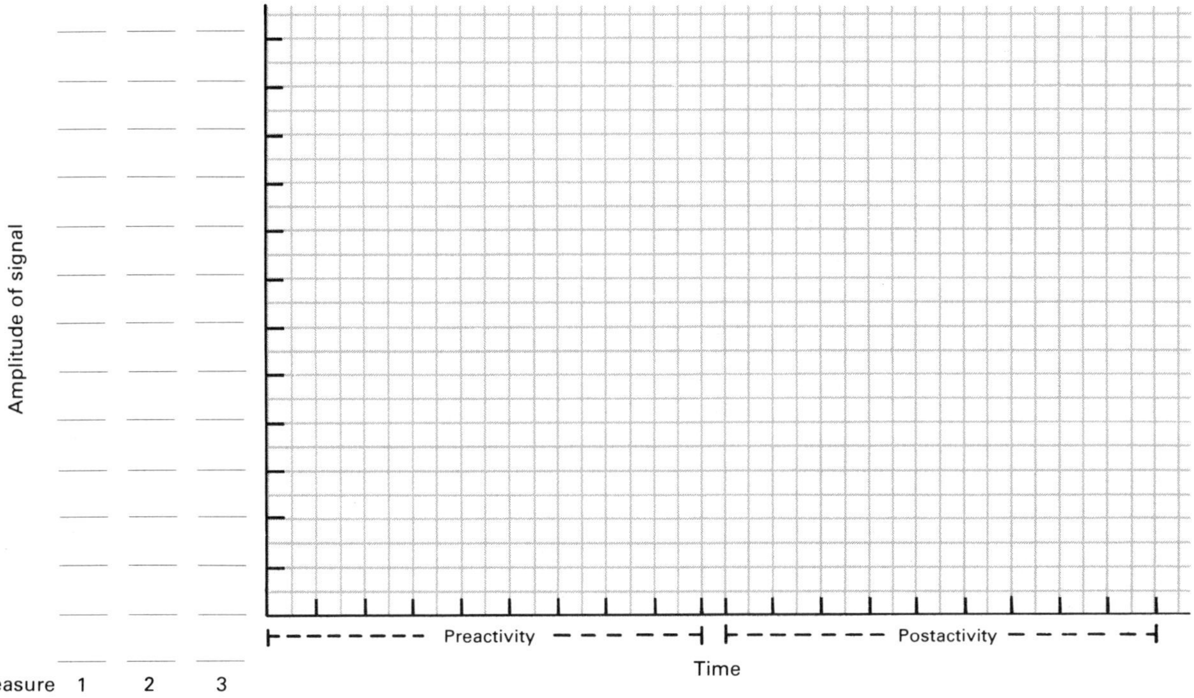

Name of measure: (1)__________ (2)__________ (3)__________

Color of line used for each measure: (1)__________ (2)__________ (3)__________

Trainee ______________________

Date ___________

LAB XXI QUESTIONS—ACTIVITY 2

1. How did you respond physically to the serial seven test (with what systems, intensity of response), i.e., what is your stress profile?

2. Was there much variation among systems in the length of time required to return to preactivity levels?

3. With what attitude did you approach this activity (fear, apprehension, enthusiasm, etc.) and how did you subjectively experience this activity?

4. Describe the difference in how you responded to a primarily physical stressor (cold pressor test) and how you responded to a psychological stressor (serial seven test).

5. Comments:

Trainee ______________________

Date __________

LAB XXI DISCUSSION AND CONCLUSIONS

1. Was there a difference among members of your group in their stress profiles for Activity 1, and if so, how were the differences related to age, sex, and common pathologies?

____

____

____

____

____

2. Was there a difference among members of your group in their stress profiles for Activity 2, and if so, how were the differences related to age, sex, and common pathologies?

____

____

____

____

____

3. Generally, did the members of your group respond differently to the cold pressor test and the serial seven, i.e., were their stress profiles different for the two activities? If so, how were their responses different? Can you explain these differences?

____

____

____

____

____

4. In what ways were the attitudes by which group members approached the activities and the way they experienced the activities related to their stress

profiles? For example, were those persons who experienced fear before and during the activity those who responded with the greatest increase in blood pressure?

5. Often one is again challenged by a stressor before one's physiological response to a previous stressor has returned to prestressor levels. What are the implications of this for health? Draw a graph of this concept.

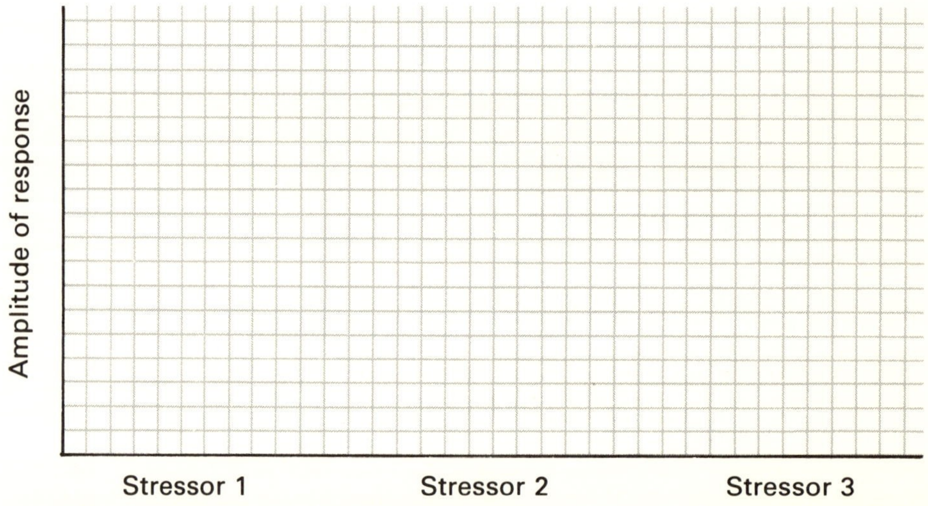

SUGGESTIONS FOR FUTURE RESEARCH

1. Evaluate other situations as a stressor test. For example, present someone with an unsolvable block puzzle. Inform them after a few minutes that your 5-year-old niece finished the puzzle in 4 min. Monitor response.
2. Develop strategies to teach people to inhibit their stress response (stress inoculation training).

Appendices

APPENDIX A: INTRODUCTION TO ELECTRICITY
APPENDIX B: GRAPHING YOUR DATA
APPENDIX C: USING THE SPHYGMOMANOMETER
APPENDIX D: EQUIPMENT PROBLEM SOLVING
APPENDIX E: BIOFEEDBACK RESOURCES
APPENDIX F: BIOFEEDBACK EQUIPMENT AND SUPPLIES
APPENDIX G: GLOSSARY

APPENDIX A
Introduction to Electricity

The following is a presentation of some basic concepts of electricity relevant to the understanding of the biofeedback signal.

THE ATOM

The *atom* is the basic unit of matter. It consists of *neutrons* (particles carrying no charge), *protons* (particles carrying positive charges), and *electrons* (particles carrying negative charges). Most atoms carry equal numbers of electrons and protons—hence, equal amounts of positive and negative charge; they are thus electrically neutral. If an electron is removed from or added to an atom, the atom then carries a net charge and is called an *ion*.

ELECTRIC CURRENT (DESIGNATED *I*)

Electric current is the flow of electric charge from one place to another. In metal conductors (such as copper wire), the movement of electric charge is in the form of electrons, whereas in liquid conductors (such as body fluids), the movement of electric charge is in the form of ions.

The magnitude of electric current is the amount of charge that passes a given point per unit time.

$$\text{Current } (I) = \frac{\text{Amount charge}}{\text{Unit time}}$$

The unit of measurement of current is the *ampere* (A).

VOLTAGE (DESIGNATED *V*)

Electrons and ions are set into motion and give rise to electric currents because of the action of electric forces. *Voltage* is the electrical ''pressure'' or potential difference that causes electric current to flow.

Unlike charges attract (positive charges are attracted to negative charges and negative charges are attracted to positive charges), while like charges repel each other (negative charges repel negative charges and positive charges repel positive charges). These forces of attraction and repulsion are the electrical forces. For example, referring to Figure 26, we see that the positive charge is attracted to position A, which is negative, and repelled by position B, which is positive. To move the positive charge from position A to position B requires work and generates voltage, a potential difference.

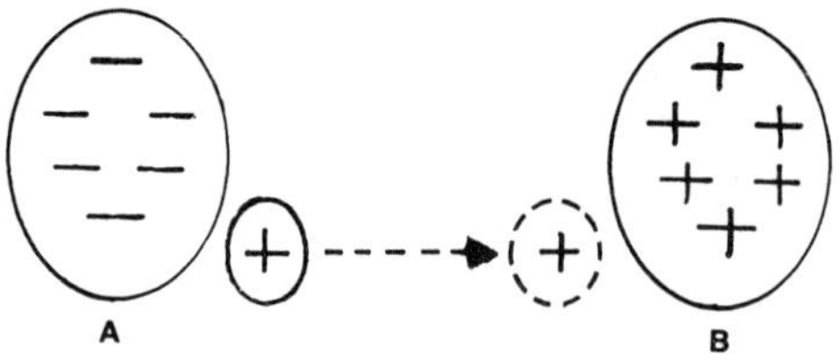

FIGURE 26. The movement of a positive charge from position A to B generates a voltage.

$$\text{Potential difference (or voltage)} = \frac{\text{Work}}{\text{Charge}}$$

The unit of measurement of voltage is the *volt* (V).

RESISTANCE (DESIGNATED *R*)

The *resistance* offered by a conductor is the ratio between the potential difference across it and the resulting current that flows through it.

$$\text{Resistance } (R) = \frac{\text{Potential difference } (V)}{\text{Current } (I)}$$

The unit of measurement of resistance is the ohm (Ω).

WATER FLOW ANALOGY AND OHM'S LAW

Imagine the flow of water (as shown in Figure 27) to be analogous to the flow of electrons through a metal wire (I). The force exerted on the piston on the top is then analogous to voltage (V), and the resistance offered by the spout is analogous to the resistance (R) of a wire. If a force F is exerted, water will flow out the spout at a certain rate (Figure 27A). If the diameter of the spout is increased, there is less resistance to the

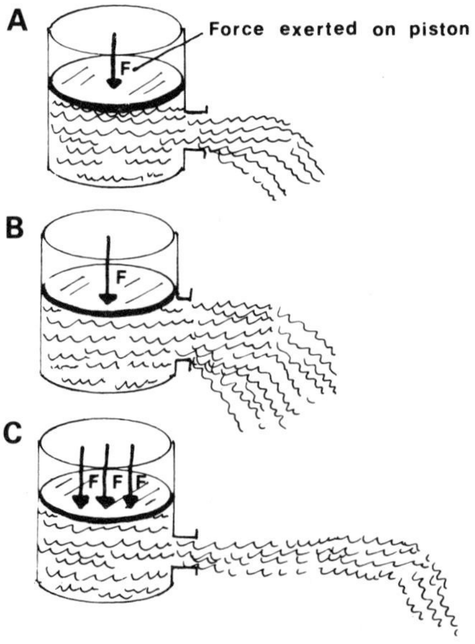

FIGURE 27. An illustration of Ohm's law with the water flow analogy. (A) With a given force and a given spout size, there is a given flow of water. (B) If the spout size increases, the resistance to flow decreases and the flow of water increases. (C) If the force increases, the flow of water increases.

flow of water and increased water flow (Figure 27B). Similarly, if a larger force is exerted, the rate of water flow is increased (Figure 27C).

This relationship between current, voltage, and resistance is given by *Ohm's Law,* which states:

$$\text{Current } (I) = \frac{\text{Voltage } (V)}{\text{Resistance } (R)}$$

Thus either an increase in V (analogous to Figure 27C) or a decrease in R (analogous to Figure 27B) results in an increase in current.

APPLICATION TO THE BIOFEEDBACK SIGNAL

Dissolved within the fluid of the body are ions (e.g., sodium, potassium, calcium, magnesium) vital to survival. Certain physiological processes (e.g., muscle contraction, nerve impulse transmission) involve the shift of these ions, such that one part of the body may be more negative than another at any point in time. Electrodes are used to monitor these shifts or changes in potential.

APPENDIX B
Graphing Your Data

The graphing of data is often important in demonstrating trends or relationships that may not be obvious from a data sheet. The following is a brief introduction to graphing.

THE AXES

The horizontal axis is traditionally referred to as the *x axis* and the vertical axis as the *y axis*. Usually one is looking at how the variable plotted along the *y* axis changes as a function of the variable plotted along the *x* axis. Almost all of the graphs in this manual have the measure of some physiological process plotted along the *y* axis and time plotted along the *x* axis. Thus one is looking at how some physiological process changes over time. For example, Figure 28 shows how one trainee's muscle tension as measured by the EMG changed over a period of 2 min.

DETERMINATION OF VALUES FOR THE *y* AXIS

The values along the *y* axis will vary depending upon the range of recorded values. To determine these values along the *y* axis, begin by looking at the data sheet and noting the smallest and greatest recordings. Table 4 gives sample EMG data to be used as an example of this graphing process.

For our example, 0.2 μV is the smallest recorded EMG value and 2.5 the largest, the range of values being from 0.2 to 2.5 μV. To determine the value of each increment on

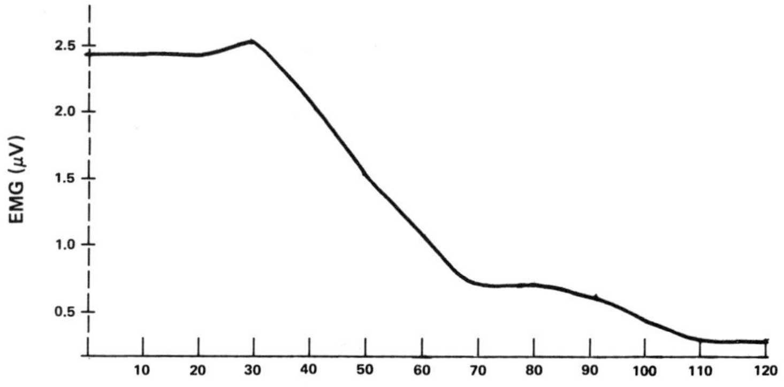

FIGURE 28. Sample graph.

TABLE 4
Sample Data

Time (sec)	EMG measurements (μV)
0	2.4
10	2.4
20	2.4
30	2.5
40	2.0
50	1.5
60	1.1
70	0.7
80	0.7
90	0.6
100	0.4
110	0.2
120	0.2

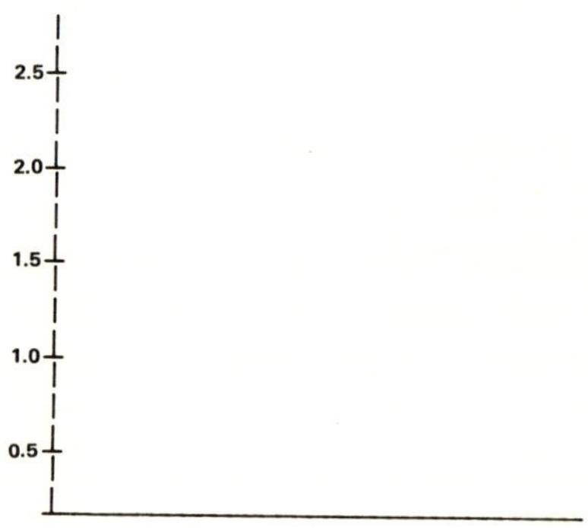

FIGURE 29. Increments along *y* axis labeled.

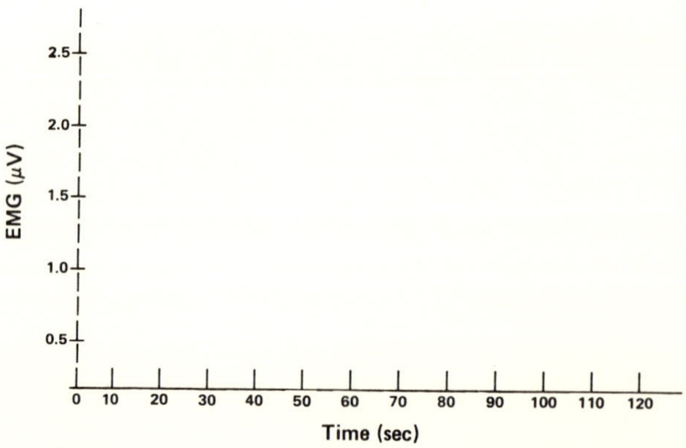

FIGURE 30. Increments along *x* and *y* axes labeled.

the y axis, first note the number of divisions printed along the y axis of the graph (if this is given). In this case assume 5 divisions are given. Next subtract the smallest value on the y axis from the largest value. In our example $2.5 - 0.2 = 2.3$. Then divide this difference by the number of divisions on the graph. In our example, $2.3 \div 5 = 0.46$. For ease of plotting on graph paper (usually with subdivisions into 10's) round the number up to 0.5 or a multiple of 0.5. In our example, 0.46 is rounded to 0.5. To determine the upper and lower values along the y axis, round the smallest and largest numbers to multiples of 0.5 also—in this case, 0 and 2.5. The value of each increment in our example is 0.5, that is, each value along the y axis is 0.5 μV larger than the preceding one. Thus, the values along the y axis are 0, 0.5, 1.0, 1.5, 2.0, and 2.5 μV, as shown in Figure 29.

DETERMINATION OF VALUES ALONG THE x AXIS

The values along the x axis will be those times at which measurements were taken. Continuing with the above example, the values are 0, 10, 20, 30, 40, 50, 60, 70, 80, 90, 100, 110, and 120 sec, as shown in Figure 30.

THE POINTS OF THE GRAPH

The points of the graph are determined by finding the correct measurement along the y axis at each time interval. For example, at 10 sec the EMG level recorded was 2.4 μV, so the correct point would be at the intersection of an imaginary line drawn across from 2.4 on the y axis and up from 10 sec on the x axis, as shown on Figure 30.

CONNECTING THE POINTS

Once the points have been put on the graph, they are often connected to make clear any trend or relationship. See Figure 28.

APPENDIX C

Using the Sphygmomanometer[1]

The following is a brief introduction to concepts basic to understanding blood pressure and a description of the use of the sphygmomanometer in measuring blood pressure.

SYSTOLE AND DIASTOLE

The normal heart beats in a rhythmic, cyclic fashion. The cardiac cycle consists of a period of relaxation called *diastole* followed by a period of contraction called *systole*.

BLOOD PRESSURE

Blood pressure is actually a measurement of the force exerted by the blood against the vessel wall. It is usually measured in millimeters of mercury (mm Hg). If, for example, the pressure is 80 mm Hg, this means the pressure exerted is sufficient to push a column of mercury up 80 mm. Blood pressure is usually given as a ratio (such as 120/80 mm Hg). The numerator (120) refers to the *systolic pressure* (the blood pressure corresponding to systole), and the denominator (80) refers to the *diastolic pressure* (the blood pressure corresponding to diastole).

USING THE SPHYGMOMANOMETER

Sit comfortably with one arm free and slightly flexed at the elbow (palm facing up) resting on a flat surface at heart level. Be sure to keep the arm and shoulder relaxed. Place the cuff around the upper arm so the lower edge of the cuff is about 2.5 cm above the elbow crease (see Figure 31). You will be measuring the pressure from the brachial artery (the main artery of the upper arm). Place a stethoscope firmly, but without undue pressure, over the brachial artery in the elbow crease. This point is usually found just medial (toward the center of the body) to the biceps tendon. (If you make a fist and flex your arm, you can see the biceps; the tendon attaches the biceps to the forearm.) (See Figure 32.)

Continue to monitor the brachial pulse with your stethoscope. Inflate the cuff until the pulse is no longer audible (i.e., sufficient pressure is applied to occlude blood flow). In most cases you will not need to go above 180 mm. Then deflate the cuff slowly, allowing the pressure to drop at the rate of about 3 mm Hg/sec. Note the level of Hg at which you hear the first sound. The pressure of the blood in the artery is approximately equal to that being applied by the cuff. This level of Hg at the time of the first sound is a measure of systolic pressure. Continue to lower the pressure slowly until the sounds become suddenly muffled. This is a measure of the diastolic pressure. Continue to decrease the pressure until all sounds disappear. After a minute of rest, repeat to confirm your measurements. Remove the cuff.

[1]REFERENCE: *Mind/body integration*, pp. 527–528.

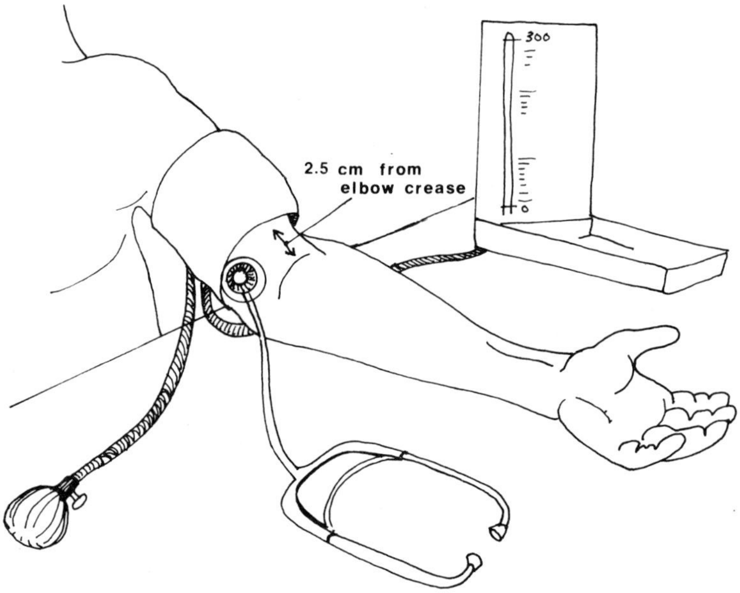

FIGURE 31. Use of the sphygmomanometer—location of cuff.

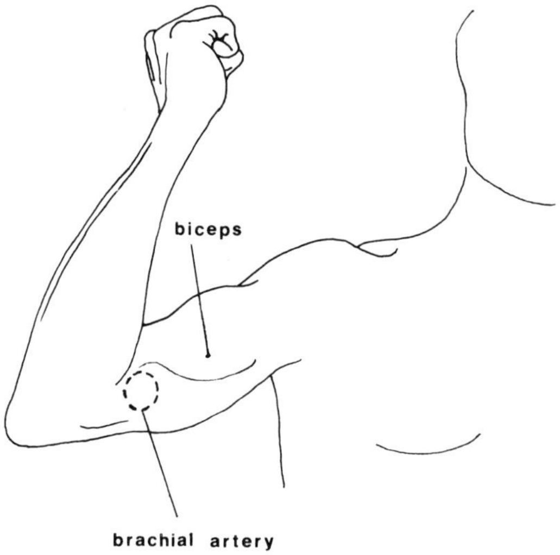

FIGURE 32. Location of brachial artery for placement of stethoscope.

APPENDIX D

Equipment Problem Solving[1]

Difficulties and problems often occur when one uses biofeedback devices: the equipment appears not to work or the monitored reading appears random. The basis of most equipment problems is often

1. Breakage in the electrode assembly.
2. Problems in electrode/skin interface.
3. Dead batteries.
4. Switches turned to incorrect setting.
5. Misunderstanding of equipment manual.

Before sending the equipment back to the manufacturer, check the following:
If the battery test does not work, then

- Check to see if the machine is turned on.
- Check to see if you have pushed the correct buttons. (Did you press the electrode check button by mistake?)
- Check your batteries. They may need to be replaced.

If the electrode test check indicates too high a resistance, then

- Check to see if the machine is turned on.
- Check to see if the electrode wires are broken.
- Check to see if the skin was properly prepared.
- Check to see if the electrode cable is plugged into the machine.
- Repeat electrode application.

If the meter moves to the left and stops there

- Check to see if the machine is turned on.
- Check amplification and/or filter range.
- Check to see if batteries are too low.
- Check to see if electrodes are touching each other.
- Check other feedback modalities (e.g., threshold, integration).

If the meter moves to the right and stays there

- Check amplification and/or filter range.

[1]REFERENCE: *Mind/body integration,* pp. 231–240.

- Check to see if the electrodes are making proper contact with the skin.
- Check to see if batteries are too low.
- Check to see if you are near other electrical appliances.
- Check other feedback modalities (e.g., threshold, integration).

If there is no auditory feedback

- Check to see if the machine is turned on.
- Check to see if the volume switch is turned to maximum.
- Check to see if the speaker is plugged in.
- Check other feedback modalities (e.g., threshold, integration).

If the meter moves erratically

- Check to see if the meter moves appropriately during the behavioral test.
- Check to see if the electrodes are appropriately attached.
- Check for other electrical artifacts (TV, CB radio, etc.).
- Check to see if the integration switch is set for direct, instantaneous feedback.

In order to determine if the problem is due to equipment or electrode assembly

- Substitute another feedback unit with the same electrodes.
- Substitute another electrode assembly with the same feedback unit.

APPENDIX E
Biofeedback Resources

ORGANIZATIONS

Biofeedback Society of America

Founded in 1969, the Biofeedback Society of America presently is composed of a membership at large and two divisions: applied and experimental. These divisions reflect the dual focus of the Society. Many state societies have recently been founded and are recognized as chapters of this national organization.

Membership in the Biofeedback Society is open to professionals and students interested in the investigation and application of biofeedback. Membership includes subscriptions to *Biofeedback and Self-Regulation,* the official journal of the Society, and *Biofeedback,* a quarterly newsletter that serves as an informal medium for information exchange for the Society. In addition, other relevant publications are available through the Society.

The Society regularly sponsors an annual scientific meeting emphasizing both basic research and clinical applications of biofeedback. In addition, Biofeedback Workshops for professionals are sponsored. These programs cover the general area of applied biofeedback, emphasizing the most current information on the use of biofeedback in the treatment of psychophysiological problems. Research findings and applications are discussed in depth by an outstanding faculty.

For more information contact:

Francine Butler, Ph.D.
Executive Director
Biofeedback Society of America
4301 Owens Street
Wheat Ridge, CO 80033
(303) 420-2889

State Societies

Most states now have state biofeedback societies. These are responsible for certification of biofeedback competence. For information regarding any of these, write Dr. Francine Butler at the address above.

LITERATURE ON BIOFEEDBACK AND RELATED AREAS

Journals

Biofeedback and Self-Regulation
Biofeedback Society of America
4301 Owens Street
Wheat Ridge, CO 80033

Psychophysiology
The Society for Psychophysiological Research
2380 Lisa Lane
Madison, WI 53711

Brain/Mind Bulletin
P.O. Box 42211
Los Angeles, CA 90004

Bibliographies

F. Butler, *Biofeedback and self-regulation: A guide to the literature*. New York: Plenum, 1978.

D. Waterman, B. Tandy, & E. Peper, *Relaxation: A bibliography*. Denver: Biofeedback Society of America, 1978.

Indexing Services

Computer searches of these indexes can be ordered through most university libraries.

Biological Abstracts (biological literature)
ERIC (educational and psychological testing literature)
Index Medicus/MEDLARS (medical and psychiatric literature)
Psychological Abstracts/PASAR (psychological literature)

APPENDIX F

Biofeedback Equipment and Supplies

The following manufacturers are only a few of the many companies that produce quality biofeedback equipment[1]:

American Biofeedback Corporation
Hunter Brook Road
Yorktown Hights, NY 10598
(914) 962-4694

Autogenic Systems Inc.
809 Allston Way
Berkeley, CA 94710
(415) 548-6056

Biofeedback Research Institute
6325 Wilshire Boulevard
Los Angeles, CA 90048
(213) 933-9451

Biofeedback Systems Inc.
2736 47th Street
Boulder, CO 80301
(303) 444-1411

Cyborg Corporation
342 Western Avenue
Boston, MA 02134
(617) 782-9820

J&J Enterprises
22797 Holgar Court NE
Poulsbo, WA 98370
(206) 779-3853

OTHER RELEVANT EQUIPMENT SOURCES

The specific equipment needed for the labs and the tapes for Instruction Set A may be ordered from

Biofeedback and Family Therapy Institute
2236 Derby Street
Berkeley, CA 94705
(415) 841-7227

Small hand thermometers can be ordered from

Consciousness Living Foundation
P.O. Box 513
Manhattan, KS 66502

Bio-Temp Products, Inc.
3266 N. Meridian
Indianapolis, IN 46208

[1]A detailed listing of biofeedback companies can be found in *Mind/body integration: Essential readings in biofeedback*, pp. 568–571.

APPENDIX G
Glossary

Terms in this glossary are defined with *specific* reference to their usage in biofeedback training.

AC—See *alternating current.*

active electrode—The electrode placed over the tissue whose electrical activity is being monitored.

alarm reaction—See *fight-flight response.*

alpha waves—A waveform generated by the brain with a frequency between 8 and 13 Hz, usually associated with relaxed wakefulness.

alternating current (AC)—An electrical current whose direction of flow shifts back and forth in a periodic manner.

ampere—The unit of measurement of electrical current.

amplifier—An electrical device that converts a small signal into a larger one.

amplitude—A measure of the intensity of an electrical signal; the unit of measurement is the volt.

ANS—See *autonomic nervous system.*

apocrine gland—A type of sweat gland located predominantly in the armpits and genital region.

arteriole—A small branch of an artery, especially one just proximal to a capillary.

artery—Any vessel carrying blood away from the heart.

artifact—Any part of a biofeedback signal not generated by the physiological system being monitored; for example, an EKG signal in an EMG recording is an artifact.

autogenic training—A system of psychophysiological relaxation originally developed by J. Schultz and W. Luthe. Frequently used as an adjunctive technique with biofeedback training.

autonomic nervous system (ANS)—That portion of the nervous system that controls visceral functions of the body, such as arterial pressure, gastrointestinal motility and secretion, urinary output, and sweating and body temperature. It is traditionally considered to act independently of volition. Autonomic impulses are transmitted to the body through two major subdivisions, called the *sympathetic* and *parasympathetic nervous systems.*

average—A type of processed biofeedback signal in which feedback represents the *mean* signal over a certain time period, i.e., the sum of multiple measurements divided by the number of measurements taken.

bandpass—Those frequencies of an electrical signal that are passed unmodified by a filter. For example, a filter with a bandpass of 100–200 Hz allows signals between 100 and 200 Hz to pass unmodified.

baseline—Measurements of a physiological function taken in the absence of some task or technique; comparison of baseline values with values generated during the task allows for determination of the effect of the task on the system being monitored.

battery test—A test to determine if a battery is charged.

behavioral test—A test during which the trainee is asked to perform some behavioral task to verify if equipment is working (for example, a trainee with EMG electrodes on his/her forehead is asked to furrow his/her brow). An increase in intensity of the feedback signal would indicate that the equipment is working.

beta waves—A waveform generated by the brain with a frequency greater than 13 Hz, usually associated with an alert state.

bioelectric potential—The electrical potential created by biological system.

biofeedback—The process of monitoring a changing physiological process and feeding back the generated signal to the individual being monitored.

bipolar recording—The process of recording electrical activity from one active electrode with reference to a second active electrode via differential amplification.

caliber—The diameter of a canal or tube.

calibration—The determination or correction of the scale of a measurement tool.

cholinergic blocking agent—A substance that blocks the action of the neurotransmitter acetylcholine.

conductance—A commonly used measure of electrodermal activity; the reciprocal of resistance, measured in mhos: $C = 1/R$.

conductor—A material that easily allows the flow of electricity.

current—Flow of electrical charge from one place to another (see Appendix A).

DC—See *direct current.*

delta waves—A waveform generated by the brain with a frequency between 1 and 3 Hz, usually associated with deep sleep.

derivative—A type of processed biofeedback signal in which feedback is given only when there is a *change* in the level of activity of the physiological system being monitored; the intensity of the signal reflects the rate of change in the level of activity.

differential amplification—(1) A process in which the difference between two electrical signals is amplified. (2) A process in which only the voltages not common to two electrodes are amplified.

direct access—The capacity to receive the physiological signal that has been amplified but not processed further—the "raw signal."

direct current (DC)—An electrical signal that does not reverse direction of flow in a periodic manner.

discharge—The spontaneous occurrence of sensations, images, feelings, thoughts, and/or movements, during the process of relaxation.

"dummy" subject—Resistors that are used to simulate the resistance qualities of the skin but that generate no electrical signal of their own.

dysponesis—From the Greek *dys* (bad) and *ponesis* (exertion). Misplaced efforts or energy expended during some activity that is not required for the performance of that activity.

eccrine gland—A type of sweat gland located over the entire body.

efferent oculomotor commands—Neural elicitation of eye movements.

electricity-shielded room—A room with sheet metal facing (usually copper) that shields it from external electromagnetic signals. Also referred to as a *Faraday cage.*

electrocardiograph (EKG)—A device that records the electrical activity of the heart.

electrode—A device for detecting changes in bioelectric potential. An electrode converts ionic bioelectric potentials generated by the body into electrical potentials required by conventional measuring devices at the tissue/electrode interface.

electrodermograph (EDG)—A device that records the electrical activity of the skin.

electrode test—A test to determine the resistance offered by an electrode assembly (electrode and leads) and the tissue/electrode interface.

electroencephalograph (EEG)—A device that records the electrical activity of the brain.

equilibrium—The state in which the feedback signal is stable or unchanging.

ergotrophic response—See *fight-flight response.*

Faraday cage— See *electricity-shielded room.*

fight-flight response—A response to stress in which large portions of the sympathetic nervous system are generally activated simultaneously, resulting in increased arterial pressure, increased cardiac output, increased blood flow to muscles, decreased blood flow to organs that are not needed for rapid activity (viscera), increased cellular metabolism throughout the body, increased muscle strength, and increased mental activity—all of which prepare the body for vigorous muscle activity. Also referred to as the *alarm reaction* or *ergotrophic response* (from the Greek *ergos,* work).

filter—An electronic device that attenuates or rejects certain components of the electrical signal while passing others unmodified.

frequency—A measure of the number of times per given time interval that a waveform reverses polarity (i.e., the number of oscillations), expressed as cycles per second or Hertz (Hz).

fugue state—A period of time during which an individual behaves in a rational, purposeful manner, yet after which s/he has no conscious remembrance of his/her actions.

gain—The factor by which an amplifier amplifies an electrical signal.

generalization—Application of skills learned in an office or laboratory situation to the "real world."

ground electrode—An electrode placed over some "neutral" tissue that is connected to the earth or to the metal framework of an electrical circuit for purposes of artifact rejection.

habituation—The process by which, after repeated exposure to a stimulus, an organism no longer responds to the stimulus.

Hertz (Hz)—The unit of measurement of the frequency of a waveform; cycles per second. 60 Hz is the predominant powerline frequency and is often a problem as an artifact in biofeedback work.

homeostasis—The maintenance of stable, constant conditions in the internal environment of an organism.

hypnogogic images—Dreamlike images not consciously generated that appear when falling asleep.

hypnopompic images—Dreamlike images not consciously generated that appear when awakening.

impedance—A measure of resistance to current flow in an AC circuit.

inion—The most prominent point of the external occipital protuberance (back of the head).

innervated—Activated or supplied by a nerve.

input—(1) The electrical signal fed into biofeedback equipment. (2) The terminal of a device into which input is fed.

instantaneous feedback—A process in which a signal is not processed with regard to time, i.e., not averaged or integrated; rather, feedback is given immediately to the trainee.

integration—A method of processing the biofeedback signal so that the feedback represents the area under the curve of the signal over a certain period of time.

interface—The region of contact between two systems; for example, the *electrode/tissue interface* refers to the region of contact between electrode and tissue.

invasive—A technique is considered *invasive* if it involves crossing normal boundaries of the body. Thus, needle electrodes are invasive, whereas surface electrodes are noninvasive.

latency—The period between the time when a stimulus is given and the time when the feedback signal reflects the trainee's response to that stimulus.

law of initial values—The intensity of a response of the autonomic nervous system to stimulation is dependent upon the prestimulus level; the higher the prestimulus level, the less intense will be the response to stimulation.

law of reverse effort—The harder you try in learning autonomic control, the less successful you are; in fact, autonomic control is most rapidly learned with an attitude of passive attention.

mantra—A word with special and/or spiritual significance used as the center of focus in meditation.

mindfulness—An attitude of remaining present, watchful, and aware of what is happening without becoming involved or captured by images, thoughts, or feelings; the attitude implies the absence of either anticipation or rumination.

modified progressive relaxation (MPR)—An abbreviated and shortened form of progressive relaxation (see *progressive relaxation*).

monopolar recording—The process of recording electrical activity from one active electrode and one reference electrode via differential amplification.

motor unit—The functional unit of a voluntary muscle, consisting of a number of muscle cells, innervated by a single nerve cell (motor neuron).

narcolepsy—A condition marked by an uncontrollable desire for sleep, or by sudden attacks of sleep.

nasion—The depression at the bridge of the nose.

noise—A signal generated by biofeedback equipment itself.

nonjudgmental acceptance—An attitude of not explaining, interpreting, or judging an experience as good or bad, but rather letting it be, without judgment.

ohm (Ω)—The unit of measurement of electrical resistance or impedance. A *kilohm* ($k\Omega$) is one thousand (10^3) ohms. A *megaohm* ($M\Omega$) is one million (10^6) ohms.

output—(1) The electrical signal produced by biofeedback equipment. (2) The terminal of a device from which output issues.

palpation of a muscle—The location of the belly of a muscle by the application of light finger pressure to the surface of the body.

parasympathetic nervous system—A major subdivision of the autonomic nervous system. Increased parasympathetic activity occurs in periods of rest and tranquility and is characterized by slowing of the heart and enhancement of visceral functions leading to digestion, growth, and repair. Movement toward deep relaxation is referred to as a *trophotropic response* (from the Greek *trophos,* nutrition) or *relaxation response*. The parasympathetic system is relatively specific in its influences and selective in its activation of the organs it controls.

phasic changes—Rapid, transient changes in the feedback signal that occur within a few seconds in response to some stimulus.

physiological systems—Functional units into which the human body is organized: integument (skin), and skeletal, muscular, circulatory (heart, vessels, circulatory fluids), respiratory, digestive, urinary, reproductive, endocrine, and nervous (including sense organs) systems.

photoplethysmograph—An instrument sensitive to changes in light transmission and used to measure changes in blood flow (hence, vascular changes).

plateau—A stable or unchanging signal.

polarity—The direction of current flow.

preauricular depression—The slight depression just in front of and above the earlobe.

progressive relaxation—A technique of muscular relaxation originally developed by Edmund Jacobson. The procedure consists of alternately contracting and relaxing all the muscles of the body. Progressive relaxation is frequently used as an adjunctive technique with biofeedback training.

proprioceptive—Receiving stimulations arising within the body.

Raynaud's disease—A pathology of the circulation in the hands and feet characterized by excessive vasoconstriction in the presence of cold or other stressors; later vasoconstriction is followed by vasodilation and intense reddening of the extremity.

"real time" feedback—Feedback characterized by a minimal lag between the change in the physiological system and the feedback signal reflecting that change.

recovery—The period between the time when the feedback signal indicates a response to a stimulus and the time when the signal returns to the prestimulus level.

reference electrode—An electrode located over an "electrically neutral" area.

relaxation response—See *parasympathetic nervous system*.

resistance—The measure of resistance to the flow of electricity in a circuit (see Appendix A).

resistor—A device used in a circuit primarily to provide resistance.

sensitivity—A measure of the ability of an instrument to detect signals of small amplitude.

sensorimotor rhythm—A waveform generated by the brain with a frequency of 12–15 Hz, measured from the scalp over the sensorimotor (central) cortex, and associated with suppression of movement.

subjective units of disturbance (SUD)—A subjective measure of the intensity of distress in response to some stimuli used in systematic desensitization. The SUD system employs a scale of 0 to 100, from "no distress" to "extreme distress."

sympathetic nervous system—A major subdivision of the autonomic nervous system. Increased sympathetic activity occurs in response to stressful situations such as intense muscular exercise, extreme cold or fatigue, fear, or anger. The response tends to be a generalized discharge (see *fight-flight response*).

systematic desensitization—A behavior therapy technique frequently used in conjunction with biofeedback by which a trainee becomes desensitized to previous anxiety-provoking stimuli. The trainee first develops a graded hierarchy of anxiety-producing stimuli and then, while remaining relaxed, visualizes each, from the least to the most anxiety-producing.
systems—See *physiological systems*.
thermal lag—The time lag between the change in temperature of a body part and the registration of that change in the feedback signal.
thermistor—A sensor used to detect and monitor changes in skin temperature.
theta—A waveform generated by the brain with a frequency between 4 and 7 Hz, usually associated with falling asleep (hypnogogic imagery).
threshold—A criterion value often employed in processing a biofeedback signal. Feedback is given only when the level of physiological activity being monitored is above or below the threshold value.
tonic changes—Gradual changes in the baseline level of feedback signal, which occur over a long period of time.
trophotropic response—See *parasympathetic nervous system*.
vasoconstriction—The constriction (decrease in caliber) of a blood vessel, especially of arterioles, leading to decreased blood flow to a body part.
vasodilation—The dilation (increase in caliber) of a blood vessel.
volt (V)—The unit of measurement of voltage. A *millivolt* (mV) is one thousandth (10^{-3}) of a volt. A *microvolt* (μV) is one millionth (10^{-6}) of a volt.
voltage—Electrical "pressure" or the potential difference that causes electrical current to flow (see Appendix A).

Renita Kitchens